"The Bullets Flew Like Hail"

Cutler's Brigade at Gettysburg
From McPherson's Ridge to Culp's Hill

James L. McLean Jr.

Savas Beatie
California

Library of Congress Cataloging-in-Publication Data

Names: McLean, James L., Jr., 1951- author.
Title: "The Bullets Flew Like Hail": Cutler's Brigade at Gettysburg from
  McPherson's Ridge to Culp's Hill / James L. McLean Jr.
Other titles: Cutler's Brigade at Gettysburg | Cutler's Brigade at
  Gettysburg from McPherson's Ridge to Culp's Hill
Description: Third edition. | El Dorado Hills, CA: Savas Beatie, [2023] |
  Includes bibliographical references and index. | Summary: "An expanded,
  revised edition of James L. McLean's *Cutler's Brigade at Gettysburg*.
  This unit history explores the composition and personalities of the
  first Union infantry to relieve General Buford's hard-pressed cavalry on
  the western outskirts of Gettysburg on the first day of the battle. The
  brigade's stubborn defense, with the arrival of the famous Iron Brigade,
  stopped the Confederate advance on the town and set the tone for the
  three-day battle"— Provided by publisher.
Identifiers: LCCN 2023009074 | ISBN 9781611216677 (hardcover) |
  ISBN 9781954547599 (ebook)
Subjects: LCSH: United States. Army. Cutler's Brigade. | Gettysburg, Battle
  of, Gettysburg, Pa., 1863. | United States—History—Civil War,
  1861-1865—Regimental histories.
Classification: LCC E475.53 .M474 2023 | DDC 973.7/349—dc23/eng/20230308
LC record available at https://lccn.loc.gov/2023009074

First Savas Beatie Edition, First Printing

SB

Savas Beatie
989 Governor Drive, Suite 102
El Dorado Hills, CA 95762
916-941-6896 / sales@savasbeatie.com / www.savasbeatie.com

All of our titles are available at special discount rates for bulk purchases in the United States. Contact us for information.

Proudly published, printed, and warehoused in the United States of America.

To Judy and Drew, for their love, patience, and understanding.

To Courtney, Camden, Lincoln, and Weston,
for enriching our family's happiness.

To my family, both past and present.

AND

To the men of Cutler's Brigade,
Whose valor and accomplishments continue to be
Wrongfully ignored or misrepresented by historians.

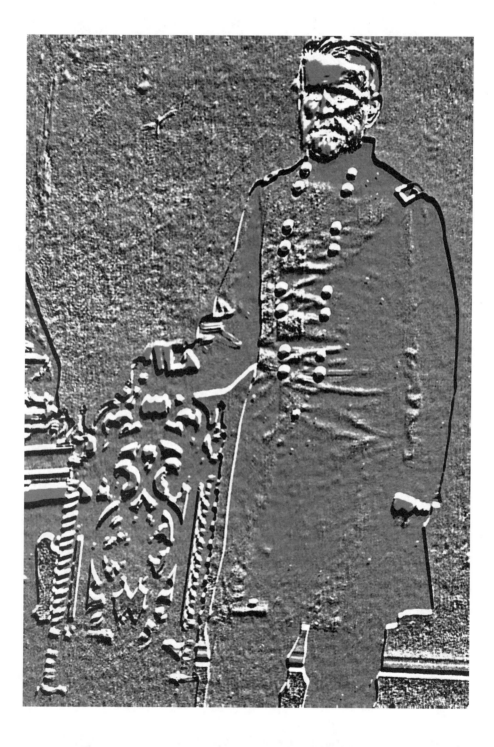

Table of Contents

List of Maps

Photos have been placed throughout the text for the convenience of the reader.

Preface to the
Savas Beatie Edition

In November 1963, at the age of twelve, I attended my first meeting of the Baltimore Civil War Round Table. Soon thereafter I became a member of the organization, and over the next fifteen years I delivered several talks to the group. Around 1978, I decided my next presentation to the renamed Round Table of American Military History would cover the performance of a single brigade during the Battle of Gettysburg. I intentionally avoided the obvious, well-known outfits like the Iron Brigade or Hood's Texans. At the same time, I needed to select a brigade for which I could find a reasonable amount of detail. My Civil War library at the time was quite small, but it contained a set of *New York at Gettysburg*. Scanning the pages of the three massive volumes, my attention was drawn to the accounts of the 76th, 95th, and 147th New York Volunteers as well as to the dedication material pertaining to the 14th New York State Militia (also known as the 14th Brooklyn or the 84th New York Volunteers). Those units, together with the 56th Pennsylvania and the 7th Indiana, comprised Lysander Cutler's brigade at Gettysburg.

My research began in earnest. My wife, Judy, and I made multiple trips to the MOLLUS Civil War Library and Museum in Philadelphia, the War College Library in Carlisle, and the Gettysburg National Military Park Library. Within those institutions, we found a great deal of information relating to Cutler's regiments. I quickly realized it would be difficult to tell the story of Cutler's brigade at Gettysburg without mentioning the exploits of John Buford's cavalry during the morning of July 1, 1863. In February 1979, I purchased my first regimental history from Dave Zullo, owner of Olde Soldier Books. Compiled by C. V. Tevis and D. R. Marquis to commemorate the 50th anniversary of the 14th Brooklyn's muster into United States service, *The History of the Fighting Fourteenth* provided a great deal of data on the regiment's role in the battle. The third Thursday of September 1979 I presented the culmination of my research to the Round Table. Although the talk was well received, I felt I needed to spend more time delving into the topic. I submitted an article, "The First Union Shot at Gettysburg," to the *Lincoln Herald*; it appeared in the Spring 1980 issue.

My interest in the Civil War and my desire to obtain unaffordable books on the subject led to the creation of Butternut and Blue. My wife and I started the book business in 1983; over the years we expanded it to include the reprinting of old volumes and the publication of original works. In 1987, my continued study of the brigade led to our company's release of 300 copies of *Cutler's Brigade at Gettysburg*. Sturdily bound in blue cloth, the print was set on a typewriter, and I drew the maps by hand. Over the next few years, the book sold out.

Much of my analysis of the brigade's performance was ignored by historians, who continued to snub the unit's contributions at the railroad cut and on Culp's Hill. I amassed a substantial amount of new information relating to the brigade, so I decided to issue a revised edition of the book.

The second iteration of *Cutler's Brigade at Gettysburg*, published in late December 1994, benefitted from additional source material, computerized typesetting, additional photographs, and professionally updated maps drawn by the late Blake Magner.

The second edition received complimentary comments. Historian Harry Pfanz graciously agreed to look at my manuscript prior to its publication and offered this assessment: "I have read and enjoyed the Cutler's brigade study very much. It is an excellent account. I don't know of anything relating to the first day to quite match it within its scope." A reviewer critiqued *Cutler's Brigade at Gettysburg* for the Civil War News. "Historical studies of this quality," he noted, "greatly enhance the understanding of the Civil War on the small unit level. To date, this volume is the definitive account of the battle for the railroad cut on July 1 and the part played by Lysander Cutler's fine brigade during its tenure at Gettysburg. It is one of the best studies of a small unit action of the Civil War." Also, a satisfied customer sent a letter praising the book. He wrote, "It is without doubt one of the most clear and concise books I have read on the Civil War. The way the maps explained each part of the action made it very clear indeed."

By the year 2000, the last copies of the second edition had been sold. *Cutler's Brigade at Gettysburg* has been out of print for more than 20 years. To my great surprise, in July 2020, Theodore P. Savas, from Savas Beatie, contacted me to express interest in reprinting the title. I agreed as long as I could correct some misspellings, a few grammar and punctuation errors, and revise some of the text. Ted agreed, and the task was made easier when I located the text of the second edition still in my computer.

I immediately went to work to deal with spelling, grammar, and punctuation miscues. In addition, a few directional errors received attention. At Ted's prompting, I changed the format of the footnotes to a more conventional style. Also, I reworked a number of the sentences in order to make the text flow more smoothly or to clarify the event being discussed. Finally, I added some analysis to a few footnotes to further emphasize points I made in the text.

Cutler's Brigade at Gettysburg contained a few historical flaws. Colonel Ira Grover and his 7th Indiana guarded the 1st Corps wagon train and cattle herd during the morning of July 1. In the afternoon, Grover moved his regiment toward Gettysburg without waiting to be relieved. Based on commentary in a published diary, I mentioned that Grover was court-martialed for leaving the train unattended. During my subsequent research for a regimental history of the 14th Brooklyn, I located Grover's court-martial in the National Archives. The colonel did not receive a reprimand for his July 1 march to Gettysburg. Instead, Lysander Cutler preferred charges against Grover for disobeying marching orders on June 12 and July 18, 1863. Jim Heenehan, in an article in *The Gettysburg Magazine*, pointed out my error. The incorrect statement has been eliminated from the current edition.[1]

Also, I erred in my alignment of two of Brigadier General James J. Archer's Confederate regiments. Research by later authors, particularly Marc and Beth Storch, convinced me that the placements I had for the 1st Tennessee and 13th Alabama should be reversed. Also, the 5th Alabama Battalion served as skirmishers and did not hold a spot in Archer's main battle line. Cartographer Mike Priest corrected the positions of the 13th Alabama and 1st Tennessee on the updated maps for this new edition.

---

1 Court-martial of Colonel Ira Grover, RG 153, Box 1510, NN-0072, National Archives and Records Administration [NARA]; Jim Heenehan, "Correcting the Error: The Court-Martial and Acquittal of Col. Ira Grover, 7th Indiana Infantry," *The Gettysburg Magazine*, Issue Number 45, (July 2011), pp. 71-83.

In Chapter 4, I used a quote by a soldier in the 147th New York to describe how the dreadful heat impacted the 1st Corps troops as they marched to Gettysburg. I mistakenly identified the Yankee as the regiment's chaplain, which was not quite true. The Confederates captured the New Yorker during the July 1 retreat through Gettysburg. During the night, the fellow wandered away from his captors and met a brave town lady. She slipped him a suit of clothes and led him to her home. After a wash and a shave, the New Yorker put on the civilian outfit and posed as a Methodist clergyman. The ruse worked, which enabled the soldier to rejoin his regiment after the battle. His comrades dubbed him "chaplain" because of his ingenious escape.

When I started my research on this project, historians referenced the timber south of the McPherson farm as McPherson's Woods. I used that name for the grove and kept it in this current edition. More recent writers refer to the area as Herbst's Woods.

I relied heavily on historian John Bachelder's correspondence with battle participants. I used typescript versions of the letters copied by the late Sam Hubbard from those housed at the Gettysburg National Military Park Library. At the time of my research, the three volumes of Bachelder correspondence, edited by David and Aubrey Ladd and recently reissued by Savas Beatie LLC, had not been published.

Another statement in *Cutler's Brigade at Gettysburg* needs clarification. On June 30, 1863, Confederate Brig. Gen. James J. Pettigrew marched three of his regiments to Gettysburg in order to gather supplies. Based on William Fox's history of the battle in volume 1 of *New York at Gettysburg*, I stated that Pettigrew halted his men near the Lutheran Theological Seminary. Pennsylvania historian Samuel Bates, in his 1875 recounting of the campaign, likewise placed Pettigrew on Seminary Ridge. Sarah Broadhead, who lived on Chambersburg Street near the west edge of town, made the following June 30 diary entry: "This morning the Rebels came to the top of the hill [Seminary Ridge] overlooking the town," she recorded, ". . . and looked over at our place. We had a good view of them from our house." Also, Michael Jacobs, a professor of mathematics and chemistry at Pennsylvania (now Gettysburg) College, observed the approach of the Southern troops. The professor started to accumulate notes concerning what he saw and heard during the eventful days before, during, and after the battle. Jacobs compiled his notes into a history of the campaign that was published in October 1863. According to Jacobs, Pettigrew's men advanced "as far as the crest of the Seminary hill, one-half of a mile northwest of Gettysburg, throwing about two dozen infantry pickets as far as Mr. Shead's house [also on Chambersburg Street]. Several officers on horseback were seen reconnoitering with their field glasses, and engaged in conversation with the people residing near the road on the hill."[2]

Since the release of the second Butternut and Blue edition, a 1905 newspaper article surfaced describing Dr. John O'Neal's ordeal on June 30, 1863. The Gettysburg physician claimed he ran into Pettigrew's column at Herr's Tavern. The doctor inferred that the Confederates never made it past Willoughby Run. In fact, he avowed that Union cavalry intervened between the Southerners and the town. Historians Harry Pfanz and Allen Guelzo used the article to conclude that Pettigrew's men never moved east beyond the stream.

I disagree. I believe Pettigrew and at least some of his men made it to Seminary Ridge. The contemporary accounts by Sarah Broadhead and Michael Jacobs during those stressful days seems more plausible than a tale told 42 years after the battle. Also, Confederate sources mentioned they observed the arrival of Brigadier General John Buford's cavalry south of town. The Rebels could have spotted the Union troopers from Seminary Ridge, but it is doubtful whether they could have seen the horsemen from Herr's Ridge.[3]

I have included some new material in this third edition. In Chapter 1, I added a few comments to the capsule histories of Cutler's regiments. My ongoing research into the exploits of the 14th Brooklyn led to my discovery of daily field returns for the brigade throughout the campaign. The documents, housed in the National Archives, specify the number of men present for duty, on detached service, sick, or in arrest. I used these numbers for the regiments' July 1 strengths instead of the counts I had in the second edition. Also, I adjusted the 14th Brooklyn's casualties at the Battles of 1st and 2nd Bull Run based on extensive research I have done the past 25 years.

I added three new appendices to this edition. The first is a July 5, 1863, letter written by a soldier in the 95th New York. Sources for the 95th New York are scarce. This document, found in the infantryman's pension file, provides a wonderful description of the opening of the battle. It is especially valuable for the New Yorker's rendition of the charge on the railroad cut.

2 Samuel Bates, *The Battle of Gettysburg* (Philadelphia, 1875), p. 54; Sarah Broadhead, *The Diary of a Lady of Gettysburg* (Hershey, 1990), p. 11; Michael Jacobs, *Notes on the Rebel Invasion of Maryland and Pennsylvania and the Battle of Gettysburg, July 1, 2, and 3, Accompanied by an Explanatory Map* (Gettysburg, 1909), p. 18.

3 "Battle 42 Years Ago," *Gettysburg Compiler*, July 5, 1905; Harry Pfanz, *Gettysburg—The First Day* (Chapel Hill, 2001), pp. 25-27; Allen Guelzo, *Gettysburg, The Last Invasion* (New York, 2013), pp. 129-130.

Chapter 8 of *Cutler's Brigade at Gettysburg* covers the difficulties experienced by John Jochum, a 14th Brooklyn soldier wounded on the morning of July 1. Jochum's pension file provided most of the details about the chasseur's recovery as well as his efforts to obtain reasonable compensation from the government due to his injury. Recently, I discovered an 1893 newspaper article Jochum wrote detailing his ordeal: his response to his injury while still on the battle field; his evacuation from the combat zone; and his subsequent treatment and partial recovery. The column enriches the effort I made in explaining the trials of a soldier wounded at Gettysburg. The second appendix added to this edition is a transcription of Jochum's article.

The final addition to the appendix is a letter written by a soldier in the 76th New York to his hometown newspaper. I discovered this letter after the second edition of my book was published. I included it in this edition for two reasons. It offers an interesting, contemporary account of the part played by the 76th New York during the march to the battlefield and during the first day's fight. In addition, the list of casualties, by company, affords a grim look at the terrible human cost of the battle.

In Chapter 3, I noted the apparent, nonchalant attitude displayed by the Federal cavalrymen encamped near the Lutheran Seminary on the morning of July 1. Large numbers of horsemen left their bivouacs and wandered into town to obtain a meal or to engage in friendly conversation. To emphasize why I found this behavior surprising, I included the tale of John Buford's conversation with Thomas Devin the previous evening. Buford predicted the Southern troops would "come booming" the next day. He asserted the Yankee cavalry would have to "fight like the devil" to hold back the advancing Confederates. Perhaps the Union cavalry should have spent more time organizing a defense instead of grabbing a good breakfast.

When I completed the first edition of the manuscript in 1986, it filled a void in the study of the battle. The book was one of the earliest attempts to detail the performance of a single brigade on those hallowed fields. Prior to my book, few titles focused on small unit actions: John Bigelow's *The Peach Orchard*, Oliver Norton's *The Attack and Defense of Little Round Top*, and David Riggs's *East of Gettysburg* were notable exceptions. Several authors concentrated on a single day: Warren Hassler's *Crisis at the Crossroads*, James K. P. Scott's *The Story of the Battles at Gettysburg* (first day), and George Stewart's *Pickett's Charge*. The manuscript preceded the first issue of *The Gettysburg Magazine* by nearly three years. A large number of books focusing on small unit actions at Gettysburg have emerged since 1987.[4]

I was one of the first writers to correctly locate the position held by the 147th New York during its July 1 morning fight. Prior to the release of my first edition, historians placed the 147th New York on the middle ridge, in line with the 56th Pennsylvania and 76th New York. A thorough examination of firsthand accounts written by Oswego men who served in the regiment, however, convinced me that the 147th New York formed on the eastern slope of the western ridge. Subsequent historians have validated this placement. My research also led to a better understanding of the alignment and service of Cutler's brigade in the July 1 afternoon fight and during its assignment to Culp's Hill.

I always believed the best military studies required solid scholarship, gifted writing, and the inclusion of ample maps. Maps are especially useful when an author describes detailed troop maneuvers in the text. John Bigelow's monumental *The Campaign of Chancellorsville: A Strategic and Tactical Study* (New Haven, 1910) set an early standard with 47 maps, plans, and sketches. Although Bigelow set the bar for campaign study maps, no Gettysburg books came close to matching his efforts for nearly three-quarters of a century. When *Cutler's Brigade at Gettysburg* was first published, it contained 38 maps showing the intricate troop movements on the battlefield. Since the publication of the initial two editions of my book, several excellent Gettysburg titles have been issued that enhance the cartography of the battle.[5]

---

4 John Bigelow, *The Peach Orchard, July 2, 1863* (Minneapolis, 1910); Oliver Norton, *The Attack and Defense of Little Round Top, July 2, 1863* (New York, 1913); David Riggs, *East of Gettysburg: Stuart versus Custer* (Bellevue, 1970); Warren W. Hassler, Jr., *Crisis at the Crossroads: The First Day at Gettysburg* (Montgomery, 1970); James K. P. Scott, *The Story of the Battles at Gettysburg* (Harrisburg, 1927); George R. Stewart, *Pickett's Charge: A Microhistory of the Final Attack at Gettysburg, July 3, 1863* (Boston, 1959). The first issue of *The Gettysburg Magazine* appeared in July 1989. An excellent, chronological list of Gettysburg histories can be found in Richard Sauers, *The Gettysburg Campaign, June 3-August 1, 1863: A Comprehensive, Selectively Annotated Bibliography*, Second Edition (Baltimore, 2004), pp. 543-553.

5 The following Gettysburg books contain superior battle maps: John Imhof, *Gettysburg: Day Two, A Study in Maps* (Baltimore, 1999); Bradley M. Gottfried, *The Maps of Gettysburg: An Atlas of the Gettysburg Campaign, June 3-July 13, 1863* (El Dorado Hills, 2007); Philip Laino, *Gettysburg Campaign Atlas: 421 Maps Encompassing the March to Gettysburg, the Battle, and the Retreat* (Dayton, 2009); and Carol Reardon and Tom Vossler, *A Field Guide to Gettysburg: Experiencing the Battlefield Through its History, Places, and People* (Chapel Hill, 2013). Gottfried, with publisher Savas Beatie LLC, has produced a series of map studies covering Eastern Theater campaigns. Since 1989,

My research uncovered manuscript material Civil War historians continue to overlook. The John Vliet Correspondence in the Brooklyn Historical Society provides an excellent take on soldier life in the Army of the Potomac. On August 1, 1865, Edward Brush Fowler sent Abner Doubleday an extract on the battle based on his diary. Gettysburg historians have seldom cited this document. The worthy John William Hofmann Papers in the Society Small Collection, housed at The Historical Society of Pennsylvania, are also infrequently sourced.

Much to my dismay, many historians continue to denigrate or diminish the role of the 14th Brooklyn during the assault on the railroad cut. They claim that the Brooklyn lads, often referred to as chasseurs or Red Legs because of their unique uniform, began their charge well after the 6th Wisconsin started its attack. Some historians believe the 14th Brooklyn merely served in a mop-up capacity. More than 100 bleeding chasseurs lying between Chambersburg Pike and the railroad cut seem to refute that interpretation. My views, expressed in the book, lean toward John Bachelder's interpretation of the events. He concluded the attack represented the "accidental meeting and voluntary union of two gallant commands from different brigades, moving from a half mile asunder, whose objective point was the enemy." Hopefully, the 14th Brooklyn history I am currently writing will strengthen the arguments I present in *Cutler's Brigade at Gettysburg*.[6]

Since the release of the second edition, I have continued to research the role played by Cutler and his men—and especially the 14th Brooklyn—in the battle. None of the new material I have found contradicts the assessments I made in my earlier work. Hopefully, a new generation of readers will find this current edition to be an enjoyable and informative read.

James L. McLean Jr.

January 29, 2023

The Gettysburg Magazine has included hundreds of excellent maps, many drawn by John Heiser, Philip Laino, and Hal Jespersen. In the revised edition of this book, Mike Priest consolidated a few of the maps. This new volume contains 26 well-crafted pieces of cartography.

6   David and Aubrey Ladd, ed., *John Bachelder's History of the Battle of Gettysburg* (Dayton, 1997), p. 226. The following source is an example of an author diminishing the role of the 14th Brooklyn at the railroad cut: Robert W. Sledge, "The Railroad Cut Reconsidered," *The Gettysburg Magazine*, Issue Number 52, (January 2015), pp. 25-40. Sledge suggested the 14th Brooklyn would have provided more help if the regiment had formed perpendicular to the railroad grade, thereby preventing the escape of the Rebels out of the west end of the cut. The suggestion lacks merit. Fowler's letter to Doubleday mentioned the Confederates extended beyond his left flank. A maneuver across the railroad cut would have exposed the backs of his men to retreating Southern infantry and to Heth's massed artillery on Herr's Ridge.

Preface to the First
Butternut and Blue Edition

During the Civil War, several units achieved great renown. Commands such as the Iron Brigade, the Irish Brigade, Hood's Texan Brigade, the Stonewall Brigade, the Louisiana Tigers, and Pickett's Virginia Division developed reputations since perpetuated by Civil War historians. However, the fighting qualities of the soldiers that composed these units and the consistently excellent leadership displayed by their officers only partially accounts for the fame that these groups achieved. Why, then, have other units that also displayed laudable courage been ignored? The question is not easy to assess.

One potential reason why certain organizations achieved acclaim can be attributed to the historian of the unit. An individual who fought with a command and later eloquently reminisced about his group's experiences consequently enhanced the reputation of that unit. Rufus Dawes, who masterfully penned the regimental history of the 6th Wisconsin, exemplifies such a writer. A second reason why some units gained acclaim can be attributed to their nicknames. The names Iron Brigade, Stonewall Brigade, and Louisiana Tigers conjure well-earned notions of invincibility. Additionally, outfits with a common ethnic background obtain followers who have a similar heritage. What wearer of the Shamrock and Kelly green does not read of the Irish Brigade with a sense of pride? State affiliation ranks as another means by which units achieve recognition. Brigades and even divisions recruited from one state have an immediate following from Civil War enthusiasts within that state. Finally, the flamboyance of leaders such as George Pickett embellishes the reputation of the outfits that served under them.

One additional strain of similarity exists between units such as the Iron Brigade, the Irish Brigade, and Hood's Texan Brigade. Throughout a major portion of the war, the regimental constitution of the organizations remained intact. A regiment that was part of a brigade or division that maintained such stability developed a trust in its supporting units that further enhanced the larger unit's fighting qualities. The Union army had a particularly nasty habit of tinkering with brigades, divisions, and even corps. Regiments were added or switched with no thought given to stability. Reasons abounded why this transpired — the expiration of enlistments, the whims of a new commander, the influx of newly-raised regiments, and battlefield attrition. The common strain in all of these factors was the federal government's short-sighted [and political] policy of raising new regiments rather than feeding recruits into existing commands. Hence, brigades often became temporary arrangements of regiments. Nonetheless, these short-lived brigades frequently served well but without the recognition of their more stable counterparts. As a result, the history of these brigades has been overlooked and/or misunderstood by generations of writers to such an extent that many students of the Civil War have developed a distorted concept of what really occurred.

The purpose of this book is to bring attention to the misunderstood exploits of a Union brigade during the Battle of Gettysburg, with an emphasis on the morning fight of July 1, 1863. Most authors equate that morning's fight with the heroics of the Iron Brigade. Certainly, accolades are well-deserved for that valorous unit. Nevertheless, another brigade made solid, if not significant, contributions to the Union cause that morning. Commanded by Brigadier General Lysander Cutler, it led the 1st Division of the 1st Corps onto the battlefield; it was the first infantry to make contact with the Rebel forces; it helped repel both Archer's and Davis's Brigades; and it suffered tremendous casualties. Additionally, it produced one of the most heroic stands made by a regiment during the entire war. During the next two days, the brigade was actively engaged, making it one of the few units that saw action all three days of the battle. Its exploits, nonetheless, have been ignored or misunderstood over the years. The reasons are several. Only three of its six regiments have histories. Although well-written, they do not achieve the style of a Rufus Dawes or a Joshua Chamberlain. The brigade has no nickname nor was it composed of a particular nationality. Its regiments came from three states— Pennsylvania, New York, and Indiana. Additionally, the six regiments served as a brigade for only a brief time. Lysander Cutler had no West Point background, was not flashy, but was tough as nails. Finally, the official reports by the regimental officers were brief. One regiment, which lost its commander, made no report. Cutler's report, based on sketchy material, is additionally limited since his brigade was separated into three parts. Several official and other reports, especially those by Captain James A. Hall, misled later historians as to what really happened on the morning of July 1.

Out of necessity it was essential to describe the cavalry action during the morning of July 1 to see how it was related to the approach of Cutler's Brigade. Very little detailed information has been printed on the subject and much of it is misleading, contradictory, or inaccurate. Hopefully, the reader will obtain a clearer picture concerning the operations of Buford's cavalry on the morning of July 1.

To complete the story of Cutler's brigade at Gettysburg, the July 1 afternoon action on Seminary Ridge and the July 2-3 fighting on Culp's Hill have been discussed in detail. The role of Cutler's regiments in those parts of the battle has been virtually ignored despite the important service they rendered in those areas.

In writing this book, I would like to thank my wife, Judy, for her help in research and proofreading. She has spent innumerable hours the past eight years doing the "little" things that make a project like this a reality.

Three libraries were particularly helpful: the MOLLUS Library in Philadelphia, the War College Library in Carlisle, and the library at the Gettysburg National Military Park. At Gettysburg, Kathy Georg Harrison and John Heiser were particularly sharing of their time and expertise.

Finally, two good friends played a major role in the completion of this project. Richard Sauers provided a great deal of assistance locating much of the valuable source material used to research this book. Rick has an almost uncanny knack of finding primary source material. His annotated bibliography of Gettysburg sources was a tremendous reference tool. The other individual who played a large part in the production of this book was the late Sam Hubbard. Sam and I spent hours discussing conflicting reports and viewpoints. Visits to the battlefield enhanced our discussions. Most importantly, Sam assisted me with my map design. He had been working on a project to plot troop movements during the battle on an hourly basis. The insights he learned from his efforts greatly assisted me in developing my maps.

Final special thanks are extended to all those customers who have supported Butternut and Blue. Without you, the production of this book could not have been possible.

James L. McLean Jr.

July 26, 1986

Preface to Second
Butternut and Blue Edition

Several years ago, a reprint of a centennial-era book was published. In the new Foreword, the author claimed that in the past 30 years he had found nothing new to add to his work. This revised edition of *Cutler's Brigade at Gettysburg* does not fall into the same category.

Some changes have been subtle and others have been less so. Many comments and corrections suggested by readers concerning the first edition have been incorporated. Chief among these is a North-South orientation now found on all maps. The maps in the second edition were superbly redrawn by Blake Magner; he kindly altered a few troop placements at the last minute. The text of the second edition is now professionally typeset. At the end, there are several new appendices. Also, the number of photographs has been increased and a new index provided.

Changes in the interpretation of the morning cavalry action and of Cutler's operations have been few. I have repositioned the gun that Hall abandoned during his retreat. The section on the charge on the railroad cut has been expanded. This was done partially in response to the excellent book *In the Bloody Railroad Cut* which was published after Cutler's Brigade. It is still my impression that the charge was made collectively by the 14th Brooklyn, 95th New York, and 6th Wisconsin.

On the other end of the fight, new research indicates that Cutler's Brigade fought on Culp's Hill facing eastward. The usual interpretation is that the unit faced north. Hence, Cutler's men played more of a role in supporting Greene's troops than is normally suggested.

In 1987, when the first edition was published, I felt that I had been relatively thorough. However, I kept stumbling across information that led me to the quest of publishing a revision of the first edition. The bibliography of the second edition is 70% larger. Most of these new sources are primary accounts. The result, I hope, is a fuller and slightly more accurate interpretation of the part played by Cutler and his brigade at Gettysburg.

This revised edition could not have been possible without the assistance of numerous historians, institutions, and Civil War enthusiasts. Rick Sauers has continued to make available any material he finds on Cutler's Brigade. His friendship and assistance has been a cornerstone to this effort.

Five institutions played a major role in this revision. The Historical Society of Pennsylvania in Philadelphia provided very helpful John William Hofmann Papers. The New Hampshire Historical Society, which houses the ultra-important John B. Bachelder Papers, granted permission to quote from the letters. Similar thanks are due the Oswego County Historical Society. That organization allowed access to the vital Henry Harrison Lyman Collection. The Brooklyn Historical Society and the New York State Library also allowed access to manuscript material.

Additional photographic materials were obtained from numerous sources. The Civil War Library and Museum in Philadelphia granted permission to use several images in their collection. Individual enthusiasts granted permission to use photos in their personal collections. These people, to whom I am deeply indebted, are Craig Johnson, Rick Carlisle, Allan Zellnock, David Cutler Ahlgren (a relative of Lysander), and Bill Howard.

Individuals who provided letters, articles, or reference material to support my research include Paul Meuse, Marc and Beth Storch, Dan Lorello, Dick Bridgeman, Lance Herdegen, Jim Madden, John Fuller, Robert K. Krick, Bill Mason, John Hennessy, and Stewart Harkness.

Harry Pfanz was gracious enough to read my manuscript and make suggestions. I am very flattered that he would take the time to review my work.

Lance Ingmire was helpful in providing an important newspaper article and in discussing the action at the railroad cut. Lance is passionately researching the 95th New York Infantry Regiment and seeks any materials concerning that unit. His goal is to write a unit history.

If I have failed to recognize any person or institution, please accept my apologies.

James L. McLean Jr.
September 1994

Cutler's Brigade at Gettysburg
From McPherson's Ridge to Culp's Hill

CHAPTER ONE

A Profile of Lysander Cutler and His Brigade

Lysander Cutler pursued several diverse and unrelated careers prior to the Civil War.

He was born on February 16, 1807, in Worcester, Massachusetts. As a young boy, Cutler strove to improve his education despite protests from his farmer father. He studied both the clothier trade and surveying, and at the age of 21 assumed the position of headmaster of a Maine school. Rowdy pupils had driven the previous instructor from this job. Cutler dealt with the problem in a direct and firm manner that was later reflected in his future endeavors. To assert his control, Cutler spent the first day at the school whipping the troublemakers!

As a young man, Cutler advanced swiftly through the ranks of the Maine militia. When a border controversy between Maine and Canada led to the bloodless Aroostook War, Cutler served as a lieutenant colonel in the militia from February 20 – April 25, 1839. Four years later he established a woolen mill and earned a fortune within ten years. However, a fire destroyed his mill and left him financially destitute. Undeterred, Cutler not only rebuilt the mill but participated in the development of a foundry, a grist mill, and a sawmill as well as some tenements. By the mid-1850s, Cutler's business acumen had earned him another small fortune and a stellar reputation. He became a selectman, a railroad director, a trustee for Tufts College, and a state senator.

Unfortunately, the Panic of 1856 wiped out Cutler's fiscal security. Broke, he moved to Milwaukee, Wisconsin, where a mining company hired him. His work utilized surveying skills he had learned 20 years earlier and also required him to travel alone through Indian country. When the war began in 1861, Cutler was employed as a grain broker and a fish inspector.[1]

Cutler had not mellowed in his 53 years. He was still a tough and active individual. His experience with the Maine militia led to his colonelcy of the 6th Wisconsin. During the next year and a half he helped mold the western regiment into a competent fighting force that would become part of the famed Iron Brigade, one of the most renowned fighting outfits in the Army of the Potomac. His personality made an immediate impression. According to Rufus Dawes, who later commanded the same regiment, Cutler was "rugged as a wolf." Another officer of the regiment described Cutler as "gruff and gouty and when roused . . . emitted a grunt, like an enraged porker." When the 6th Wisconsin reached Washington, Cutler pinpointed line officers he felt were unacceptable and administered a test to eliminate seven captains and lieutenants "under the thin disguise of failure to pass the exam."

Another incident further illustrates Cutler's mettle. When President Abraham Lincoln relieved Maj. Gen. George B. McClellan from command of the Army of the Potomac in November 1862, widespread dissatisfaction gripped the army. Some officers in the Iron Brigade thought about resigning their commissions. When Cutler caught wind of the rumor, he let it be known that anyone considering a resignation in the face of the enemy would be recommended for dismissal— which effectively ended the demonstration. "Cutler had in all matters of command and discipline the courage of his convictions," explained Dawes. Occasionally, the crusty colonel displayed a tender side. November 28, 1861, was the first Thanksgiving away from home for many of the boys in the 6th Wisconsin. To help alleviate their anxiety and homesickness, Cutler bought 20 mince pies for each company in his regiment [about ¼ of a pie per man]. Cutler's nickname, "Old Graybeard," was almost certainly one of affection.[2]

---

1 Ezra Warner, *Generals in Blue: Lives of the Union Commanders* (New Orleans, 1964), p. 110; Jesse B. Young, *The Battle of Gettysburg* (New York, 1913), p. 386; Alan T. Nolan, *The Iron Brigade, A Military History* (Madison, 1975), pp. 16, 34; *Aroostook War, Historical Sketch and Roster of Commissioned Officers and Enlisted men Called into Service for the Protection of the Northeastern Frontier of Maine* (Augusta: Kennebec Journal Print, 1904), p. 22.

2 Nolan, *The Iron Brigade*, pp. 16, 53, 64-67, 88-96, 112, 170; Rufus Dawes, *Service with the Sixth Wisconsin* (Marietta, 1890), pp. 26, 27, 31; John Tregaskis, comp., *The Battlefield of Gettysburg* (New York, 1888), no page nos.; Glenn Tucker, *High Tide at Gettysburg: The Campaign in Pennsylvania* (Dayton, 1973), p. 114.

Oil painting of Lysander Cutler

Courtesy of David Cutler Ahlgren

Cutler's military record prior to Gettysburg was excellent. On August 5, 1862, he commanded an independent wing during the Frederick Hall Raid. Under his leadership, the 6th Wisconsin, a squadron of cavalry, and a section of artillery penetrated enemy lines, wrecked two miles of track along the Virginia Central Railroad, destroyed some Confederate supplies and warehouses, and eluded a Rebel cavalry force led by Maj. Gen. J. E. B. Stuart. In all, Cutler's group marched 90 miles in just three-and one-half days while fulfilling their mission.[3]

Later that same month, on August 28 during the Second Bull Run Campaign, Cutler suffered a severe leg wound during the battle at Brawner's Farm when a bullet struck him in the upper right thigh. The wound continued to cause him great pain after he returned to duty that November. According to one of Cutler's staff officers, "Old Graybeard" frequently required assistance to mount his horse due to lameness and stiffness in his injured thigh. On at least one occasion in 1864, the lingering effects of his wound led to temporary paralysis. E. B. Wolcott, a Wisconsin surgeon and prewar friend, believed Cutler's death in 1866 was "clearly traceable to the effects of the wound and exposure in the service."[4]

Soon after Cutler returned to duty with the 6th Wisconsin, his brigade commander, John Gibbon, received a promotion to lead a division. For a brief time Cutler replaced Gibbon in charge of the collection of western regiments now nicknamed "the Iron Brigade." Many felt "Old Graybeard" deserved to remain in command. However, politics intervened as it often did in the Army of the Potomac, and Solomon Meredith was put in command of the brigade. It was not a smooth transition. At Fredericksburg, Brig. Gen. Abner Doubleday became irritated with Meredith when the subordinate failed to move his brigade quickly enough to satisfy him. Doubleday relieved Meredith, and Cutler once again found himself in temporary command of the brigade. Cutler made an immediate impact. During the December battle, the 19th Indiana held an advanced picket line and was nearly left behind when the army retreated across the Rappahannock River. Only Cutler's vigilance prevented the Hoosiers from being stranded on the wrong side of the river.

During the winter months of early 1863, President Lincoln removed Ambrose Burnside and put Maj. Gen. Joseph "Fighting Joe" Hooker in command of the

---

3 Nolan, *The Iron Brigade*, pp. 64-68.

4 Nolan, *The Iron Brigade*, pp. 88-96; Lysander Cutler Pension File, National Archives & Records Administration, hereafter cited as NARA; Jack D. Welsh, M.D., *Medical Histories of Union Generals* (Kent, OH, 1996), pp. 88-89.

Army of the Potomac. It was the beginning of a major reorganization. Cutler was promoted to brigadier general, dating back to November 29, 1862, and assumed command of the 2nd Brigade, 1st Division, 1st Corps in Brig. Gen. James S. Wadworth's division. Cutler's mixed brigade of five regiments consisted of the 76th New York, 56th Pennsylvania, 95th New York, and 7th Indiana regiments, as well as the newly added 147th New York. The 1st Corps saw but limited action during the disastrous Chancellorsville Campaign that unfolded in late April and early May of 1863.[5]

The Army of the Potomac underwent further changes soon after the conclusion of the devastating spring campaign. Attrition, battle casualties, and the discharge of 58 regiments whose enlistment terms had expired necessitated the major reorganization of Wadsworth's division. The unit had dwindled from 19 to just 11 regiments and was consolidated from four brigades into two. The Western Iron Brigade became the 1st Brigade, 1st Division, 1st Corps, and Cutler's command remained the 2nd Brigade, 1st Division, 1st Corps. Fortunately for Cutler, he picked up an additional regiment in the 14th Brooklyn. Chasseur John Vliet commented favorably about Cutler soon after his regiment joined the brigade. Vliet maintained that Cutler made frequent visits to the New Yorkers' camp and seemed to show more interest in the Brooklyn boys than any previous general. Although the 76th and 95th New York and 56th Pennsylvania had served together for about a year, Cutler's brigade as a whole entered the summer of 1863 campaign having never cooperated as a consolidated unit. It is important to understand each regiment's unique history prior to being brigaded under Cutler.[6]

---

5 For more on the reorganization that winter, see Al Conner and Chris Mackowski, *Seizing Destiny: The Army of the Potomac's "Valley Forge"* (Savas Beatie, 2016).

6 Nolan, *The Iron Brigade*, pp. 170, 180-184, 196, 197, 233; Henry J. Hunt, "The First Day at Gettysburg," in Robert U. Johnson and Clarence C. Buel, eds. *Battles and Leaders of the Civil War*, 4 vols. (New York, 1956), vol. 3, *Retreat From Gettysburg*, p. 258; Young, *The Battle of Gettysburg*, p. 386; Warner, *Generals in Blue*, p. 110; John Vliet Letter, June 6, 1863, John Vliet Collection, Brooklyn Historical Society. In May 1861, the 14th Brooklyn mustered in "for the war." After First Bull Run the regiment was brigaded with the 22nd, 24th, and 30th New York regiments, all two-year outfits. The 2nd United States Sharpshooters joined the brigade in March 1862 and left the unit in January 1863. In April 1862, the brigade made a grueling march from Catlett's Station to Falmouth, which earned the command the nickname "Iron Brigade." The Eastern Iron Brigade fought well at Second Bull Run, South Mountain, and Antietam. Throughout May 1863, the 22nd, 24th, and 30th New York regiments headed back to the Empire State when their terms of service expired. The 14th Brooklyn, a regiment without a brigade, was then assigned to Cutler's brigade.

The 76th New York, nicknamed the "Cortland County Regiment," recruited its members primarily from Cortland, Otsego, and other central New York counties. The enlistees mustered into service on January 16, 1862, and departed for the capital the following day. The experience of the 76th offers a good illustration of how Federal regiments were often shifted within the army's command structure. From January to March 1862, the regiment was part of the 3rd Brigade, Casey's division, Army of the Potomac. During March, April, and May, the central New York outfit fell under Wadsworth's command in the Military District of Washington. During May through June the regiment came under the jurisdiction of the Department of the Rappahannock, and from June to September 1862, the 76th New York was in Abner Doubleday's 2nd Brigade of Maj. Gen. Irvin McDowell's 3rd Corps, part of Maj. Gen. John Pope's Army of Virginia. It was during its time under Pope that the regiment fought its maiden battle. On August 28 it was ordered, together with the 56th Pennsylvania, to reinforce Brig. Gen. John Gibbon's Western Brigade, which had been attacked by several Confederate divisions in the wing of the Confederate Army of Northern Virginia led by Maj. Gen. Thomas J. "Stonewall" Jackson. The Battle of Brawner's Farm was a stand-up, slug-it-out affair at close range. The fighting cost the 76th New York about 100 casualties. Soon after the campaign, the New York regiment became a portion of the 2nd Brigade, 1st Division, 1st Corps, Army of the Potomac, and would remain in that capacity until January of 1864.[7]

By May 13, 1863, the 76th New York was a skeleton of its former self. Disease and battle attrition had severely depleted its ranks. To compensate for its losses the regiment received recruits from two disbanded regiments: about 50 men from the 24th New York and about 205 officers and men from the 30th New York. As a result, the 76th New York would enter the July 1, 1863, battle at Gettysburg with 375 officers and men.[8]

---

7 *New York Monuments Commission for the Battlefields of Gettysburg and Chattanooga, Final Report on the Battlefield of Gettysburg* (Albany, 1900), p. 612 [hereafter noted as *New York at Gettysburg*]; Nolan, *The Iron Brigade,* pp. 88-96; Bruce Catton, *Mr. Lincoln's Army* (New York, 1951), pp. 21-23; William F. Fox, *Regimental Losses in the American Civil War, 1861-1865* (Albany, 1889), pp. 31, 209; Frederick H. Dyer, *A Compendium of the War of the Rebellion* (New York, 1959), p. 1434.

8 Adam Smith, *History of the 76th Regiment, New York Volunteers* (Cortland, 1867), p. 223 [hereafter cited Smith, *76th New York*]; John Busey and David Martin, *Regimental Strengths at Gettysburg* (Baltimore, 1982), p. 24; *New York at Gettysburg,* p. 611; Warren W. Hassler, *Crisis at the Crossroads* (Tuscaloosa: Univ. of Alabama Press, 1970), p. 143; Cutler's Field Return, RG 393, Part 2, NARA.

The 56th Pennsylvania history closely paralleled that of the 76th New York. The regiment was recruited for a three-year enlistment term and organized and trained at Camp Curtin, Harrisburg, Pennsylvania. Its colonel, Sullivan Amory Meredith, was a prominent Philadelphian. Like the 76th New York, the command traveled to the capital in early 1862. During April 1862, the Pennsylvanians guarded government property and stores left behind by Brig. Gen. Joseph Hooker's Peninsula-bound division. On the 24th of April, the unit was transferred to Aquia Landing, a Union supply port and depot near Fredericksburg, Virginia. While there, the regiment was kept busy repairing wharves, cutting wood, rebuilding the railroad, and performing other "'unsoldierly'" duties. From May to June, the regiment was designated as part of the Department of the Rappahannock. The 56th Pennsylvania and 76th New York, brigaded together in the 1st Division, 3rd Corps, Army of Virginia under John Pope, encountered their initial enemy fire at Brawner's Farm. The fighting cost the 56th Pennsylvania 61 out of 300 men engaged. Both regiments would continue to serve together throughout the war.[9]

Colonel John William Hofmann led the 56th Pennsylvania during the 1863 summer campaign. Hofmann was born in Philadelphia on February 18, 1824, the son of a German immigrant. As a youth he joined the Military Company of Junior Artillerists and remained with the organization from 1840-1843. He switched allegiance in 1843 to the Artillery Corps of Washington Grays and served in that unit until the Civil War erupted. As a member of these militia groups, Hofmann participated in suppressing four riots in the Quaker City (August 1842, January 1843, May 1844, and July 1844). Service in these quasi-military groups earned him a captaincy in the 23rd Pennsylvania in 1861 and later an appointment as major of the 56th Pennsylvania. His efforts in recruiting the 56th Pennsylvania, together with his soldierly bearing, led to his promotion to lieutenant colonel. When Col. Sullivan Meredith was wounded during the Second Bull Run Campaign, Hofmann assumed control of the regiment. During the Antietam Campaign, battle casualties and seniority temporarily elevated Hofmann to command of the brigade. On January 8, 1863, the Philadelphian was promoted to colonel of the 56th

---

9 *Pennsylvania at Gettysburg, Ceremonies at the Dedication of the Monuments Erected by the Commonwealth of Pennsylvania* (Harrisburg, 1904), pp. 339-347; Nolan, *The Iron Brigade*, pp. 88, 95, 96; Dyer, *A Compendium of the War of the Rebellion*, p. 1593; Catton, *Mr. Lincoln's Army*, pp. 21-21; *Military Record of Brevet Brig. Gen. John William Hofmann, United States Volunteers* (Philadelphia, 1884), pp. 3-5; William B. Frankin, "Notes on Crampton's Gap and Antietam," in Robert U. Johnson and Clarence C. Buel, eds., *Battles and Leaders of the Civil War*, 4 vols. (New York, 1956), vol. 2, p. 598; Warner, *Generals in Blue*, p. 320.

Pennsylvania. Hofmann was never wounded, never reported sick, and was almost constantly with his command. His regiment entered the Gettysburg fight with 17 officers and 235 men.[10]

The 95th New York, also known as the "Warren Rifles," was raised from November 1861 through March 1862. Seven companies came from New York City, one from Haverstraw, one from Sing Sing, and one from Westchester County. A sprinkle of enlistees, who simply joined the first regiment that struck their fancy, hailed from Newark, New Jersey. On March 6, 1862, the 95th New York mustered into service with George H. Biddle commissioned as colonel, James B. Post as lieutenant colonel, and Edward Pye as major. Approximately 1,000 strong, the "Warren Rifles" reached the capital on March 19, 1862, and bivouacked at Camp Thomas. During May and June 1862, the regiment became part of Abner Doubleday's brigade, Department of the Rappahannock, where it united with the 76th New York and 56th Pennsylvania. The brigade was later designated the 2nd Brigade, 1st Division, 3rd Corps of Pope's Army of Virginia. The 95th New York saw limited action at Brawner's Farm on August 28 but was actively engaged the next evening on a ridge overlooking Groveton. The regiment lost more than 100 men during the three days of fighting at Second Bull Run. In September of 1862, the 56th Pennsylvania, 76th New York, and 95th New York became the 2nd Brigade, 1st Division, 1st Corps, Army of the Potomac. Colonel Biddle, a 61-year-old Mexican War veteran, led the "Warren Rifles" when the Gettysburg Campaign opened. Major Edward Pye, a 40-year-old graduate of Rutgers College and a pre-war New Jersey lawyer, was second in command. On July 1, 1863, the regiment carried into battle 21 officers and 218 men.[11]

The 7th Indiana Regiment's career began differently from the experiences of the previous three regiments. This unit originally mustered in as a three-month organization. During its term of enlistment, the Hoosiers toiled in western Virginia to help neutralize the Confederate threat in the region. When their term of service expired, the regiment boarded Baltimore and Ohio Railroad passenger cars to head

10 *Military Record of . . . Hofmann*, pp. 3-5; *North to Antietam*, p. 598; Busey and Martin, *Regimental Strengths at Gettysburg*, p. 24; Frank Taylor, *Philadelphia in the Civil War* (Philadelphia, 1913), p. 76; Hassler, *Crisis at the Crossroads*, p. 143; *Pennsylvania at Gettysburg*, p. 312; 56th Pennsylvania Battlefield Marker; Cutler's Brigade Field Return, RG 393, Part 2, NARA.

11 *North to Antietam*, p. 497; *New York at Gettysburg*, p. 737; Dyer, *A Compendium of the War of the Rebellion* p. 1442; Nolan, *The Iron Brigade*, pp. 89-90; Busey and Martin, *Regimental Strengths at Gettysburg*, p. 24; Edmund Raus, *A Generation on the March* (Lynchburg, 1987), pp. 74-75; Cutler's Brigade Field Return, RG 393, Part 2, NARA.

home. During their return, Col. Ebenezer Dumont organized a meeting in his headquarters car where he and his officers and some of the men discussed reenlistment. They agreed to reorganize the regiment as a three-year outfit and to retain their numerical designation. On September 13, 1861, after a brief period of recruitment, the 7th Indiana Volunteers committed to a three-year enlistment. The regiment promptly returned to western Virginia, and on October 3, 1861, participated in its first combat at the Battle of Green Briar.[12]

With some fighting under its belt, the outfit was transferred to the Shenandoah Valley to serve under Maj. Gen. Nathaniel Banks. On March 23, 1862, the 7th Indiana fought against Stonewall Jackson's troops at the First Battle of Kernstown. That June, the Indiana regiment met Jackson's veterans again at Port Republic. Not long thereafter, it became part of Pope's Army of Virginia. Service at Cedar Mountain on August 9 followed as did combat on August 30 at the Second Bull Run debacle. When George McClellan quickly reorganized the defeated Union forces around Washington and moved westward to pursue General Lee's Confederate army in Maryland, the 7th Indiana was attached to the 2nd Brigade, 1st Division, 1st Corps, Army of the Potomac, which also contained the 76th and 95th New York and 56th Pennsylvania regiments. By that September, four of the six units that would comprise Cutler's brigade at Gettysburg had banded together. During the Army of the Potomac's next four battles—South Mountain, Antietam, Fredericksburg, and Chancellorsville—the brigade saw scant action. Limited casualty totals from those fights confirm that the command had been spared from serious combat. At Gettysburg, Col. Ira G. Grover, a 31-year-old college graduate and prewar lawyer and politician, commanded the 7th Indiana. The outfit entered the battle with 437 officers and men.[13]

The 147th New York was added to Cutler's brigade before Chancellorsville. The 147th New York, nicknamed "The Plowboys" and the "Oswego Regiment," hailed from Oswego County. The northern New York enlistees had answered President Lincoln's July 1862 call for 300,000 additional troops. The regiment recruited from the third week of August 1862 until it mustered into service on September 22 and 23, 1862. The New York outfit had a distinctive ethnic flavor

12 Orville Thomson, *Narrative of the Service of the Seventh Indiana Infantry in the War of the Rebellion* (n.p., n.d.), pp. 4-42.

13 Dyer, *A Compendium of the War of the Rebellion*, p. 1120; *Report of the Adjutant General of the State of Indiana, Vol. 2* (Indianapolis, 1865), p. 47; *North to Antietam*, p. 598; *Retreat from Gettysburg*, pp. 145, 234; Raus, *A Generation on the March*, p. 19; Busey and Martin, *Regimental Strengths at Gettysburg*, p. 24; Cutler's Brigade Field Return, RG 393, Part 2, NARA.

with entire companies containing either Irish or German recruits. Under Col. Andrew S. Warner, a former assemblyman with no military experience, the regiment left for Washington on September 27. The next day, 837 enlisted men received their Enfield rifles at Elmira, New York. The regiment arrived in the capital on September 29, and it was attached to Washington's defenses.

Camp life appeared pleasant and easy, but it soon took a destructive turn. Many raw recruits, not realizing the importance of sanitation, contracted malaria or suffered from dysentery. Indeed, "the dead march" soon became as familiar as reveille. The inexperienced Colonel Warner failed to recognize the importance of drill and discipline. In addition, the 147th New York spent much of its time working on fortifications or building roads. The construction work, disease, and lack of drill disillusioned the regiment.[14]

Not all the time spent in Washington was boring or dangerous. During off-duty hours, soldiers visited the Capitol, the White House, various parks, the Patent Office, and the Smithsonian Institution. On November 2, President Lincoln and Secretary of State William Seward reviewed the regiment during a dress parade. Later in the month, near Thanksgiving, Company K received a 300-pound box of cooked turkeys, chickens, mince pies, and other delicacies from their Oswego families and friends. The next day the regiment dined on this splendid repast. When the Oswego boys finished their feast, seven baskets of food remained.[15]

The regiment received its marching orders the same day its members were enjoying their food from home. Colonel Warner exhibited his inexperience by drawing so many supplies and so much equipment that 33 six-mule teams were needed to haul his requisitions—and 10 loads still had to be left behind. Serving as part of the provost guard of the Army of the Potomac, the 147th New York marched to Port Tobacco and was ferried to the supply base at Aquia Landing. Once there, the men unloaded barges, performed picket duty, or guarded the bridge and rail line connecting Aquia Creek to Fredericksburg. Good fortune was their lot at the Battle of Fredericksburg, where the 147th New York was not engaged.

Soon after the battle, the regiment marched to Union headquarters at Falmouth. The Oswego unit guarded the railroad and helped the injured soldiers embark on the cars. The sight of ghastly battle wounds, the inexperienced conduct

---

14 Snyder, Charles, *Oswego County, New York in the Civil War* (Oswego County, 1962), pp. 54- 55; *New York at Gettysburg*, pp. 997-998; Dyer, *A Compendium of the War of the Rebellion*, p. 1460.

15 Snyder, *Oswego County, New York in the Civil War*, pp. 55-56.

of its officers, and the laborious and seemingly non-military duties to which the regiment had been assigned caused a general despondency throughout the ranks. These disheartening circumstances reached a climax in January 1863 when the Army of the Potomac's commander, Maj. Gen. Ambrose Burnside, ordered a winter offensive. Soon after the Yankees dismantled their camps and started their march, chilling rains poured from the sky and drenched the troops. The precipitation transformed the roads into boggy quagmires that made marching nearly impossible. For four days the troops endured the rain, the cold, and the muck before returning to their camps. The weather took its toll on the 147th New York. The elements contributed to new cases of typhoid fever, pneumonia, and dysentery, which resulted in 44 deaths. Ironically, Burnside's "Mud March" eventually strengthened the Oswego outfit. Colonel Warner, four captains, and three lieutenants who were either ill or dissatisfied exercised their option to resign. Major Francis C. Miller became the regiment's lieutenant colonel, and Captain George Harney assumed the rank of major. These officers, as well as the replacements at the captain and lieutenant levels, would prove to be much better leaders.[16]

After the "Mud March," the 147th New York resumed its fatigue duty on the docks. The labor ended in March 1863 when the regiment was assigned to Cutler's command, swelling his brigade to five regiments. The 147th New York benefitted greatly from the change. "Old Graybeard" drilled the outfit constantly and stressed discipline. New Yorker George Harney would later boast that within a month the regiment was transformed "from its indifference and demoralization into one of the best organizations in the army." The Oswego boys saw scant action during the Chancellorsville Campaign in May, losing two killed or mortally wounded. As a result, the 147th entered the summer campaign having never "seen the elephant." The lieutenant colonel, a 33-year-old prewar carpenter named Francis Miller, led the regiment throughout the Gettysburg Campaign. Miller entered the first day's battle with 27 officers and 403 enlisted men.[17]

16 Snyder, *Oswego County, New York in the Civil War,* pp. 56-57; *New York at Gettysburg,* pp. 998-999.

17 Snyder, *Oswego County, New York in the Civil War,* pp. 56-57; *New York at Gettysburg,* pp. 998-999; Dyer, *A Compendium of the War of the Rebellion,* p. 1460; Busey and Martin, *Regimental Strengths at Gettysburg,* p. 24; Fox, *Regimental Losses in the American Civil War,* p. 31; Hassler, *Crisis at the Crossroads,* p. 143; Raus, *A Generation on the March,* p. 83; Cutler's Brigade Field Returns, RG 393, Part 2, NARA.

The final regiment added to Cutler's ranks before Gettysburg was the 14th Brooklyn (also known as the 14th New York State Militia or the 84th New York Volunteers) in June of 1863. It became the longest serving and the most experienced regiment within the brigade. Prior to the war, the outfit operated as a militia regiment in Brooklyn, New York. Six days after the firing on Fort Sumter, the 14th New York State Militia answered President Lincoln's call for 75,000 three-month troops. Governor E. D. Morgan, for political or other reasons, refused to call out the regiment. For nearly a month the militia group remained in Brooklyn drilling daily. Finally, Congressman Moses Odell (who represented the Brooklyn district), together with a committee from New York's Union Defense Committee and Alfred M. Wood, the 14th Brooklyn's colonel, met with President Lincoln in Washington. The lobbying effort worked, and Lincoln used his power as commander-in-chief to call up the militia outfit. The enlistment term, however, was "for the war" instead of three months. On May 18, 1861, the regiment received orders to report to the capital. New York City's Union Defense Committee provided the transportation funds for the excursion.[18]

The Brooklyn soldiers had two sources of extreme pride. One was their uniform. Prior to the war, the militia group had switched to a colorful chasseur outfit. As the regiment recruited to wartime status, the city of Brooklyn gladly furnished its enlistees with the special clothing. The uniform consisted of a blue cap trimmed with red, a short blue jacket lined with two rows of bell buttons, scarlet loose-fitting pants, white gaiters, and a red breast piece or vest also decorated with a column of bell buttons. Its participation at First Bull Run that July wore out the 14th Brooklyn's red trousers. Much to the regiment's disgust, the government supplied the Brooklyn lads with blue pants. The chasseurs raised such a fuss that they received red trousers thereafter.

The regiment's numeral was another source of pride. At the end of 1861, New York's Governor Morgan decided to change the 14th Brooklyn's numeric designation. When the state raised two-year regiments in 1861, it branded one of them as the 14th New York State Volunteers. To prevent confusion, Morgan decided to alter the 14th New York State Militia's number and designation to the 84th New York Volunteers. This act, with the support of the War Department, caused turmoil within the Brooklyn regiment that continued for months. Finally,

---

18 C. Tevis and D. R. Marquis, *The History of the Fighting Fourteenth* (New York, 1911), pp. 15-16; *New York at Gettysburg*, pp. 686-687. The War Department later defined "for the war" as a 3-year term of service.

through the intervention of Maj. Gen. Irvin McDowell, who had mustered in the 14th New York State Militia on May 23, 1861, the War Department relented and allowed the Brooklyn boys to retain their original number. Throughout the war, regimental officers avoided using "84," which is why all correspondence, payrolls, and official reports bear the heading "14th New York State Militia" or "14th Brooklyn."[19]

These were not the only features that made the 14th Brooklyn colorful. After the war, Surgeon Algernon S. Coe of the 147th New York penned a tribute to the regiment that appeared in the *National Tribune*. "Probably no regiment in the war of the rebellion," began Coe, "took a more conspicuous part, engaged in so many battles, and did so much to enliven the spirit of the boys and keep them from falling into despondency on the weary march, in advance or retreat, in bivouac or dreary monotony of Winter quarters." The surgeon continued:

> A true history of the regiment, with a little coloring, would read like a romance, rivaling the fictions of the days of chivalry and of Charles Lever. Not much can be said in respect to the discipline of the regiment, and, indeed, a too rigid discipline would have materially impaired its efficiency, which fact seemed to be well understood by the officers in command. Their enterprise and fertility of resources in supplying themselves and comrades with comforts and necessities in the most difficult situations [and] reckless bravery in battle . . . endeared them to all who knew them; hence they very naturally became pets, and even in a measure privileged, without exciting the jealousy or envy of other regiments."[20]

The 14th Brooklyn saw action at First Bull Run, where it fought well. The former militia group made three determined charges up Henry Hill in an attempt to retake two batteries captured by the Rebels. The chasseurs nearly outflanked Brig. Gen. Jackson's Virginia brigade holding the ground opposite the Federal guns. More than 150 Brooklyn lads fell killed or wounded during the engagement. Its conspicuous gallantry earned the regiment the nicknames "Fighting Fourteenth"

---

19 Tevis and Marquis, *The History of the Fighting Fourteenth*, pp. 15, 237 and 252; "14th Regiment New York State Militia, 1861-1864," *Military Collector and Historian, Vol. 10, No. 3* (Fall 1958), pp. 80-82. The 14th Brooklyn's chasseur uniform looked similar to a Zouave outfit. One difference was that the red chasseur trousers featured loose-fitting legs while Zouave pants sported an exaggerated, baggy fit. Also, Zouaves wore fezzes; chasseurs donned kepis. Throughout the war, the 14th Brooklyn received issues of both blue and red trousers. The regiment saved the red pants for parade and battle.

20 A. S. Coe, "The 14th N. Y. Zouaves," *National Tribune,* August 13, 1885. Charles Lever was an Irish novelist whose protagonists were lively, devil-may-care heroes.

and "Red-Legged Devils." The unit went on to serve with McDowell's command in northern Virginia in early 1862, which later became part of John Pope's Army of Virginia. The "Fighting Fourteenth" saw action on all three days at Second Bull Run, sustaining nearly 150 casualties. The Brooklyn boys also fought at South Mountain, Antietam, Fredericksburg, and Chancellorsville. After the latter campaign, the term of enlistment of the two-year regiments brigaded with the 14th Brooklyn expired, so the "Red-Legged Devils" were assigned to Lysander Cutler's brigade in June.

On July 1, 1863, Col. Edward Brush Fowler led 26 officers and 331 veterans from their Marsh Creek bivouac to Gettysburg.[21]

21 Tevis and Marquis, *The History of the Fighting Fourteenth*, pp. 24-74; *New York at Gettysburg*, p. 687; Dyer, *A Compendium of the War of the Rebellion,* p. 1438; Busey and Martin, *Regimental Strengths at Gettysburg*, p. 24; 14th Brooklyn Battlefield Marker; Hassler, *Crisis at the Crossroads*, p. 143; Cutler's Brigade Field Return, RG 393, Part 2, NARA.

CHAPTER TWO

The March to Gettysburg

Following the May 1863 Chancellorsville Campaign, the Rappahannock River in the Falmouth-Fredericksburg region separated Robert E. Lee's Army of Northern Virginia from Joseph Hooker's Army of the Potomac. As the Union army was recovering from its latest defeat, Confederate President Jefferson Davis approved General Lee's proposal to seize the initiative and move his army north across the Mason-Dixon Line through Maryland and into Pennsylvania.

General Lee based his decision on several factors. The march would draw Union troops out of war-ravaged Virginia and allow farmers to harvest their crops. Lee also sought a decisive Confederate victory on Northern soil that might terminate hostilities. In addition, the general hoped an invasion would stall inevitable Union offensives in other theaters and possibly relieve Federal pressure against the strategic stronghold of Vicksburg, Mississippi, which was under siege by a Union army commanded by Maj. Gen. Ulysses S. Grant.

On Wednesday morning, June 3, Major General Lafayette McLaws's Division of Lt. Gen. James Longstreet's First Corps secretly initiated the movement. By June 5, a large portion of Lee's army had crossed the Rappahannock-Rapidan river line. Hooker realized that same day that portions of Lee's army had abandoned their camps, but he did not know they were beginning a large-scale offensive. By June 10, he forwarded reports to Washington indicating that some of Lee's men had moved around his right flank and north of the Rappahannock River. President Abraham Lincoln refused Hooker's suggestion that he advance upon the enemy capital by declaring, "Lee's army, and not Richmond, is your sure objective point." Rebuffed, Hooker issued orders to pursue the Rebel force.[1]

The 1st Corps, which included Cutler's brigade, received its marching orders on June 12. A man in the 14th Brooklyn grumbled that it marked the fifth time his unit had "struck tents and loaded the wagons before finally marching." Major General John F. Reynolds had been ordered to shift his 1st Corps toward the Orange and Alexandria Railroad to discourage any potential Rebel cavalry expeditions across the Rappahannock from Brandy Station. Burdened with seven days of rations and approximately forty pounds of equipment, Cutler's men departed their camp near White Oak Church around 2:00 a.m.

From June 12 through June 15, temperatures soared into the 90s, which caused severe discomfort to the woolen-clad troops. Water was scarce, and the marching soldiers churned clouds of dust that made breathing difficult. About noon on the first day's march, Brig. Gen. James Wadsworth's 1st Division of Reynolds's corps halted at Hartwood Church. The division formed a hollow square, with one open end. On this open side, a blindfolded deserter named Private John Wood of the 19th Indiana, his arms secured, sat on his coffin. When an officer dropped a handkerchief, the firing squad completed its gruesome task. The "deliberate and ghastly preparation" for Wood's execution, wrote the historian of the 14th Brooklyn, "affected scores of men throughout the division more than any fight which they had ever participated in had been able to do." Many hardened veterans turned their heads rather than watch the depressing affair. After the execution, the 1st Corps resumed its march. Cutler's men eventually halted near Deep Run, Virginia, at 6:00 p.m., having logged 21-24 miles.[2]

1 Edwin Coddington, *The Gettysburg Campaign: A Study in Command* (New York, 1968), pp. 3-10; *War of the Rebellion: A Compilation of the Official Records of the Union and Confederate Armies*, 128 vols. (Washington, D.C., 1880-1910), Series 1, vol. 27, pt. 1, pp. 30, 34, 35, 38, 140, and vol. 27, pt. 2, pp. 293-294, hereafter OR. All citations are to vol. 27, pts. 1, 2, and 3; Henry G. Pearson, *James S. Wadsworth of Geneseo, Brevet Major-General of United States Volunteers* (London, 1913), pp. 194-195.

2 Kenneth Bandy, ed., *The Gettysburg Papers*, 2 vols in 1 (Dayton, 1978), p. 290; *New York at Gettysburg*, pp. 735, 1000; Smith, *76th New York*, p. 225-228; Tevis and Marquis, *The History of the Fighting Fourteenth*, pp. 75-82; OR pt. 1, pp. 141-144; Snyder, *Oswego County, New York in the Civil War*, p. 58; John Kress, "Tales of the War. Thrilling Description of Scenes and Incidents at Gettysburg," *Missouri Republican*, December 4, 1886; Thomson, *7th Indiana*, p. 160. Thomson wrongly claimed Wood robbed a dead Rebel of his uniform at Chancellorsville, traveled to Washington, and surrendered as a deserter. John Vliet letter, June 19, 1863, John Vliet Collection. For details on Wood's execution, see James L. McLean, Jr., "The Execution of John Wood on the March to Gettysburg," *The Gettysburg Magazine* (Issue 45, July, 2011).

Brigadier General James Wadsworth

Author's Collection

Two of Cutler's regiments, the 56th Pennsylvania and 76th New York, took a different route. The Pennsylvania outfit had been detached from Cutler on June 7 and participated in the large cavalry battle at Brandy Station on June 9. The Pennsylvanians rejoined the brigade four days later at Bealeton Station, missing the tiresome June 12 march entirely. The 76th New York was less fortunate. When orders for the June 12 march arrived, the regiment was performing advanced outpost duty, so its line stretched several miles beyond the rest of the brigade. To catch up with its parent unit, the New Yorkers had to first consolidate their ranks before tramping from first light until 9:00 p.m. They covered a remarkable 35 miles during those 19 torturous hours. "No man who endured that march will readily forget it," recorded the regimental historian. "The weather was hot, the roads dusty, and many men, with great difficulty, managed to keep up with the regiment. Yet with blistered feet and aching shoulders they plodded on."[3]

The next day offered no rest for the weary soldiers. In an effort to overtake Lee's army, Hooker demanded another forced march. Cutler's men covered between 15 and 20 miles along Warrenton Road on June 13 in spite of the heat and the dust. Cases of sunstroke were common, and straggling could not be prevented. To make matters worse, roads clogged with other troops and supply trains impeded progress. Often the men stood in readiness to march, "the wearying effects of standing about equaling those of actual marching." The 1st Corps reached Bealeton Station at 6:00 p.m.

The advance continued on Sunday, June 14. Following the line of the Orange and Alexandria Railroad, Cutler's men passed Warrenton Junction before halting at 9:00 p.m. for coffee. After the liquid refreshment, the troops resumed their march, though not without difficulty. Lieutenant Samuel Healy of the 56th Pennsylvania recorded in his diary that the column appeared to get lost and was in confusion throughout this night march. Nonetheless, the troops splashed through Kettle Run in the darkness. Later, they crossed the more formidable Broad Run on an improvised bridge of rails, aided by light from torches and from bonfires built along the banks. The division continued past Bristoe Station. The fatigued soldiers gradually jettisoned extra clothes and any nonessentials to lighten their burden. Straggling continued to be a problem. Soldiers who left the column without permission were subject to arrest on grounds of desertion. Sergeant Bristol of the

---

3 Smith, *76th New York*, pp. 225-228; *Pennsylvania at Gettysburg*, pp. 339-340; Bvt. Brig. Gen. J. W. Hofmann, "The Fifty-Sixth Regiment Pennsylvania Volunteers in the Gettysburg Campaign," *Philadelphia Weekly Press,* January 13, 1886, p. 1, hereafter cited as Hofmann, *PWP;* Coe, "The 14th N. Y. Zouaves."

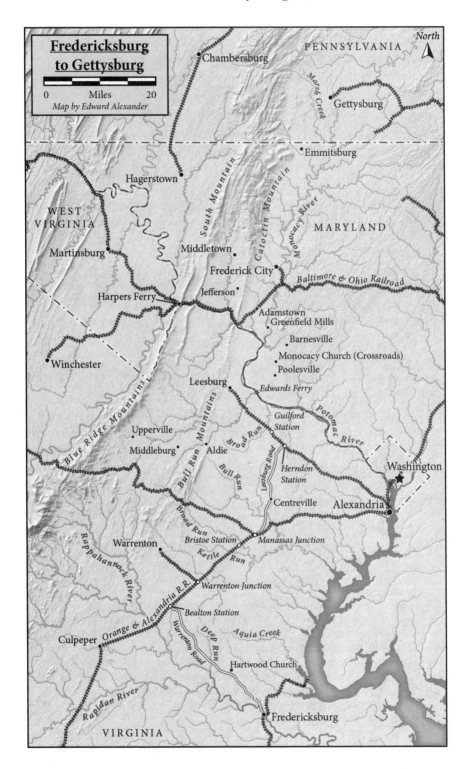

Fredericksburg to Gettysburg

0   Miles   20

Map by Edward Alexander

147th New York had trouble obtaining passes for those unable to continue. "Some doctors," he derisively reflected, "have as much heart as the horse they ride on."

Near daybreak on June 15, the troops were granted a three-hour respite near Manassas Junction. The march resumed at 7:00 a.m. Once again, the heat caused much suffering. The march carried them across the hallowed ground of First Bull Run, where the first major battle of the war had been fought. The men received another brief rest along the banks of the lazy Bull Run tributary. The historian of the 14th Brooklyn described the disturbing landscape:

> Evidences of that tragedy were to be seen at every hand. But the most striking and the most gruesome symbolism of battle was the hundreds of skeletons lying about. The dead of both armies had been buried hastily in shallow graves and the rains had uncovered them. To the newer men in the division the sight of those bare bones sticking out of the earth or partially covered by it, was an eloquent reminder that there is more of the pitiful and terrible than of the grand and spectacular in the game of war.

Some members of the 56th Pennsylvania took advantage of the interlude to bathe in Bull Run to get some relief from the heat. Once it was time to move out, the troops crossed the stream at Blackburn's Ford and continued on until Wadsworth's division finally stopped near Centreville. The men had covered 64 miles in just 78 hours, an incredible marching feat.[4]

For the first time since it left White Oak Church, Reynolds's 1st Corps was granted a one-day breather. While Hooker attempted to pinpoint the whereabouts of Lee's army, stragglers reunited with their units. Water, at last, was plentiful. The Federals drank their full and washed their bodies and clothes. While at Centreville,

---

4 Snyder, *Oswego County, New York in the Civil War*, p. 58; Tevis and Marquis, *The History of the Fighting Fourteenth*, p. 77; Smith, *76th New York*, p. 226; Bandy, ed., *The Gettysburg Papers*, p. 290; *OR* pt. 1, p. 141; Pearson, *James S. Wadsworth of Geneseo*, pp. 195, 196; "The Civil War Journal of Samuel Healy," Vertical File, GNMP Library. Surgeon Coe of the 147th New York recalled an interesting incident during the June 13 march: "General Reynolds, after the column got in motion, rode from the foot to its head. He found the 14th Brooklyn boys scattered along the line until he reached the head of the regiment. He examined each one he met and inquired of him if he was ill, and when told that he was not, asked if he had a permit to fall out. He found each one armed with a permit, duly signed by the Surgeon of the regiment. When he came up to the Colonel in command of the regiment (there were about six of the men with the Colonel) he directed him to put his Surgeon under arrest and have another Surgeon detailed to take care of the regiment. My assistant, accordingly, was so detailed. . . . It seems that the Surgeon was prepared with printed blank permits, which he had signed in blank, and gave them to his Hospital Steward, with instructions to fill in the name of the soldier, as he called for it on the march." Coe, "The 14th N. Y. Zouaves."

Col. William P. Wainwright relinquished command of the 76th New York due to sickness. Major Andrew Jackson Grover, a 33-year-old Mexican War veteran and ordained Methodist minister succeeded him.[5]

Reveille at 3:00 a.m. on June 17 initiated what may have been one of the most difficult marches of the war. The men sweltered in the intense heat, and by the hundreds they fell from sunstroke and exhaustion. Even mounted officers were overcome by the soaring temperatures and thick dust, with some falling from their horses. Abram Smith, the historian of the 76th New York, described the difficult march. "After leaving Centerville, on the seventeenth, the army moved toward Leesburg. The day was extremely hot," recalled Smith after the war. "The march," he continued,

> was made through a dense forest of pine shrubs, which, while furnishing no shade to protect from the scorching rays, prevented any good effects from cool breezes, if any existed, in that sultry climate. The roads were filled with wagons, batteries, cavalry, infantry, artillery, all rushing, halting, sweating. The dust arose in suffocating clouds, was inhaled at every breath, and settling upon faces from which the perspiration flowed at every pore, soon rendered the face of the most intimate friend indistinguishable in the surging crowd.

In his diary, Lieutenant Healy of the 56th Pennsylvania described the severity of the march. He commented about the heat and dust, and he noted that much of the movement was conducted in double-quick time. Healy also heard rumors that five men in the division had suffered from sunstroke and that three had died under the broiling conditions. Other gossip suggested that the heat had "broken" a 14th Brooklyn captain. The scuttlebutt about the chasseur officer was true. Adolphus Gill succumbed to some form of heat exhaustion and had to be evacuated in an ambulance. He missed the rest of the campaign. During the march, men simply dropped out along the way, unable to maintain the demanding pace. John Vliet alleged the severe marching conditions caused his teeth, bones, and head to ache. After a 20-mile tramp, the 1st Corps finally bivouacked at Herndon Station, a depot along the Loudon and Hampshire Railroad near Leesburg, Virginia.[6]

---

5 Snyder, *Oswego County, New York in the Civil War*, p. 58; Tevis and Marquis, *The History of the Fighting Fourteenth*, pp. 77-78; OR pt. 1, pp. 141-142; Bandy, ed., *The Gettysburg Papers*, p. 290; Smith, *76th New York*, pp. 226-227; Raus, *A Generation on the March*, pp. 70-71.

6 Tevis and Marquis, *The History of the Fighting Fourteenth*, pp. 77-78; Smith, *76th New York*, pp. 221-228; OR pt. 1, p. 142; Pearson, *James S. Wadsworth of Geneseo*, pp. 196-197; Healy Journal; John Vliet Letter, June 19, 1863, John Vliet Collection.

During the next several days, the foot-weary soldiers of the 1st Corps enjoyed a period of relative rest. They spent June 18 at Herndon Station. The heat remained oppressive, but an afternoon shower provided temporary relief. The next day the corps marched just four to six miles to Guilford Station, where it bivouacked until June 25. Rain continued on June 19, followed by a terrific two-day thunderstorm. On June 20, a cavalry brawl broke out at nearby Aldie. The 76th New York received orders to aid the Federal horsemen, but the instructions were soon countermanded. The clash was a red flag that danger was ever-present, and the 14th Brooklyn performed picket duty two miles from camp.

Local partisans proved to be another source of irritation. One man of Cutler's brigade suggested the guerrillas were "thick as snails." Another wrote in a letter home, "This forest region is full of guerrillas, who shoot at our men when they catch one of them out alone. Several have been shot by them, but none . . . seriously injured." Despite this threat, the lure of foraging kept many men occupied during the encampment.

Once the weather cleared, inspections, dress parades, company drills, and battalion drills filled the days. Despite these time-consuming activities, men in the 56th Pennsylvania found time on June 24 to participate in a game of base ball.[7]

The march resumed on June 25. The 1st Corps traveled eight miles to Edward's Ferry, where it crossed the Potomac River on long pontoon bridges. The men shouted with joy upon entering Maryland. "What joy it gives the soldier to walk again on loyal soil. We are now among friends," exalted one soldier in a letter home to his parents. Inspired to be once again on Union turf, the troops continued their march. A steady rain began to fall soon after they crossed the Potomac, continuing throughout the day. The route taken was "by way of Poolesville, Monocacy Crossroads, to Barnesville." After a hike of 18 to 20 miles, Cutler's brigade was ordered to make camp in a muddy cornfield. In some areas, puddles of water stood three to six inches deep between the corn rows. Rather than spend a miserable night in the muck, most of the troops wandered to a patch of woods on a knoll across the road. To make his men more comfortable, General Wadsworth purchased a stack of straw for them to use as a buffer against the wet ground.

At 9:00 a.m. the next day, the men rolled their wet blankets and continued their pursuit of Lee's Army of Northern Virginia. Rain persisted. The dirt roads, already

---

7 Smith, *76th New York*, pp. 228-229; Tevis and Marquis, *The History of the Fighting Fourteenth*, p. 78; Pearson, *James S. Wadsworth of Geneseo*, p. 199; Healy Journal; Thomson, *7th Indiana*, pp. 159-160. During the Civil War, the national pastime was not yet a compound word and was spelled "base ball."

churned into a muddy pulp, worsened as hoofs, feet, and wheels penetrated, agitated, and deepened the mire. Despite the elements, patriotic citizens from little villages like Adamstown turned out to cheer the Federal troops. They often offered food and drink to the weary travelers, which boosted the spirits of the exhausted men. After another march of 15 or 16 miles, the 1st Corps went into camp at Jefferson, Maryland.[8]

On Saturday, June 27, Lysander Cutler's brigade left Jefferson about 6:00 a.m. Second Lieutenant Henry H. Lyman jotted in his diary that the column "passed through very nice country." When the brigade approached Middletown, Col. Edward Fowler of the 14th Brooklyn "ordered the remains of the drum corps up to the front of the regiment and the men, tired though they were from forced marches, all braced up and entered the place with flags flying and stepping out to the music with vim and spirit." The day's eight-mile jaunt left the brigade within a mile and a half of the South Mountain battlefield. Some of the men in the 147th New York consumed contaminated water and became ill that afternoon and evening.[9]

The kindness and enthusiasm of patriotic citizens made the march through Maryland much more palatable. John Vliet commented that civilians lining the route often served water to the soldiers from tubs and pails. Fresh baked bread, pies, and biscuits were either given to the soldiers or sold at a "very low price." Despite these gestures, Union soldiers scoured the Maryland countryside for additional food. Vliet recalled that hungry Federals "appropriated" livestock, especially pigs, sheep and chickens. Guards were eventually posted to control unauthorized foraging.[10]

Cutler's men resumed their journey between 2:30 p.m. and 3:00 p.m. on June 28. Many soldiers took time during the morning respite to scribble letters to loved ones. As spectators came out to cheer the north-bound troops, many soldiers left the ranks to ask the well-wishers to mail their hastily written notes. The march was a short one of five to eight miles, with the men stopping at Frederick. The only

8 Smith, *76th New York*, p. 229; Tevis and Marquis, *The History of the Fighting Fourteenth*, p. 78; Pearson, *James S. Wadsworth of Geneseo*, p. 199; Uberto A. Burnham Letter to his Parents, June 25, 1863, Uberto A. Burnham Papers, New York State Library.

9 Tevis and Marquis, *The History of the Fighting Fourteenth*, pp. 78-80; Smith, *76th New York*, p. 229; excerpt from Henry Lyman Diary, Vertical File, Gettysburg National Military Park Library

10 John Vliet Letter, July 2, 1863, John Vliet Collection.

difficult stretch occurred when the troops crossed the Catoctin Mountain range. It was another wet evening, but General Wadsworth once again came to the rescue.[11]

Henry Lyman of the 147th New York explained, "Existing general orders were strict that the troops should not forage, or burn the fences of civilians. It looked like having to lie down all night in wet clover, in damp clothing, and without coffee." Lyman continued:

> General Wadsworth could not and would not stand that. Sending for the old farmer,he asked how much was the value of the rails around that field. The farmer said he didn't want to sell them at any price, and pleaded the general orders for protection. General Wadsworth's reply was: 'I am a farmer myself; your fence won't be needed to protect the clover which is already flat and ruined; my men are tired, wet and hungry and must have coffee; your rails will be burned by either Union or Rebel soldiers in the next ten days; they're worth about $250; here it is; take it or take your chances.' The farmer took the money which the general paid from his own pocket, and orders were given to use the rails for fire. In less than three minutes every rail had left the fence, and in ten minutes a thousand cheerful fires were blazing and giving warmth and comfort to 8,000 or 10,000 wet and weary men, whose prolonged cheers for General Wadsworth fairly rent the heavens.[12]

Another incident demonstrated Wadsworth's concern for his troops and his "persuasive powers" with civilians. Long difficult marches had destroyed the soldiers' shoes. Wadsworth took measures to alleviate this problem by confiscating every pair of boots and shoes that could be found along the road. "They were frequently taken from the feet of citizens and transferred immediately to the pedal extremities of bare-footed soldiers," recalled John Kress, who continued his reminiscence:

> The general and his staff officers rode up to a fine stone flour mill, the proprietor of which sat on the steps looking at the troops marching past. The miller was a middle-aged man of well-to-do appearance, fairly well dressed in flour-dusted gray clothing. General

---

11 Wadsworth was always thinking of the welfare of his troops. Prior to the Chancellorsville Campaign, General Hooker ordered each soldier to carry 10 days' rations, 100 cartridges, extra shoes, an overcoat, a blanket, a tent, a canteen, and a musket—in all about 95 pounds. Wadsworth doubted the practicality of hauling such a load, so he had his orderly equip him with the aforementioned gear. The general paced his tent for an hour with this burden, determined the folly of the order, and directed his men to pack in a more reasonable manner. Smith, *76th New York*, p. 255; Tevis and Marquis, *The History of the Fighting Fourteenth*, p. 80; Lyman Diary.

12 *New York at Gettysburg*, pp. 1000-1001. Wadsworth was born to affluent landowning parents in western New York State and had inherited significant wealth.

Wadsworth bade him 'good morning,' and as he did so, noticed that the miller wore an excellent pair of shoes. The general halted, and not having time to make examinations, asked him if he had any boots or shoes. The miller said he had none. 'You have a fine pair of shoes on your feet, sir, I will take them, if you please, for one of my bare-footed soldiers.' 'No, sir; you shall not take the shoes off my feet; I am a free American citizen, the owner of this mill and of much property hereabouts. I will not submit to such an outrage.' 'I must have the shoes and cannot waste time parlaying with you.' Turning to an aid, the general directed him to have two or three of the orderlies dismount and remove the man's shoes. The miller concluded that discretion was the better part of valor and gave up his shoes.[13]

Before the 1st Corps troops moved out on June 28, a momentous decision had been made in Washington and carried out in Frederick. Army commander Joseph Hooker, displeased with what he considered to be undue interference from General-in-Chief Henry Halleck and President Lincoln, offered to relinquish his command. Lincoln happily obliged. Early that morning, Col. James A. Hardie, a member of Halleck's staff, delivered an order from the president directing the commander of the 5th Corps, Maj. Gen. George Gordon Meade, to assume command of the Army of the Potomac. A surprised Meade spent the day assessing the position and condition of his army. Although Meade issued a statement concerning the change in command, it is hard to determine when the troops realized the succession had occurred. In fact, rumors surfaced that Maj. Gen. George B. McClellan had been placed in charge of the army. By June 30, news of the command switch had filtered through to the ranks of the army.[14]

By the evening of June 28, Meade was aware the bulk of Lee's army had penetrated Pennsylvania north of Hagerstown and that part of it had passed through Gettysburg marching toward York. In an effort to catch the Rebels, Meade ordered his army to advance the next day toward the Pennsylvania border north of Frederick. The 1st Corps troops rose at 3:00 a.m. on the 29th to begin their hike. Rain once again made marching miserable. Thirsty Union troops dried wells along

---

13 Kress, "Tales of War."

14 Coddington, *The Gettysburg Campaign*, p. 209; OR pt. 1, p. 114; J. H. Stine, *History of the Army of the Potomac* (Philadelphia, 1892), p. 447; Harwell, Richard, ed., *Two Views of Gettysburg* (Chicago, 1964), pp. 67-68; *Retreat from Gettysburg*, p. 301. Hooker's lack of popularity is illustrated by the following newspaper excerpt: "The 14th boys learned on the march that Hooker had been displaced, and General Meade substituted for him. Of the new commander the 14th knew but little, but they considered almost any change an improvement. There were rumors that McClellan was in command. Nine-tenths of the Regiment heard this news with great gratification." "The Story of a Member of the 14th Captured at Gettysburg," *The Brooklyn Daily Eagle,* July 7, 1863.

the route. Fortunately, patriotic women continued to line the way, distributing loaves of bread, ripe cherries, and dippers full of milk or water. A few profiteers sold foodstuffs to the men at exorbitant prices. The Federals had little time for rest and no dinner during the 26-mile march. The exhausted troops camped in wet fields near Emmitsburg between 9:00 p.m. and 11:00 p.m.[15]

The activities on the last day of June were not as tiresome. The men marched five miles to Marsh Creek, leaving the vanguard of the Union 1st Corps about four miles shy of Gettysburg. Cutler's brigade rested in a cultivated field south of the creek while the Iron Brigade bivouacked north of the stream. When the 56th Pennsylvania crossed the Maryland-Pennsylvania border, "they sent up a cheer, showing their appreciation of 'Home, sweet, sweet home.'" Since June 30 was the last day of the fiscal year, officers spent the afternoon filling out payrolls and muster rolls, as well as commissary, ordnance, and other regimental returns. While the officers were thus engaged, the men in the ranks bathed in a nearby mill dam, rested, or foraged. Chickens, in particular, were fair game. Practically everyone in the 14th Brooklyn and some fellows in the 147th New York dined on fowl that evening. The only interruption occurred prior to nightfall when the brigade was ordered to form a line to resist a potential attack. The threat failed to materialize, and the troops returned to their camps.[16]

The evening of June 30, few, if any, of Cutler's men had any inclination that they were about to play a pivotal role in one of the crucial battles of the war. They probably did not even know that the destination of their next day's march was Gettysburg.

15 Coddington, *The Gettysburg Campaign*, pp. 224, 225, 228-229; Tevis and Marquis, *The History of the Fighting Fourteenth*, p. 80; Smith, *76th New York*, p. 232; Lyman Diary.

16 Hofmann, *PWP*, p. 1; Bandy, ed., *The Gettysburg Papers*, p. 367; *Pennsylvania at Gettysburg*, p. 315; Tevis and Marquis, *The History of the Fighting Fourteenth*, pp. 80-81; Lyman Diary; Smith, *76th New York*, p. 233; J. Wm. Hofmann, *Remarks on the Battle of Gettysburg* (Philadelphia, 1880), p. 3; According to Sgt. C. W. Cook of the 76th New York, because it was late in the day and because one company was on picket, his regiment's certificates of muster were not signed by Major Grover. C. W. Cook, "A Day at Gettysburg," *National Tribune*, April 7, 1898.

CHAPTER THREE

The Union Cavalry
and John Reynolds

When General Robert E. Lee realized how rapidly George Gordon Meade's Army of the Potomac had advanced, he decided to concentrate his army at Cashtown, Pennsylvania.

While Maj. Gen. Henry Heth, a division commander in Ambrose Powell Hill's 3rd Corps, waited for the remainder of the Confederates to arrive there, he received permission from Hill to send Brig. Gen. James Johnston Pettigrew's North Carolina brigade seven or eight miles east to the town of Gettysburg. Heth instructed Pettigrew to search for supplies (especially shoes) and to return the same day.

On the morning of June 30, Pettigrew's men tramped toward Gettysburg along Cashtown (Chambersburg) Pike. They reached a ridge west of and overlooking the crossroads town around 10:00 a.m. The prominent feature on the long north-south ridge was the Lutheran Theological Seminary. From the elevation, Pettigrew and other officers carefully examined the village through their field glasses. Interviews with local citizens and personal observation convinced the wary brigadier general of the proximity of Union soldiers.

About an hour after stopping on Seminary Ridge, Pettigrew's Confederates spotted Federal cavalry approaching Gettysburg from the south via Emmitsburg Road. Rather than risk an engagement with a Yankee detachment of unknown size and composition, Pettigrew wisely withdrew his men without obtaining the desired

Major General Henry Heth

Courtesy of Civil War Library and Museum, Philadelphia, PA

supplies. After retracing its morning route, the large Tar Heel brigade encamped just west of Marsh Creek.[1]

1 Coddington, *The Gettysburg Campaign*, pp. 234-236,263-264; James L. McLean, Jr., "The First Union Shot at Gettysburg," *Lincoln Herald*, Vol. 82, No. 1 (Spring 1980), p. 319; Tucker, *High Tide at Gettysburg*, p. 98. Cashtown Pike is the same thoroughfare as Chambersburg Road or Chambersburg Pike.

The Union troopers entering Gettysburg belonged to Brig. Gen. John Buford's cavalry division, spearheaded by the 8th Illinois. Loyal citizens lined the streets to welcome the Union horsemen with ovations, food and drink, and the patriotic waving of handkerchiefs and flags. The exuberant display of affection by Gettysburg's residents touched the troopers. In 1913, a veteran of the 8th Illinois related that he still cherished a purple ribbon given to him by a young girl that afternoon. According to another member of the 8th Illinois, "When our cavalry advance reached the city, and passed on through the streets, men, women, and children crowded the sidewalks and vied with each other in demonstrations of joyous welcome." He continued:

> Hands were reached up eagerly to clasp the hands of our bronzed and dusty troopers; cake, beer, wine and milk were passed up to the moving column as we marched slowly along the crowded streets; doors, windows, and balconies were filled with ladies waving handkerchiefs. . . Altogether it was one of the most touching, spontaneous, and heartfelt demonstrations my eyes ever witnessed. . . . To receive such a reception . . . was an inspiration.[2]

Meade, as his June 30 instructions to Maj. Gen. John Reynolds indicated, was anxious for Federal cavalry to make contact with the enemy. Buford fulfilled Meade's wish when he filed his troopers west out of Gettysburg along Chambersburg Pike in the direction of Pettigrew's retreat. Buford quickly notified Reynolds of the presence of the enemy. The 1st Corps commander, in turn, relayed the information to Meade. Using this and other reconnaissance reports, the Union army commander issued orders to his various corps during the early morning hours of July 1 for a general advance that day toward Gettysburg. Reynolds's 1st Corps was the first infantry scheduled to arrive.[3]

Meanwhile, Buford was busy at Gettysburg. He realized the ground south and west of the town offered excellent opportunities for defensive operations. As a result, he deployed his men to the west to counter any Rebel advance from that

2 Colonel William Gamble to W. S. Church, March 10, 1864, Vertical File, GNMP; Newel Cheney, *History of the Ninth Regiment New York Volunteer Cavalry* (Jamestown, 1901), p. 102; Morgan Hughes, "People of Gettysburg," *National Tribune*, March 24, 1892; Frank Willett, "Another Gettysburg," *National Tribune*, December 1, 1892; Handwritten transcript of an article in the July 1, 1913, *New York Times*, Vertical File (8th Illinois Cavalry), GNMP.

3 Tucker, *High Tide at Gettysburg*, pp. 91, 101-102; Coddington, *The Gettysburg Campaign*, p. 237; *OR* pt. 3, pp. 414-416, 458-459.

Brigadier General John Buford

Courtesy of Civil War Library and Museum, Philadelphia, PA

direction. In order to fully understand Buford's deployment and what happened at the beginning of the battle, a survey of the terrain is necessary.

Chambersburg Pike was one of ten roads emanating from Gettysburg. The pike connected Gettysburg with Cashtown and Chambersburg, both of which lay to the northwest. Just north of the road, an unfinished railroad cut essentially paralleled the pike. Near the town, the railroad cut was about 250 feet from the road. The distance between the road and unfinished railroad gradually increased to

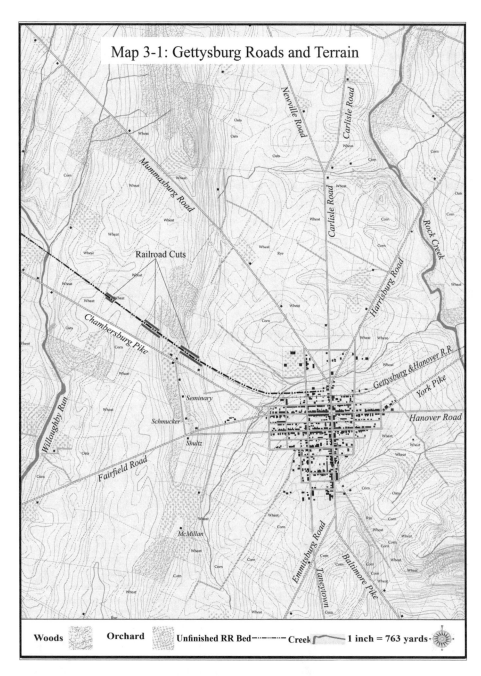

Map 3-1: Gettysburg Roads and Terrain

Newville Road

Carlisle Road

Mummasburg Road

Carlisle Road

Rock Creek

Railroad Cuts

Harrisburg Road

Chambersburg Pike

Gettysburg & Hanover R.R.

York Pike

Seminary

Hanover Road

Willoughby Run

Schmucker

Shultz

Fairfield Road

McMillan

Emmitsburg Road

Taneytown

Baltimore Pike

Woods   **Orchard**   **Unfinished RR Bed** ‒‒‒‒ **Creek**   **1 inch = 763 yards**

about 400-550 feet as one traveled west toward Willoughby Run, a fordable stream with a north-south orientation. Between Willoughby Run and Gettysburg, a distance slightly over one mile, three ridges roughly paralleled the stream. The ridge closest to town, about 2,400 feet from its outskirts, was named after the Lutheran

Theological Seminary located upon it. Partially wooded Seminary Ridge rose 50 feet above the town's center. The second, or middle, ridge was about 1,300 feet west of, and slightly lower than, Seminary Ridge. The third ridge, about 700-800 feet farther west, was roughly the same height as the middle ridge. Because of its gentle slopes, an individual standing halfway down the eastern side of the ridge could easily see the head and shoulders of a person standing on the western decline.

Along the top and the eastern slope of the third ridge, south of Chambersburg Pike, stood a house, barn, and several outbuildings owned by Edward McPherson. The western slope of this ridge dropped down to Willoughby Run. A grove of trees popularly known as McPherson's Woods stood just south of the McPherson buildings and extended from the middle ridge west to Willoughby Run. Together, the second and third elevations have been commonly referred to as "McPherson Ridge."

The final terrain features of importance were the three railroad cuts. The unfinished railroad grade north of the pike was cut into the earth, and thus sat below ground level. This depressed railroad bed could be crossed, with minor difficulty, at almost any spot except where the ridges intersected the grade. At those three places, the height of the banks of the cut prevented individuals from crossing. Anyone caught in the railroad bed at those locations would be hard-pressed to climb out.[4]

Buford's cavalry force consisted of two brigades and a battery of artillery. Colonel William Gamble commanded the 1st Brigade, which included the 8th New York, the 8th Illinois, three squadrons of the 3rd Indiana, and two squadrons of the

---

4 Hassler, *Crisis at the Crossroads*, pp. 17, 21-23; McLean, "The First Union Shot at Gettysburg," p. 319; Coddington, *The Gettysburg Campaign*, pp. 265-266; J. W. Hofmann, "Gettysburg Again," *The National Tribune,* June 5, 1884; Capt. Calvin D. Cowles, comp., *Atlas to Accompany the Official Records of the Union and Confederate Armies* (New York, 1983), Plate 95. Hereafter cited as *Official Military Atlas.* Ascertaining exact distances between the ridges is difficult because the ridges are not exactly parallel. Most of my measurements were taken along the line of Cashtown (Chambersburg) Pike. I used my odometer, a plate from the *Official Military Atlas*, and a blueprint of a scale map prepared by my late friend Sam Hubbard. I also consulted two letters found in the Gettysburg Vertical Files, one from Frederick Tilberg to Alan Nolan, March 3, 1960, and the other from Tilberg to Warren Hassler, February 23, 1951. Seminary Ridge and the middle ridge are closest along the pike. At the time of the battle, McPherson rented his 119-acre farm to the John Slentz family. Kathleen George, "Edward McPherson Farm: Historical Study," typescript in GNMP Library. When the first edition of this book was published in 1987, scholars commonly identified the grove south of the McPherson buildings as McPherson's Woods. Current scholarship has corrected the name of the patch of timber to Herbst's Woods. Any mention of McPherson's Woods in the text or on the maps refers to Herbst's Woods.

Colonels William Gamble (left)
and Thomas Devin (below)

*Courtesy of the
Library of Congress*

12th Illinois. Colonel Thomas C. Devin's 2nd Brigade contained the 6th and 9th New York, the 17th Pennsylvania, and one squadron of the 3rd West Virginia. Lieutenant John H. Calef's Battery A, 2nd US Artillery, which contained six 3-inch rifles, provided artillery support. Gamble's troopers and Calef's cannoneers camped just west of the Lutheran Seminary. Devin's men bivouacked to the north and northwest of the unfinished railroad.

Scouting parties and picket outposts deployed along the numerous roads emanating from Gettysburg. Colonel Gamble dispatched a portion of the 8th New York through McPherson's Woods to the southwest with orders to picket along Fairfield Road. He also sent a squadron of the 8th Illinois under Capt. Daniel W. Buck about two miles west along Chambersburg Pike. Buck divided his men into seven outpost groups and deployed them east of Marsh Creek: three south of the pike, one outfit on the road itself, and two groups north of the thoroughfare. Captain Buck stationed his final outpost, under Lt. Marcellus Jones, farther west. It occupied a low ridge next to a blacksmith shop, near the bridge spanning Marsh Creek on Chambersburg Pike. Finally, videttes from the 12th Illinois and the 3rd Indiana picketed the area north of Buck's line.

Colonel Devin also sent out pickets. Devin's outpost line extended Gamble's front and concentrated on guarding the Carlisle, Harrisburg, and York approaches into Gettysburg. Companies A and H of the 9th New York patrolled Harrisburg

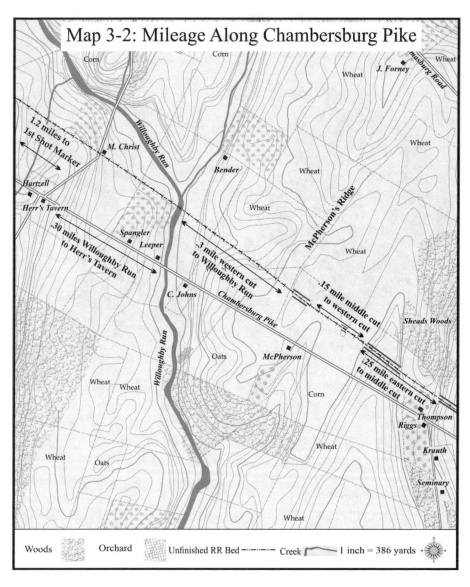

Map 3-2: Mileage Along Chambersburg Pike

and Hunterstown roads while Companies C and M camped on the grounds of the Pennsylvania (now Gettysburg) College at the northern edge of town. Three companies of the 17th Pennsylvania Cavalry also served as outposts. Companies E, F, and M under Maj. J. Q. Anderson covered Newville and Carlisle roads. Apparently, a portion of the 6th New York Cavalry also served as pickets. Buffered

Brigadier General J. Johnston Pettigrew

Generals in Gray

by this wide arc of mobile Yankee outposts, General Buford was prepared to hold his ground until General Reynolds arrived with his 1st Corps infantry the following morning.[5]

The Confederates also had plans. When General Pettigrew returned from his June 30 expedition, he informed General Heth, his division commander, about the arrival of Yankee cavalry in Gettysburg. Ambrose Powell Hill, Heth's corps commander, arrived while Pettigrew was describing the morning's events. Neither Hill nor Heth believed the detachment Pettigrew observed was part of the Army of the Potomac. As a result, Heth secured permission from General Hill to march his division the next day into Gettysburg to obtain the supplies Pettigrew had failed to procure. Hill further instructed Heth to determine the size and composition of the enemy force that had moved into Gettysburg. On the slight chance that he encountered enemy infantry, Hill ordered Heth not to force an engagement. A number of the officers in Pettigrew's command concurred with the conclusions reached by Hill and Heth. On the

---

5 McLean, "The First Union Shot at Gettysburg," pp. 319-321; Bandy, ed., *The Gettysburg Papers*, p. 171; Luther Minnigh, *Gettysburg: "What They Did Here"* (Gettysburg, 1924), p. 15; OR pt. 1, pp. 924, 938, 1030; Coddington, *The Gettysburg Campaign*, p. 266; *New York at Gettysburg*, pp. 1138, 1145; Cheney, *History of the Ninth Regiment New York Volunteer Cavalry*, p. 103; H. P. Moyer, *History of the 17th Regiment Pennsylvania Volunteer Cavalry* (Lebanon, 1911), p. 60; Augustus Clark, "The 6th New York Cavalry, Its Movement and Service at the Battle of Gettysburg," *United Service Magazine*, Vol. 16, 1896, p. 413; Willett, "Another Gettysburg;" John Beveridge, "First Shot at Gettysburg," *National Tribune*, July 31, 1892. Those troopers assigned to picket duty were denied the attention of the Gettysburg citizens. According to Thomas Day of the 3rd Indiana Cavalry, civilians continued to bring food to Buford's encamped soldiers. Many cavalrymen were invited into town for supper and, subsequently, breakfast. Thomas G. Day, "Opening the Battle. A Cavalryman's Recollections of the First Day's Fight at Gettysburg," *National Tribune*, July 30, 1903. Day also mentioned that the 8th Illinois and 3rd Indiana wore black slouch hats, "the same as the Iron Brigade."

Brigadier General James J. Archer

Courtesy of the
Library of Congress

morning of July 1, as Heth's infantry division began moving east toward town, some of Pettigrew's troops mentioned that they would find only Pennsylvania militia.[6]

Heth's command, accompanied by Maj. William J. Pegram's battalion of artillery, left its Cashtown encampment at 5:00 a.m. There was an air of indifference, perhaps even of unpreparedness, as the Confederates tramped along Chambersburg Pike. In fact, neither a cavalry escort nor infantry skirmishers preceded the head of the column. Heth later admitted that he erred by placing his batteries near the front of his advance. Another mistake Heth made was selecting Brig. Gen. James Jay Archer's Brigade, the smallest in the division, to spearhead the march.

James Archer was born in Maryland, graduated from Princeton, and was breveted for bravery at Chapultepec during the Mexican War. From 1855-1861, the Marylander served as a captain in the Regular Army. His brigade saw its first action during the Civil War on the Virginia Peninsula at the Battle of Fair Oaks on May 31, 1862. After its combat baptism, it had participated in every one of the Army of Northern Virginia's campaigns. Just two months before Gettysburg, Archer's men achieved new laurels at Chancellorsville by seizing the important Hazel Grove position. Constant campaigning during the first two years of the war, however, had depleted Archer's command. It marched toward Gettysburg comprised of the 13th Alabama (308 men), 5th Alabama Battalion (135 men), 1st Tennessee Provisional

---

6 Bandy, ed., *The Gettysburg Papers*, pp. 172, 173, 432; Stine, *History of the Army of the Potomac*, pp. 450-451; Coddington, *The Gettysburg Campaign*, pp. 264-265; Tucker, *High Tide at Gettysburg*, pp. 100-101; William Love, "Mississippi at Gettysburg," *Publications of the Mississippi Historical Society* (1906), p. 29; Colonel A. H. Belo, "The Battle of Gettysburg," *Confederate Veteran*, 40 Vols. (1900), Vol. 8, p. 165; Alexander K. McClure, ed., *The Annals of the War* (Philadelphia, 1879), p. 307; *OR* pt. 2, p. 637.

Brigadier General Joseph R. Davis

*Courtesy of Civil War Library and Museum,
Philadelphia, PA*

Army (243 men), 7th Tennessee (249 men), and 14th Tennessee (220 men). It remained a veteran and usually dependable outfit but only numbered about 1,200 men.[7]

Heth next blundered by placing Brig. Gen. Joseph Davis's inexperienced brigade behind Archer's battle-weakened command. That unit had only joined the Army of Northern Virginia on June 1, 1863, just prior to the invasion. Although the 2nd and 11th Mississippi regiments could claim veteran status, the 42nd Mississippi and the 55th North Carolina had not yet seen any appreciable action. The 55th North Carolina had served in eastern North Carolina and on guard duty in the vicinity of Petersburg, Virginia. In the spring of 1863, the North Carolina regiment participated in Lt. Gen. James Longstreet's Suffolk Campaign without seeing combat. When the well-clothed Tar Heel regiment joined Lee's army, it featured a splendid 17-piece regimental band. Two factors favored the unit. First, their colonel, John Kerr Connally, had stressed drilling and discipline during the time spent in North Carolina and Petersburg. Second, it was reported that not a man in the regiment was older than 30; such youth undoubtedly roused their enthusiasm to "see the elephant."[8]

---

7 Bandy, ed., *The Gettysburg Papers*, p. 432; Young, *The Battle of Gettysburg*, pp. 166, 442; Tucker, *High Tide at Gettysburg*, p. 101; Douglas S. Freeman, *Lee's Lieutenants: A Study in Command*, *Vol. 3* (New York, 1944), p. 78; Coddington, *The Gettysburg Campaign*, p. 266; Shelby Foote, *The Civil War: Fredericksburg to the Meridian* (New York, 1963), p. 467; *O. R.*, *Part 2*, pp. 646- 647; John B. Lindsley, ed., *The Military Annals of Tennessee, Confederate* (Nashville, 1886), pp. 227-246, 323-326; Tennessee Troops, Vertical File 7-CS 11, GNMP; Clifford Dowdey, *Death of a Nation* (New York, 1958), p. 93; T. Benton Kelley, "Gettysburg. An Account of Who Opened the Battle by One Who was There," *National Tribune,* December 31, 1891.

8 North Carolina Troops: Personal Accounts, Gettysburg Vertical File 7-CS 9b, GNMP ("Fifty-Fifth North Carolina: History of Regiment and Officers-Positions Occupied at Gettysburg," *Galveston Daily News,* June 21, 1896, p. 9); Love, "Mississippi at Gettysburg," p. 31;

General Davis, who led the brigade, was Confederate President Jefferson Davis's nephew. Devoid of any military training, Joe Davis was about to command troops in battle for the first time on this sultry July morning. His credentials for command were highly suspect. In a letter to his wife, Brig. Gen. Thomas R. R. Cobb characterized the president's nephew as pleasant, but lazy. Historian Douglas Southall Freeman described him as "inexperienced, pleasant, and unpretending." The brigadier received his education in Nashville and at Miami University in Oxford, Ohio, studied law, and served in the Mississippi senate. When the war erupted, he entered the service as a captain, rose to the rank of lieutenant colonel, and became colonel of the 10th Mississippi. He left that position to serve on his uncle's staff in Richmond. Davis's nomination to brigadier caused some controversy in the Confederate Senate when several politicians challenged the promotion on the grounds of nepotism. His commission was denied once before finally being confirmed, and he was given command of a brigade under Heth.

Joe Davis's weaknesses were exacerbated by the fact that most of his staff and many of his regimental field officers lacked combat experience. On the morning of July 1, he led the 55th North Carolina (640 men under Col. John Connally), the 2nd Mississippi (492 men under Col. John Marshall Stone) and the 42nd Mississippi (575 men under Col. Hugh Reid Miller) along Chambersburg Pike toward Gettysburg. Unfortunately for Davis, his fourth regiment, the experienced 11th Mississippi, was on detached provost guard duty and not with the brigade.[9]

*   *   *

The Confederate column advanced leisurely along Chambersburg Pike without incident until it approached the Marsh Creek Bridge about 7:00 a.m. While the massive Rebel foraging column sauntered toward Gettysburg, activity among

---

Tucker, *High Tide at Gettysburg*, pp. 113-114; Walter Clark, ed., *Histories of the Several Regiments and Battalions from North Carolina in the Great War, 1861-1865*, 5 Vols. (Raleigh, 1901), Vol. 3, pp. 290-297, hereafter cited as Clark, ed., *North Carolina Regiments*; Dowdey, *Death of a Nation*, p. 93.

9 Freeman, *Lee's Lieutenants*, Vol. 3, p. 78; Dowdey, *Death of a Nation*, p. 87; Ezra Warner, *Generals in Gray: Lives of the Confederate Commanders* (New Orleans, 1959), pp. 68-69; Young, *The Battle of Gettysburg*, p. 442; Busey and Martin, *Regimental Strengths at Gettysburg*, p. 175; Gary Gallagher, ed., *The First Day at Gettysburg* (Kent, 1992), pp. 99-102; Robert K. Krick File on Joseph R. Davis. For detailed information on Davis's Brigade, see the two-part article by Terrence J. Winshel, "Heavy Was Their Loss…," *The Gettysburg Magazine*, Issue No. 2 (1990), pp. 5-14, and *The Gettysburg Magazine, Issue No. 3* (1990), pp. 77-85.

the Union videttes heightened. The predawn mist had dissipated by the time Pvts. Thomas B. Kelley and James O. Hale of Company E, 8th Illinois Cavalry, reported for duty at 6:00 a.m. near the blacksmith shop overlooking Marsh Creek. From their advanced and elevated perch near the bridge, they caught a glimpse of the fog of dust rising above Heth's column. Private Kelley judged the dirt cloud to be two and one-half miles away. For the next 30 to 45 minutes, Kelley and Hale watched the portending spire of grime float toward them. Eventually, they discerned a Rebel flag and a few moments later the head of the infantry column led by a soldier mounted on a white or light gray horse. Kelley hurriedly surveyed the picket line but could not find his immediate superior, Sgt. Levis S. Shafer, so he dashed back to the rear to report the Confederate advance.

Moments before Kelley's arrival, Lt. Marcellus Jones had returned to the reserve after visiting his picket lines. On his way back to his post, Jones had purchased some bread and butter for his breakfast and oats for his horse. Before Jones could enjoy his meager meal, Kelley arrived with news of the Confederate approach. Another vidette galloped up to the reserve with similar tidings sent from Sergeant Shafer. Tearing a page from his memoranda book, Jones scribbled a note to Maj. John Beveridge to warn him about the approaching Confederates. As Jones mounted his horse, he ordered the rest of the reserve to follow. Then he raced to where Kelley had sighted the enemy. By now, Sergeant Shafer had also arrived. Jones dismounted, borrowed Shafer's carbine, rested the gun in the fork of a rail fence, and fired the first shot at Gettysburg.[10]

The initial contact forced the Confederates to change their deployment. General Archer detached the 5th Alabama Battalion and two companies of the 13th Alabama to serve as skirmishers while the remainder of his brigade formed a line of battle south of the pike. General Davis arranged his three regiments north of the road. Cannoneers from Capt. Edward Marye's Fredericksburg Artillery, part of Pegram's Battalion, unlimbered a single gun next to a house along the road. A moment later, Captain Marye ordered his men to fire "shrapnel shell" at the

---

10 H. O. Dodge, "Opening the Battle. Lieutenant Jones the 8th Illinois Cavalryman Fired the First Shot at Gettysburg," *National Tribune*, September 24, 1891; McLean, "The First Union Shot at Gettysburg," pp. 320- 321; OR pt. 2, pp. 646-647; Bandy, ed., *The Gettysburg Papers*, p. 173; Lindsley, *The Military Annals of Tennessee*, pp. 245-246; "Heth's Division at Gettysburg," *The Southern Bivouac*, Vol. 3 (1885), p. 385; 8th Illinois Cavalry, Gettysburg Vertical File 6-I8, GNMP; Kelley, "Gettysburg;" O. H. Ditzler, "The First Gun at Gettysburg," *National Tribune*, May 22, 1902; booklet entitled *Marcellus E. Jones, Captain, 8th Illinois Cavalry*, Vertical File 6-I8, GNMP, hereafter cited as *Marcellus Jones*. Many distances are given in rods. One rod equals sixteen and one-half feet or five and a half yards.

Yankees. Marye's piece unleashed several rounds despite protests from the homeowner, who soon thereafter fled to a safer location. When the shelling drew no response, the Confederate skirmishers advanced.

Union videttes, meanwhile, took advantage of any available cover—trees, fences, ridges, tall grass—to resist the cautiously advancing Rebels. Before long a tentative, sporadic skirmish fire erupted between the Yankee troopers and Southern infantrymen. The slow progress made by the Confederate soldiers can be attributed to several factors. First, the terrain favored skirmishers as opposed to heavy battle lines. Maintaining an orderly line while marching several miles through woods, across streams, and up and over ridges consumed time. Second, the Union troopers were armed with breech-loading carbines, which allowed a relatively small number of skirmishers to deliver a deceivingly high volume of fire. Third, the Rebels suffered from the delusion that they were facing militia, or, at worst, only Yankee cavalry. There was no need to hurry because militia always panicked, and cavalry usually yielded before a large infantry force without a hard fight.

Buford's troopers, however, only begrudgingly gave up ground. They fired long enough and at such a distance (as much as 800 yards) that the Southerners began thinking twice about just who they were facing. A final reason for the slow advance, at least partly the result of the obstinate resistance by the Yankee cavalry, was the uncertainty of what really lay ahead. No one knew what was waiting beyond the next ridgeline, so care had to be taken to prevent an ambush. The Federal troopers resisted the Confederate advance along Chambersburg Pike for about two miles.[11]

Confederate accounts offered contradictory evidence pertaining to the tenacity of the Union resistance. Colonel Birkett D. Fry of the 13th Alabama described it as "inconsequential resistance," though the existence of a hostile and tenacious force armed with breech-loading weapons must have served as a serious, if not formidable, deterrent to the Rebel advance. Several soldiers corroborated Fry's claim. W. H. Moon of the 13th Alabama recalled that the Southern skirmish line and the Yankee cavalry they faced exchanged only occasional shots. Private E. T.

---

11 "Heth's Division at Gettysburg," p. 385; *OR* pt. 2, pp. 646-649; *Marcellus Jones;* Captain W. F. Fulton, "The Fifth Alabama Battalion at Gettysburg," *Confederate Veteran, Vol. 31* (1923), p. 379; Lindsley, *The Military Annals of Tennessee*, p. 246; Coddington, *The Gettysburg Campaign*, pp. 266, 689fn; Nolan, *The Iron Brigade*, p. 235; Young, *The Battle of Gettysburg*, p. 166; Bandy, ed., *The Gettysburg Papers*, p. 174; Belo, "The Battle of Gettysburg," p. 165; James Beale, "The First Day's Fight," *Philadelphia Weekly Times,* April 27, 1878, p. 7; Hassler, *Crisis at the Crossroads*, pp. 30-32; John L. Marye, "The First Gun at Gettysburg: With the Confederate Advance Guard," *American Historical Register*, Vol. 2 (1895), pp. 1228-1229.

Boland claimed Confederate skirmishers easily drove back the Union pickets until they neared Willoughby Run. There, Boland admitted, the Union cavalry "began to get stubborn." According to Capt. J. B. Turney of Company K, 1st Tennessee, "The sharpshooters, under command of Major Buchanan, of the First Tennessee, encountered the Federal advance some three miles southwest of Gettysburg. The enemy fell back slowly, resisting our approach, until General Archer ordered a halt when we were within about one mile of the town."

William F. Fulton later wrote that when he and his comrades in the 5th Alabama, together with a portion of the 13th Alabama, moved forward as skirmishers, they drove Buford's cavalry "in gallant style." According to Fulton's recollection, "the distance over which they drove this cavalry was some three or four miles, maybe more, hardly any less. Anyway, they were driven rapidly back upon their infantry support." Fulton elaborated on this point in his postwar reminiscence:

> This battalion (5th Alabama) and fifty men drawn from the Thirteenth Alabama Regiment were deployed to the right of the road leading toward Gettysburg as skirmishers to drive in the Federal outposts. They encountered the cavalry about five miles out from Gettysburg and began to push them back. After driving them four miles the skirmish line halted west of Willoughby Run. . . . Let me emphasize the fact that the Fifth Alabama Battalion led the advance . . . (and) drove in the Federal pickets over four miles.

Although it is difficult to gauge the severity of the conflict between Union pickets and Rebel skirmishers, there can be no doubt that continual fighting took place from Marsh Creek to Willoughby Run.[12]

While the Union pickets sparred with Rebel skirmishers along Chambersburg Pike, a surprisingly nonchalant attitude prevailed throughout the cavalry encampment, especially considering the conversation Buford had with Colonel Devin the night before. Buford had told Devin the Southerners would "'come *booming*—skirmishers three deep'" along Chambersburg Pike. "'You will have to

---

12 B. D. Fry to John Bachelder, February 10, 1878; Dr. W. H. Moon, "Beginning of the Battle at Gettysburg," *Confederate Veteran*, Vol. 33 (1925), p. 449; E. T. Boland, "Beginning of the Battle of Gettysburg," *Confederate Veteran*, Vol. 14 (1906), p. 308; J. B. Turney, "The First Tennessee at Gettysburg," *Confederate Veteran*, Vol. 8 (1900), p. 535; Fulton, "The Fifth Alabama Battalion at Gettysburg," William Fulton, *The War Reminiscences of William Frierson Fulton II, Fifth Alabama Battalion, Archer's Brigade* (Gaithersburg, 1986), p. 76. An excellent account of the advance and subsequent fighting by Archer's Brigade can be found in Mark and Beth Storch's article in *The Gettysburg Magazine, Issue No. 6* (1992) entitled "'What a Deadly Trap We Were In': Archer's Brigade on July 1, 1863," pp. 13-27.

fight like the devil to hold your own until supports arrive." Thus, the veteran Buford had predicted his troopers would have a hard time holding off the Rebel advance until Reynolds's 1st Corps reached the battlefield.

Despite Buford's prophesy, troopers left their camps throughout the morning, with or without permission, to enter the town. Major John Beveridge, the commander of the 8th Illinois Cavalry, recalled that many officers and troopers ventured into Gettysburg simply to enjoy conversation with friendly civilians. Constant campaigning in Virginia had left the men thirsting for attention from the friendly Pennsylvanians. Undoubtedly, many of the cavalrymen entered the town in search of food and other supplies. Thomas Day of the 3rd Indiana Cavalry may have exemplified what frequently transpired in the camp west of Gettysburg. The previous evening he had accepted an invitation to dine in town. He acknowledged that he "had a good supper, and was invited back to breakfast." He intended to do so, but his horse was particular about the water it drank and refused to quench its thirst from Willoughby Run. The search for good water led horse and rider to a trough west of the stream. While there, Day heard the skirmishing, thereby losing his opportunity for a sumptuous breakfast. In another incident, A. R. Mix of the 9th New York Cavalry stated that he received permission from Buford to go into town in order to secure a pair of boots.

An additional witness to the flow of visitation into Gettysburg was John A. Kress, an aide to General Wadsworth. During the 1st Corps's march to Gettysburg that morning, Wadsworth instructed Kress to lead a detail to the town to obtain all the boots and shoes he could find. When Kress and his entourage arrived, they saw a party of officers, including Buford, emerge from a hotel on the main street. Even John Calef, Buford's artillery commander, acknowledged that he made plans to leave his battery to enter the town. Once he finished breakfast, he decided to "make a hasty inspection of Gettysburg, there to make some purchases for our mess." He never made it to town.[13]

Lieutenant Aaron B. Jerome served as one of Buford's signal officers. On June 30, Buford instructed him to find a good observation post, so Jerome stationed himself in the cupola of the Lutheran Seminary and waited. At 7:00 a.m. the next

---

13 Bandy, ed., *The Gettysburg Papers*, pp. 90, 91; Samuel P. Bates, *The Battle of Gettysburg* (Philadelphia, 1875), p. 55; Hassler, *Crisis at the Crossroads*, p. 19; *Illinois Monuments at Gettysburg* (Springfield, 1891), pp. 17-18; John Calef, "Gettysburg Notes: The Opening Gun," *Journal of the Military Service Institution of the U. S.*, Vol. 40 (1907), p. 47; A. R. Mix, "Experiences at Gettysburg," *National Tribune*, February 22, 1934; Day, "Opening the Battle;" Kress, "Tales of the War."

morning he spotted the Confederate advance and reported it to Buford. Not long thereafter, Captain Buck, in command of the 8th Illinois pickets, sent word that the Southerners were advancing in two mixed columns of infantry and artillery preceded by a heavy veil of skirmishers. Major John L. Beveridge received the communication. Observing no higher-ranking officers in the vicinity, he acted promptly on his own: he sent a squadron of the 8th Illinois out to support the pickets and sounded "boots and saddles." Buford and Gamble arrived as the 8th Illinois troopers broke camp. Gamble completed the troop dispositions. First, he sent three additional squadrons from the 8th New York to reinforce the Yankee skirmishers. Miss Amelia E. Harmon, who lived in a large house south and west of McPherson's Woods, recalled seeing some of Buford's men deploy:

> At nine a.m. . . . came the boom of a cannon to the west of us. We rushed to the window, to behold hundreds of galloping horses coming up the road, through the field and even past our door. Boom! again spoke the cannon, more and more galloping horses, their excited riders shouting and yelling to each other and pushing westward in hot haste, past the house and barn, seeking shelter of a strip of wood on the ridge beyond.[14]

Gamble placed his remaining force in a line along the westernmost ridge as follows: the 3rd Indiana under Col. George Chapman held the right just north of the railroad cut; the 12th Illinois (attached to Chapman's command) formed between the cut and Chambersburg Pike; the 8th Illinois aligned left of the pike; and the 8th New York deployed in the vicinity of McPherson's Woods. Gamble later explained in a letter to W. S. Church that he had 900 of his 1,600 men in line, which meant he deployed 700 of his troopers as skirmishers farther to the west.

When news of the Confederate advance reached Calef just prior to his departure for town, the artilleryman quickly arranged his battery in three sections of two guns each. He placed one section on either side of Chambersburg Pike.

14 Lieutenant A. B. Jerome to Major General Hancock, Oct. 18, 1865, Bachelder Papers Typescript, GNMP; Bandy, ed., *The Gettysburg Papers*, pp. 173, 432, 451; OR Pt. 1, pp. 927, 934, 938, 939; Stine, *History of the Army of the Potomac*, p. 452; *Retreat from Gettysburg*, pp. 274-275; James K. P. Scott, *The Story of the Battles at Gettysburg* (Harrisburg, 1927), p. 277; Calef, "Gettysburg Notes," pp. 47-49; Abner Hard, *History of the Eighth Cavalry Regiment Illinois Volunteers* (Aurora, 1868), pp. 256-258; Colonel Chapman's Letter, March 30, 1864, Bachelder Papers Typescript, GNMP; Moyer, *History of the 17th Regiment Pennsylvania Cavalry*, pp. 62, 373; *Pennsylvania at Gettysburg*, pp. 877-878; George Henry Chapman Diary, 3rd Indiana Cavalry, Robert Brake Collection; W. N. Pickerill, *Indiana at the Fiftieth Anniversary of the Battle of Gettysburg* (1913), p. 41, hereafter cited *Indiana at Gettysburg*; Occupation and Burning of the E. Harmon Building, Human Interest File, GNMP.

Colonel George H. Chapman

*Courtesy of the
Library of Congress*

Companies E and L of the 17th Pennsylvania Cavalry supported these guns. Calef unlimbered the third section near the 8th New York Cavalry. He split his battery to deceive the Confederates about the number of guns fortifying the Union line.

Devin arranged his regiments as an extension of Gamble's right flank. From left to right, he posted the 3rd West Virginia, 6th New York, 9th New York, and 17th Pennsylvania. The right flank of the 17th Pennsylvania was anchored on Mummasburg Road near the Forney farm. Devin also sent reinforcements to assist the pickets covering the northern roads. Finally, he dispatched a squadron of the 6th New York to support the Federal videttes challenging Heth's approach. In all, nearly 800 skirmishers, representing portions of the 8th Illinois, 8th New York, 12th Illinois, 3rd Indiana, and 6th New York, harassed and delayed the Rebel advance.[15]

Once formed, the main Union line awaited the enemy. Eventually, the Federal troopers saw the skirmishers' horse holders fall back over Herr's Ridge, which was west of Willoughby Run. A line of smoke rising above the crest of Herr's Ridge became visible a short time later, followed soon thereafter by the Union videttes. Gradually, Rebel skirmishers appeared. Confederate batteries wheeled into line, unlimbered, and fired. Not long thereafter, Archer's line of battle tramped into

---

15 John M. Vanderslice, *Gettysburg: Then and Now* (Dayton, 1983), pp. 70-72; Hassler, *Crisis at the Crossroads*, p. 30; *New York at Gettysburg*, p. 1145; Gamble to Church, March 10, 1864, Vertical File, GNMP; George Henry Chapman Diary, Robert L. Brake Collection; Pickerill, *Indiana at Gettysburg*, p. 41; John Busey and David Martin, *Regimental Strengths and Losses at Gettysburg, Fourth Edition* (Hightstown: Longstreet House, 2005), p. 104. The total of 800 skirmishers comes from Gamble's report of 700 videttes (letter to Church) and a squadron (or about one-third) of the 6th New York's 218 men. T. Benton Kelley, in "Gettysburg," boasted, "If any one living thinks Johnny reb got this two and a half or three miles from the 8th Ill. Cav., 'dismounted,' without winning every inch of the ground they got, he does not know the mettle we contained."

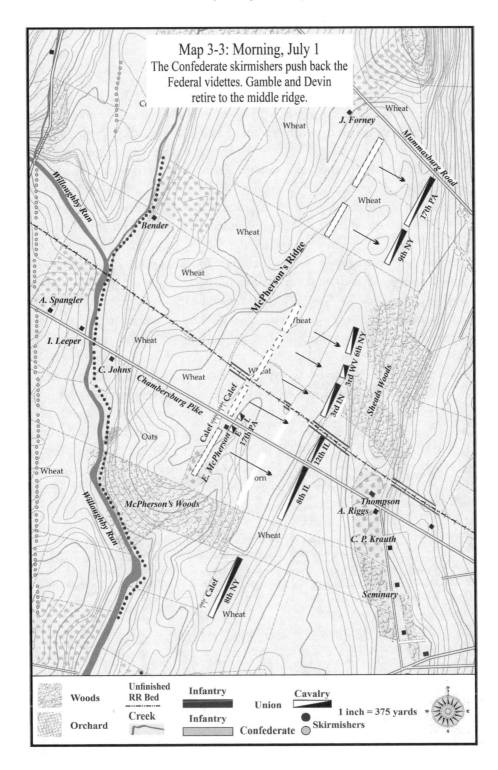

Map 3-3: Morning, July 1
The Confederate skirmishers push back the
Federal videttes. Gamble and Devin
retire to the middle ridge.

view. Federal cavalry skirmishers, meanwhile, rallied along the east bank of Willoughby Run.[16]

The stout resistance offered by the Union troopers and Calef's artillery surprised Heth. When the Confederate general reached Herr's Ridge and surveyed the terrain ahead, he became especially concerned about McPherson's Woods. Heth worried that the timber might harbor additional enemy troops, so he directed his artillery to pound the grove in order to flush out any troops that might be concealed there. Afterwards, he instructed Archer and Davis to make a "forced reconnaissance." Archer's men aligned south of the pike. The 7th Tennessee formed with its left flank anchored on Chambersburg Pike. The 14th Tennessee, the 1st Tennessee, and the 13th Alabama extended Archer's line to the south. The 5th Alabama Battalion and 50 men from the 13th Alabama continued to perform skirmish duty in front of the brigade. Davis arranged his brigade above Chambersburg Pike, with the 42nd Mississippi on his right next to the road and the 2nd Mississippi and 55th North Carolina extending the line northward.[17]

The staccato of skirmishing intensified as the Southerners closed with the cavalry. Behind a heavy screen of Rebel skirmishers waited three lines of Confederate infantry that overlapped Gamble's left flank. The "overpowering numbers" of Rebel infantry Buford had foreseen the night before, coupled with the effectiveness of the Confederate cannonade, forced Gamble to withdraw his main line to a position along the middle ridge, a difficult feat he executed with skill. Devin followed suit, dropping back one regiment at a time. Confederate skirmishers advanced more quickly on the Union right flank. Several accounts indicated that Rebel skirmishers advanced as far as the Forney farm before the Union cavalrymen repulsed them. Even though the main Union cavalry line retired,

---

16 Bandy, ed., *The Gettysburg Papers*, pp. 174, 175, 451; Scott, *The Story of the Battles at Gettysburg*, p. 277; Cavalry Battlefield Markers; David Gregg McIntosh, *Review of the Gettysburg Campaign* (Falls Church, 1984), p. 44. LeGrand Wilson, the assistant surgeon of the 42nd Mississippi of Davis's Brigade, confirmed the existence of the Federal skirmish line along Willoughby Run. LeGrand Wilson, *The Confederate Soldier* (Memphis, 1973), p. 116. When cavalry fought dismounted, every fourth trooper served as a horse holder.

17 OR pt. 2, pp. 627, 648-650; Bandy, ed., *The Gettysburg Papers*, p. 432; Hassler, *Crisis at the Crossroads*, p. 51; Scott, *The Story of the Battles at Gettysburg*, p. 278. In the first two editions of *Cutler's Brigade at Gettysburg*, I had Archer's line, from north to south, as the 7th Tennessee, the 14th Tennessee, the 5th Alabama Battalion, the 13th Alabama, and the 1st Tennessee. Research by subsequent historians has convinced me the true order of Archer's line, from north to south, is now accurately reflected in the main text. Consider the 5th Alabama Battalion to be in skirmish formation.

Major General John Reynolds

Calef maintained his position on the western ridge straddling Chambersburg Pike. The Yankee skirmishers continued offering stout resistance along the east bank of Willoughby Run.[18]

Between 9:00 and 10:00 a.m., John Reynolds, commander of the Union 1st Corps, arrived on the scene ahead of his troops. Reynolds met Buford at the Lutheran Seminary and surveyed the situation. Realizing the value of the ground held by the Yankee cavalrymen, as well as the steep odds they faced, Reynolds instructed Buford to hold at all costs. Then the 1st Corps commander rode west to inspect the cavalry line, offering encouragement to the troopers. Reynolds dispatched aides with news and orders. Through Captain Stephen Weld, Reynolds informed General Meade that he would resist the Southern attack even if it meant barricading the streets of the town. Other messengers carried orders for the 3rd and 11th Corps to hasten to Gettysburg.[19]

Once he accomplished all he could with what he had at his disposal, Reynolds returned to Emmitsburg Road near the Codori house to await the appearance of Brig. Gen. Lysander Cutler's regiments. Reynolds needed the brigade's prompt arrival to stabilize the position being defended by the hard-pressed Federal cavalry and to take possession of the favorable terrain west of town.

18 OR pt. 1, pp. 934, 939; Abner Doubleday, *Chancellorsville and Gettysburg* (New York, 1882), p. 126; Calef, "Gettysburg Notes," p. 49; Hassler, *Crisis at the Crossroads*, p. 31; *New York at Gettysburg*, p. 1153. This seems to be the most plausible explanation of Union cavalry movements. Both Gamble and Devin clearly mention falling back to the next, or middle, ridge. It would be ludicrous to believe that Calef's guns would have been left alone without the support provided by the Yankee skirmishers.

19 Hassler, *Crisis at the Crossroads*, pp. 36-38; Coddington, *The Gettysburg Campaign*, p. 267; *Pennsylvania at Gettysburg*, p. 24; Tucker, *High Tide at Gettysburg*, pp. 106-107; Oliver O. Howard, *Autobiography of Oliver Otis Howard* (New York, 1908), p. 407; Bandy, ed., *The Gettysburg Papers*, p. 454; *Retreat from Gettysburg*, p. 276; William Swinton, *The Twelve Decisive Battles of the War* (New York, 1867), p. 328; *In Memoriam, James Samuel Wadsworth, 1807-1864* (Albany, 1916), p. 37; Rosengarten to Bates, Robert Blake Collection, Reynolds File.

CHAPTER FOUR

Cutler's Brigade Arrives

On July 1, a 4:00 a.m. reveille awakened the soldiers in Lysander Cutler's encampment south of Marsh Creek. The next few hours were packed with activity.

The men ate a breakfast consisting mostly of hardtack and coffee. Tired of army rations, several members of the 147th New York visited nearby farmhouses and returned with quart pails of hot coffee and loaves of soft bread. The men also drew one day's rations and 60 rounds of ammunition. Either a morning mist or a nighttime light drizzle rendered the loaded and stacked muskets of the 76th New York unserviceable, forcing the men to remove the damp cartridges so their weapons would be ready if needed. Shelter halves, blankets, and knapsacks had to be packed. The commanders were also busy. At 6:00 a.m., Maj. Gen. John F. Reynolds sent for division commander Maj. Gen. Abner Doubleday. The 1st Corps commander read dispatches to Doubleday from Gens. George Meade and John Buford, after which he informed the division leader that he was going to advance to Gettysburg with the 1st Division. Reynolds told Doubleday to follow with the remainder of the corps.

At 7:00 a.m., an aide "galloped hurriedly" to the tent of Edward Fowler, colonel of the 14th Brooklyn, informing him to ready his command to march. The same or other aides would have repeated the process with the regimental commanders of the 95th, 76th, and 147th New York, and the 56th Pennsylvania. Minutes later bugles sounded the order to pack up and fall into marching formation. As the Union soldiers prepared to move, Reynolds rode up to Brig. Gen. James Wadsworth and directed him to start at once. The 1st Division had led the 1st Corps the previous day, so military etiquette called for the other divisions to pass it, leaving the 1st Division to bring up the rear. The protocol, however, took time to execute, and Reynolds apparently felt he had no time to waste. Wadsworth ordered 1st Lt. Clayton Rogers, one of his staff aides, to start the division toward Gettysburg. Since Cutler's brigade was closest to division headquarters, it received the orders first. As a result, Cutler's men were ready for the journey before Brig. Gen. Solomon Meredith's Iron Brigade, which had camped about 200 yards north of Marsh Creek. Cutler's men "crossed Marsh Creek by the bridge on the Emmitsburg-Gettysburg road pike . . . and passed Meredith's Brigade still in their bivouac."[1]

As the troops formed for the march along Emmitsburg Road, the heat of the day was already noticeable. Many soldiers considered the earlier blood-red sunrise to be an omen for extremely high temperatures. Reynolds and his staff led the column. The troops stretched out behind them in the following order: Wadsworth and his staff; Cutler and his staff; the headquarter guard (Sgt. H. H. Hubbard and 18 men from the 147th New York); the 76th New York; the 56th Pennsylvania; the 147th New York; the 95th New York; the 14th Brooklyn; and Capt. James A. Hall's 2nd Maine battery. Reynolds selected the 7th Indiana to stay behind to guard the 1st Division's wagon train and cattle herd. The column left its encampment between 7:30 a.m. and 8:00 a.m. Eventually, the Iron Brigade followed. Meredith had delayed the order to "fall in." According to Clayton Rogers, the gap between the two brigades grew to approximately one mile.

---

1 Bvt. Brigadier General J. Wm. Hofmann, *Remarks on the Battle of Gettysburg* (Philadelphia, 1880), p. 3; Hofmann, *PWP*, p. 1; Snyder, *Oswego County, New York in the Civil War*, p. 63; "A Chaplain at Gettysburg," *Gettysburg Newspaper Clippings Relating to the Battle*, GNMP, p. 148; Lyman Diary; J. V. Pierce, "Gettysburg, Last Words as to 'What Regiment Opened the Battle,'" *National Tribune*, April 3, 1884; Tevis and Marquis, *The History of the Fighting Fourteenth*, p. 81; Smith, *76th New York*, p. 236; Doubleday, *Chancellorsville and Gettysburg*, pp. 124-125; *New York at Gettysburg*, p. 990; Pearson, *James S. Wadsworth of Geneseo*, p. 204; J. W. Hofmann, "Gettysburg," *National Tribune*, June 19, 1884. In an 1865 letter to Doubleday, Colonel Fowler recounted that the 14th Brooklyn began the march toward Gettysburg at approximately 7:30 a.m. His recollections were based upon extracts from his diary. Colonel E. B. Fowler to Abner Doubleday, August 1, 1865, Abner Doubleday Paper, hereafter cited as Fowler Extract. Members of the Iron Brigade made many erroneous postwar claims that their unit led the march to Gettysburg and also opened the infantry engagement. Details sympathetic to the Iron Brigade can be found in Lance J. Herdegen, "Old Soldiers and War Talk," *The Gettysburg Magazine*, Issue No. 2 (1990), pp. 15-24; Earl M. Rogers, "The Second, or Fifty-Sixth—Which," *Milwaukee Sunday Telegraph*, June 22, 1884.

For the most part, Cutler's men maintained a brisk pace but felt no sense of urgency. An anxious Lt. Col. Francis Miller of the 147th New York, however, rode along his regiment ordering his men to keep "closed up." After covering one and a half miles, the troops halted for about ten minutes while Generals Reynolds, Wadsworth, Cutler and their staffs conferred, using binoculars and a map to study the ground before them. Major Andrew Grover, meanwhile, noticed men from his 76th New York eyeing with envy cherry trees loaded with fruit. "Boys," he shouted so everyone could hear, "the General charges you to be very particular to keep strictly within the rules, and not meddle with those cherry trees! Be sure you don't break the trees down!" Everyone understood the major's implication: the New Yorkers relished the cherries, but "the trees did not remain quite uninjured."

Once the brigade resumed its march, Reynolds and his staff cantered ahead to Gettysburg in advance of the column. Before long, the tramping Yankees noticed circular white puffs of smoke rising in the sky to the northwest and heard the faint rumble of distant artillery. Colonel Fowler reckoned it was 9:00 a.m. when his men spotted these first signs of battle. Cutler's troops accelerated their gait. "It looked like serious work ahead," noted the historian of the 14th Brooklyn, "and every man's veins swelled and pulsed with the thought of what he was going into." Aides and orderlies riding south past Cutler's men delivered scraps of information: Buford was hard-pressed, and the Rebels were "thicker than blackberries." Staff officers urged Cutler's men forward. One man in the 147th New York recalled, "We were being hurried at the utmost speed along the road on that hot July morning, sweltering from every pore. As for me, my clothes could not have been wetter if I had fallen into a pond of water."[2]

Cutler's brigade continued its rapid pace until it reached the Codori house, one-half to three-quarters of a mile south of Gettysburg. There, on the west side of Emmitsburg Road, sat General Reynolds. After he had finished his reconnaissance, the general had ridden back to the road to direct his troops to the battlefield by the shortest possible route. Wadsworth and Reynolds discussed briefly whether the 1st

2 Tevis and Marquis, *The History of the Fighting Fourteenth*, pp. 81-82; *New York at Gettysburg*, pp. 615, 733, 736, 988, 990, 1001; *Pennsylvania at Gettysburg*, pp. 343-344; Hassler, *Crisis at the Crossroads*, p. 38; Coddington, *The Gettysburg Campaign*, pp. 261-262; Bandy, ed., *The Gettysburg Papers*, p. 242; Captain Hall to Bachelder, December 29, 1869, Bachelder Papers Typescript; Smith, *76th New York*, pp. 236-237; Hofmann, *Remarks on the Battle of Gettysburg*, pp. 3-4; Unsigned statement, Bachelder Papers Typescript; Pierce, "Gettysburg, Last Words"; "A Chaplain at Gettysburg," p. 148; "Playing Parson," *National Tribune*, October 4, 1888; Hofmann, "Gettysburg"; Rogers, "The Second, or Fifty-Sixth—Which"; Fowler, "The Fourteenth Regiment," *The Brooklyn Daily Eagle*, July 6, 1863.

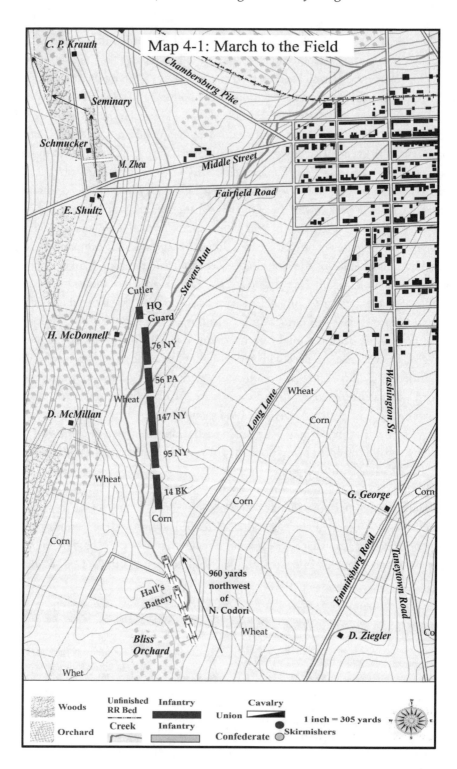

Map 4-1: March to the Field

Division should be deployed in the town proper or west of the village. Reynolds decided the ridge network west of Gettysburg offered excellent defensive terrain. He was also concerned that if the Federals held the town, Confederate shells might destroy some of the structures and injure civilians. Therefore, Reynolds ordered Wadsworth to turn his division off Emmitsburg Road so it could proceed directly toward the sound of the battle.[3]

Pioneers came forward to level the fences bordering Emmitsburg Road—a task Reynolds's escorts had already begun. Once cleared, Reynolds and Wadsworth led Cutler's vanguard, comprised of the headquarters guard and the 76th New York, off road heading northwest. Despite the best efforts of the pioneers, a member of the 76th New York remembered that his regiment "was obliged to remove fences as they led the army through fields, gardens and yards." When officers directed the column to double-quick, some of the soldiers dropped nonessential gear like knapsacks along the route. As the men hurried forward, officers ordered them to load their muskets, causing one soldier to forever recall "the wild rattle of jingling ramrods." Cutler's men crossed Stevens' Run and the fields near the McMillan home. Hall's battery overtook the Oswego boys as the 147th New York crossed the run. The head of the brigade reached Fairfield Road, scaled the sturdy post and board fences lining both sides of the lane, and pushed on. The well-built fences temporarily delayed Hall's guns, limbers, and caissons. The tramping infantry swept past the Schumacher home. Some of the men from the 147th New York had stopped to drink water handed out by two ladies at a fence gate, but officers rode up and kicked away the pails. There was no time for delay. The morning march had begun without a sense of urgency, but it was ending in crisis. Finally, after almost a mile of exhausting double-quick, the men crossed Seminary Ridge below the Lutheran Seminary buildings. It was about 10:00 a.m.[4]

---

3 Swinton, *Twelve Decisive Battles*, p. 328; Tevis and Marquis, *The History of the Fighting Fourteenth*, p. 82; Tucker, *High Tide at Gettysburg*, p. 107; Hassler, *Crisis at the Crossroads*, p. 38; *Retreat from Gettysburg*, p. 276; Coddington, *The Gettysburg Campaign*, p. 267; B. F. Parkhurst, "At Gettysburg. Heroism of the 147th NY," *National Tribune,* November 1, 1888; Pierce to Bachelder, November 1, 1882, Bachelder Papers Typescript; *In Memoriam, James Samuel Wadsworth*, p. 37.

4 Hassler, *Crisis at the Crossroads*, pp. 38, 39; *New York at Gettysburg*, pp. 615, 990; Coddington, *Gettysburg Campaign*, p. 268; Bandy, ed., *The Gettysburg Papers*, pp. 152, 242; Tevis ad Marquis, *The History of the Fighting Fourteenth*, p. 82; "A Chaplain at Gettysburg," p. 148; M. M. Whitney, "The 76th New York. How It Opened the Fight on the First Day at Gettysburg," *National Tribune,* July 21, 1887; Pierce, "Gettysburg, Last Words"; Lyman Diary; Pierce to Bachelder, Nov. 1, 1882, Bachelder Papers Typescript; Hofmann, "Gettysburg Again"; Pearson, *James S. Wadsworth of Geneseo*, p. 207.

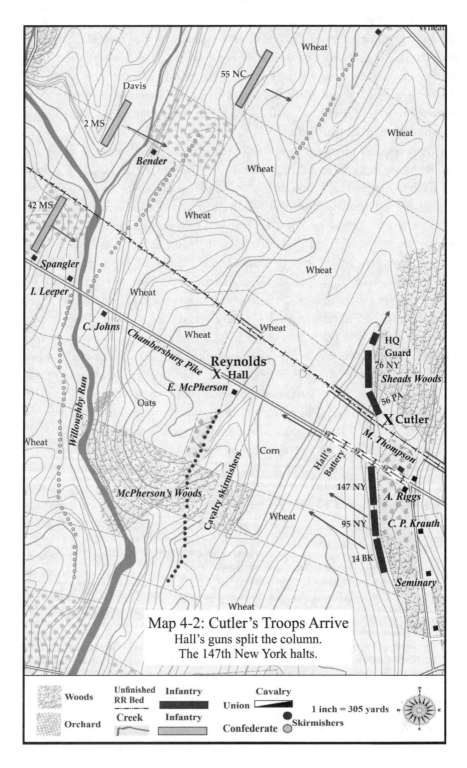

Map 4-2: Cutler's Troops Arrive
Hall's guns split the column.
The 147th New York halts.

When Cutler's regiments and Hall's battery approached the Seminary building, they deployed in different directions. As the brigade moved northward along the depression between the eastern and middle ridges, a number of Gamble's weary troopers retired to the left of the infantry. After the 2nd Maine battery reached the eastern slope of Seminary Ridge south of the theology building, Lt. Col. James M. Sanderson of Reynolds's staff informed Hall that the general wanted to see him. The artillerist galloped west to find Reynolds on Cashtown Road near the McPherson buildings. According to Hall, the corps commander instructed him to "put your battery on this ridge to engage those guns of the enemy." The position had previously been held by Calef's right section of guns north of Cashtown Pike and on the western ridge. Reynolds, Wadsworth, and Hall discussed the fact that the location was one of danger. To help protect the exposed pieces, Reynolds instructed the division commander to post three regiments to the right of Hall's guns. The 2nd Maine battery arrived moments before Cutler's men got into position, unlimbered, and began targeting the Rebel cannon positioned along Herr's Ridge. The meeting ended with Reynolds telling Wadsworth that he would take care of the left.[5]

The 76th New York and 56th Pennsylvania crossed Seminary Ridge south of the school, descended into the swale between the middle and eastern ridges, and surged toward Cashtown (Chambersburg) Pike. After the two regiments passed the Seminary building, which was to their right, "a shower of shells" from Confederate batteries on Herr's Ridge west of Willoughby Run exploded near them. Moving in a vulnerable "columns of fours," the two regiments continued northward along the swale. With shells crashing about, the regiments halted briefly to await orders. To escape the artillery barrage, Colonel Hofmann directed the men around him to lie down, which also offered a brief respite for the exhausted infantry. Veterans of the 76th New York would later tell a member of the 147th New York that they blessed the memory of Colonel Hofmann for this act of humanity.

Unfortunately for the weary infantry, the pause was but a brief interlude between fatiguing events. Wadsworth ordered Cutler to cross Cashtown Pike and

---

5 Cheney, *History of the Ninth Regiment New York Cavalry*, p. 109; Coddington, *The Gettysburg Campaign*, p. 268; Hassler, *Crisis at the Crossroads*, pp. 39-42; Jacob Hoke, *The Great Invasion, or General Lee in Pennsylvania* (New York, 1959), p. 263; Bandy, ed., *The Gettysburg Papers*, p. 454; Swinton, *Twelve Decisive Battles*, p. 329; *New York at Gettysburg*, pp. 1006-1007; Hall to Bachelder, December 29, 1869, Bachelder Papers Typescript. Hall's battery could not have unlimbered on the western ridge unless the Confederate infantry was still a substantial distance to the west. Otherwise, Hall's guns would have been quickly overrun.

This photo was taken from the crest of the westernmost ridge, facing west. Willoughby Run (unable to be seen) is at the bottom of the ridge. Herr Ridge is the height in the background. In the far background are the Blue Ridge Mountains. Hall's Battery formed to the right of this photo. *Author*

The 76th New York and 56th Pennsylvania passed over this area and then marched up the crest of the middle ridge [from which this shot was taken]. Note the Seminary buildings to the left. *Author*

The 76th New York and the 56th Pennsylvania crossed over this ground, between the middle ridge and Seminary Ridge, prior to crossing the railroad cut. The elevation and bridge to the left background locates the deep, middle cut. *Author*

the railroad grading with his three leading regiments, form a line of battle, and advance west. The brigadier promptly marched his men across the pike and the unfinished railroad bed; they continued northward for another 150-200 yards. Cutler and his staff followed the 56th Pennsylvania. At this point, Cutler ordered the two regiments in front of him, the 76th New York and the 56th Pennsylvania, to change formation from column to battle line.[6]

Meanwhile, the 14th Brooklyn and 95th New York passed around the front of the Seminary. Reynolds sent orders for the 14th Brooklyn's Col. Edward Fowler to take command of his regiment and the 95th New York; Reynolds directed Fowler to deploy this demi-brigade to the left of Hall's engaged battery. The two regiments faced left and moved toward the crest of the western ridge with the 95th New York on the right and the 14th Brooklyn on the left. While Fowler's command completed its change of direction from north to west, Reynolds and his staff

6 *Pennsylvania at Gettysburg*, pp. 316, 341; *New York at Gettysburg*, p. 615; OR pt. 1, p. 281; Hofmann, *PWP*; Hofmann, *Remarks on the Battle of Gettysburg*, p. 4; Pierce to Hofmann, August 11, 1888, J. William Hofmann Papers, Society Small Collection; Bandy, ed., *The Gettysburg Papers*, p. 175.

watched from the northeastern edge of McPherson's Woods. A veteran of the 95th New York recalled that Reynolds "hurriedly gave some direction to Colonel Fowler as we were advancing up into the orchard towards the crest of the ridge where the cavalry were skirmishing." What transpired in the conversation was never recorded, but it almost certainly included Reynolds informing Fowler of the dangers ahead.

As Colonel Gamble's troopers peeled off to the left, Confederate artillery shelled them. Some cavalrymen on the crest of the ridge continued skirmishing while Fowler's men approached. By now, Brig. Gen. James J. Archer's Confederate brigade could be seen halfway down the east slope of Herr's Ridge. Fowler's men quickly ascended the western ridge and moved through an orchard. The colonel formed his demi-brigade with its left resting against McPherson's Woods and its right anchored along the McPherson buildings. The house, barn and outbuildings prevented Fowler's men from seeing the rest of Cutler's command.[7]

The 147th New York occupied the middle of Cutler's line during the march. According to Reynolds's plan, the regiment should have accompanied the 56th

The 14th Brooklyn and the 95th New York advanced along this east slope of the middle ridge and continued to the western ridge. *Author*

---

7 *New York at Gettysburg*, pp. 616, 733; Tevis and Marquis, *The History of the Fighting Fourteenth*, pp. 82, 132; Bandy, ed., *The Gettysburg Papers*, p. 175; Pierce, "Gettysburg, Last Words."

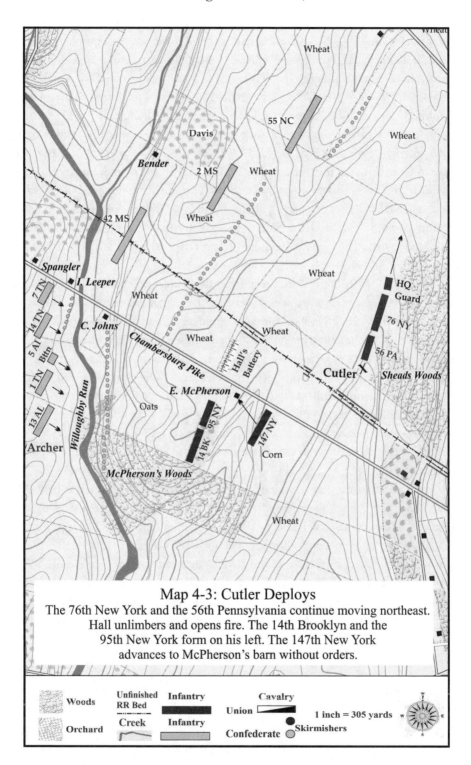

Map 4-3: Cutler Deploys

The 76th New York and the 56th Pennsylvania continue moving northeast.
Hall unlimbers and opens fire. The 14th Brooklyn and the
95th New York form on his left. The 147th New York
advances to McPherson's barn without orders.

Pennsylvania and 76th New York north of the railroad cut. Several obstructions, however, interrupted these New Yorkers. Volney Pierce, a lieutenant in the outfit, claimed the Seminary buildings presented the first obstacles to the "Oswego boys." Near Cashtown Pike, Hall's battery created another impediment. To reach its appointed position, the Maine guns broke formation, increased speed, and cut through the infantry column. According to James Coey, the 2nd Maine battery came "tearing and galloping along." Hall recalled the same events in a postwar letter to Gettysburg historian Bachelder. "My battery came over Seminary Ridge at a gallop the enemy opening on it at once. Turning from General Reynolds," continued Hall, "I met the battery, between the two ridges, and turned head of column to right, moving by a flank under protection of a crest, till in rear of position designated by General Reynolds, when I formed 'to the left in battery,' and opened."[8]

While the 147th New York waited for the battery to pass, Lt. Col. Francis Miller watched the 95th New York and 14th Brooklyn change from column to battle line as they headed toward the western ridge. Miller had yet to receive orders as he observed the brigade drifting in two distinct directions. The officer decided to advance his men at a double-quick toward the McPherson buildings. Confederate shells exploded overhead as the regiment advanced. When the 147th New York reached the structures, Miller halted it and deployed from column into line of battle near a garden fence east of the structures. The left of the regiment rested near the rear of the McPherson house. Private John Bartlett had a vivid memory of the buildings because during the lull he escaped enemy shells by entering the barn's stone basement.

There are two versions of what happened next. The first, which is probably untrue, suggested that Lieutenant Colonel Miller rode off to get orders for his regiment. The second, which is more likely, is that an aide carried instructions to Miller. According to Capt. Charles Parker of Company C, a staff officer approached the lieutenant colonel and told Miller to immediately move the 147th New York to the right of Hall's guns to prevent the 2nd Maine Battery from being overrun. Sergeant Amos Allfort identified the aide as Capt. William Bloodgood from Cutler's staff.

---

8 Pierce never clarified why the buildings caused a problem. Pierce to Hofmann, August 11, 1888, J. William Hofmann Papers, Society Small Collection; Hall to Bachelder, December 29, 1869, Bachelder Papers Typescript.

The 147th New York probably lingered in the vicinity of the McPherson buildings for about five minutes. When Miller finally ordered his command to support Hall's guns, he directed his regiment to move by flank to the right. As the men passed along the depression between the western and middle ridges, Private Bartlett recalled seeing Hall's caissons, horses, and guns. As the regiment crossed the unfinished railroad, Confederate skirmishers could be seen operating along the opposite end of the deep cut formed by the western ridge. The depth of the cut prevented the Rebels from striking Hall's flank. The moment the end of the 147th New York's column reached the north bank of the unfinished railroad, the regiment was in line with Hall's caissons to the south. Lieutenant Colonel Miller ordered "By the left flank; guide center." The 147th New York, which had never experienced enemy fire, ascended the eastern slope of the gentle ridge with the railroad cut on its left. An old rail fence perpendicularly separated the right companies from the rest of the regiment.[9]

The arrival and deployment of Cutler's brigade under a barrage of artillery fire came at a critical time for the Union cause. Its arrival allowed Buford's embattled cavalrymen, who had steadfastly delayed the Confederate advance for several hours, to pull rapidly out of their positions. The Rebels had already formed into lines of battle that surged forward to fill the void left by the departing Federal troopers. General Reynolds, according to an unidentified 1st Corps staff officer, expected the Confederates to advance along both Cashtown (Chambersburg) and Fairfield roads. Reynolds relayed this information to General Doubleday, who, after scanning the terrain west of Gettysburg, concluded that a Yankee force positioned in McPherson's Woods and along the neighboring ridge would threaten the flanks of Southern columns moving eastward on those roads.

The rapid Confederate advance toward McPherson's Woods and McPherson's Ridge jeopardized those key defensive positions. The Iron Brigade had not reached the front. Only the quick deployment of Cutler's brigade, supported by Hall's battery, could save the position. Reynolds had hurried Cutler's split brigade

---

9 *New York at Gettysburg*, pp. 991, 1001-1002; John Bartlett Letter, November 23, 1889, Vertical File, 147th New York, GNMP; Pierce, "Gettysburg, Last Words"; Pierce to Hofmann, August 11, 1888, and A. S. Coe to Hofmann, July 12, 1888, J. William Hofmann Papers, Society Small Collection; Amos Allfort, "Memory of the First Engagement of the Battle of Gettysburg," Henry Harrison Lyman Collection; Parkhurst, "Heroism of the 147th New York"; Lyman to Bachelder, no date; Coe to Bachelder, December 28, 1888, Bachelder Papers Typescript; Pierce to Bachelder, November 1, 1882, Bachelder Papers Typescript; Snyder, *Oswego County, New York in the Civil War*, p. 63; James Coey, "Cutler's Brigade. The 147th New York's Magnificent Fight on the First Day at Gettysburg," *National Tribune,* July 17, 1915.

McPherson's Barn is on the left, where the 147th New York awaited orders. Hall's battery would have been aligned along the ridge to the right of the road (near the monument of the mounted officer). *Author*

The 147th New York left the McPherson's buildings and traversed this ground before crossing the railroad cut. Note that the cut is invisible (it follows the telephone lines, which no longer exist). This view supports Hall's claim that he was initially unaware of any railroad cut. *Author*

forward to blunt the advance of a numerically superior enemy. Cutler's regiments moved without the benefit of reconnaissance and before they could shake out skirmish lines. In fact, the 76th New York was still changing from column to line when it came in contact with the enemy.

Historians usually credit Hall's battery with holding the line until the Iron Brigade arrived, but that analysis is incomplete. If Cutler's men had not been thrown forward in such a hasty and hazardous manner, the story of the Battle of Gettysburg would have been very different.[10]

10 Hassler, *Crisis at the Crossroads*, p. 42; Bandy and Freeland, *The Gettysburg Papers*, p. 243; OR pt. 1, p. 244; Hofmann, "Gettysburg"; Charles Veil to D. McConaughy, Esq., Vertical File, McPherson Farm Area Action, GNMP; E. R. Reed, "The Second Wisconsin Sticks to Its Claim," *National Tribune,* March 20, 1884; Vertical File, James W. Wadsworth, Jr. Papers, GNMP. Reed was another Iron Brigade soldier who mistakenly asserted that the Black Hat Brigade led the march to Gettysburg and that his regiment fired the first shots. He also noted that during the route to the battlefield he could see "clearly for a mile or more ahead" but observed no troops. It is unlikely anyone could have seen that far ahead on the clearest of days, but his statement does substantiate the considerable gap between the two brigades during the march to Gettysburg. Boland, "Beginning of the Battle of Gettysburg," p. 308.

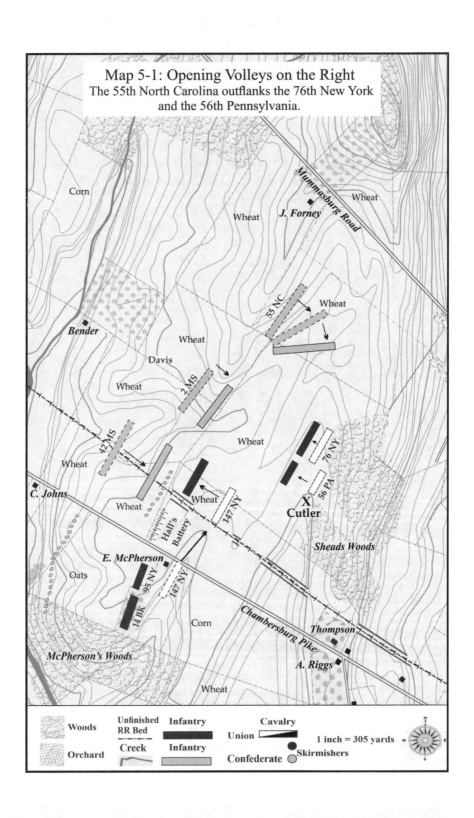

Map 5-1: Opening Volleys on the Right
The 55th North Carolina outflanks the 76th New York and the 56th Pennsylvania.

Corn

Wheat

Mummasburg Road

Wheat

J. Forney

Wheat

55 NC

Wheat

Bender

Wheat

Davis

2 MS

Wheat

Wheat

42 MS

Wheat

76 NY

C. Johns

Wheat

56 PA

X

Cutler

147 NY

Wheat

Hall's Battery

Sheads Woods

E. McPherson

Oats

95 NY

147 NY

14 BK

Corn

Chambersburg Pike

Thompson

McPherson's Woods

A. Riggs

Wheat

Woods	Unfinished RR Bed	Infantry	Cavalry
Orchard	Creek	Infantry	Union
		Confederate	Skirmishers

1 inch = 305 yards

CHAPTER FIVE

Cutler's Brigade Engages the Enemy

Lysander Cutler's two lead regiments, the 76th New York and 56th Pennsylvania, crossed the unfinished railroad and continued to advance under the partial cover of the middle ridge for perhaps 150-200 yards. The move isolated them from the rest of Cutler's regiments, which in turn placed them in great peril. The density of their columns provided Southern cannoneers posted on Herr's Ridge with an inviting target whenever they caught a glimpse of the Yankee troops. The northward march also moved the two regiments closer to a large and as-yet unseen Confederate force that had already deployed into battle line, complete with skirmishers. If Cutler's men encountered the Rebel infantry while deployed in a column, they would be subjected to a brutal musketry from the enemy without being able to effectively return fire.

Fortunately for his men, Cutler sensed the Confederate presence, so he ordered his regiments to change their alignment from column into battle line. Since Cutler was in the rear of the 56th Pennsylvania, the 76th New York necessarily received the order after the Pennsylvanians. Colonel J. William Hofmann formed his 56th Pennsylvania in line of battle along the gentle slope of the middle ridge's east side before moving his regiment west a short distance. Concurrently, the 76th New York began changing formation.[1]

As this was transpiring, Brig. Gen. Joseph Davis's Confederate brigade continued its eastward advance. Davis had placed his 42nd Mississippi on the right

---

1 *Pennsylvania at Gettysburg*, p. 341; Hofmann, *Remarks on the Battle of Gettysburg*, p. 4.

This is the terrain observed by the men of the 56th Pennsylvania and 76th New York once they crossed the middle ridge. On the left (above), the 2nd Mississippi held the reverse side of the next ridge. To the right (facing page), the 55th North Carolina appeared where the road turns. *Author*

of his brigade, its southern flank touching the turnpike, the 2nd Mississippi in the center, and the 55th North Carolina on his left. As the Rebels pressed forward, fire from Captain Hall's 2nd Maine battery apparently forced the Confederate line to drift northward. Colonel John M. Stone, the commander of the 2nd Mississippi, later remembered that his regiment "was cut in two by a lane with a post and rail fence on both sides of the road, with the larger part of the regiment on the right. . . side of the lane." After crossing a branch of Willoughby Run, the Rebels began ascending the slope beyond. Anxious to meet the enemy, the 55th North Carolina plunged forward and broke brigade formation.[2]

The western ridge temporarily separated the opposing forces. As Hofmann reached the top of the middle ridge with his Pennsylvania men, he saw a line of battle approaching well off to his right and "just rising to the crest of the swell west

[2] OR pt. 2, p. 649; Governor Stone to General Davis, Bachelder Papers Typescript, no date; Hassler, *Crisis at the Crossroads*, p. 43; Captain S. A. Ashe, "The First Day at Gettysburg," *Confederate Veteran* (1930), Vol. 38, p. 379.

of the one we were on."[3] "The atmosphere being a little thick [from the smoke from the cavalry skirmish], I took out my glasses to examine the enemy," explained General Cutler in a letter to Pennsylvania's Governor Andrew Curtin. The brigadier continued:

> Being a few paces in the rear of Colonel Hofmann, he turned to me and inquired, 'Is that the enemy?' My reply was 'Yes.' Turning to his men he commanded 'Ready, right oblique, aim, fire!' and the Battle of Gettysburg was opened. The fire was followed by other regiments instantly. . . . When Colonel Hofmann gave the command 'aim,' I doubted whether the enemy was near enough to have the fire effective, and asked him if he was within range; but not hearing my question, he fired, and I received my reply in a shower of rebel bullets.[4]

Because of the character of the ground, Hofmann's men could only spot the distant ranks of the 55th North Carolina. The 56th Pennsylvania's volley, which was delivered around 10:15 a.m., ripped through the North Carolina lines and

3 Hofmann, *Remarks on the Battle of Gettysburg*, p. 4; *New York at Gettysburg*, p. 616; Hofmann, *PWP*; *Pennsylvania at Gettysburg*, p. 341.

4 Samuel Bates, *History of the Pennsylvania Volunteers, 1861-1865*, 5 Vols. (Harrisburg, 1869), Vol. 2, pp. 219-220.

(Left) Colonel John William Hofmann
Author's Collection

(Below) Cutler's men first saw the
55th North Carolina on the ground
where the road bends to the right. *Author*

injured at least two men of the color guard. Rebel muskets retaliated. The aim of John Connally's 640 Tar Heels, firing at the enemy for the first time, was surprisingly accurate. Scores of

blue-clad soldiers fell dead or wounded. The hail of Southern lead also struck the mounts ridden by Cutler and two members of his staff, temporarily unhorsing the officers. The deadly fire notwithstanding, the 56th Pennsylvania advanced a short distance before finally halting on the western slope of the middle ridge.[5]

---

5 55th NC, *GDN*, p. 9; Busey and Martin, *Regimental Strengths at Gettysburg*, p. 175; Bates, *History of the Pennsylvania Volunteers*, Vol. 2, pp. 219-220; *New York at Gettysburg*, pp. 615-616; Clark, ed., *North Carolina Regiments*, Vol. 3, p. 297; Hofmann, *Remarks on the Battle of Gettysburg*, p. 4.

56th Pennsylvania Monument

Steven Floyd

The Confederate musketry also inflicted heavy damage on the 76th New York. Besides being closer to Davis's Rebels, Brig. Gen. James Wadsworth wrote that the New Yorkers were still not in line when the enemy fire struck them. C. W. Cook confirmed the general's observation: "Before we could come to a front we found ourselves engaged with a vastly superior force of the enemy, advancing at short range in front, and on our right flank."

At first, due to the nature of the terrain—gentle slopes and swales abound in that area—the New Yorkers were unable to spot any enemy troops. Suddenly, the left of the 2nd Mississippi, about 30 rods (165 yards) to the west and concealed in tall grass, opened a murderous fire upon the Empire State men. Major Andrew Grover, who was concerned that the musketry fire may have emanated from friendly troops, withheld the fire of his own men. As a result, the 76th New York endured three unanswered volleys before taking any defensive action. "We were exposed to their fire for several minutes before replying," lamented Capt. John Cook. About this same time, Capt. Robert Story of Company B narrowly escaped death when a cannon ball passed between his legs and plowed into the earth just behind him.[6]

The ferocity of the artillery fire and musketry is well documented. Sergeant Edgar D. Haviland, Company E, 76th New York, explained as much in a letter home to his mother:

---

6 Bates, *History of the Pennsylvania Volunteers,* Vol. 2, pp. 219-220; OR pt. 1, pp. 265-267; *New York at Gettysburg,* p. 616; Smith, *76th New York,* pp. 371-372; C. W. Cook, "Who Opened Gettysburg," *The National Tribune,* Nov. 24, 1892.

Captain Samuel M. Byram
(76th New York)

Author's Collection

During the initial action on July 1, men on the right flank of the 56th Pennsylvania and on the left flank of the 76th New York would have viewed this terrain. The 2nd Mississippi would have been in the vicinity of the tree line. *Author*

> We arrived at Gettysburg on the first day of July and we had a grand celebration of fire works. . . . We had a great many killed and wounded from the cannons before we got into the Musketry fire. After we got into the musketry the men fell like sheep on all sides of me. When we first came into line thare was a Corporal hit with a cannon ball and fell wright back into my arms.

Another New Yorker, C. W. Cook, also wrote about the deadly effectiveness of the enemy fire during the early stages of the battle. Cook's tent mate of two years, Frank Gay, was struck by a bullet and fell. When Cook stooped to assist him, a second ball struck Gay in the head. After the fight, Uberto Burnham claimed many New Yorkers discovered their clothes and equipment had been riddled with bullet holes. Some found enemy musket balls trapped in their knapsacks, canteens,

76th New York Monument

Steven Floyd

and haversacks. One soldier had his musket shattered by a bullet. It hardly seemed possible for a man to have survived such waves of lead and iron.[7]

John Connally's 55th North Carolina, meanwhile, holding the left side of Davis's brigade line, continued its fast-paced advance. The regiment's left extended well beyond Cutler's exposed right flank. When the Confederates crossed the swell where they were first observed by the 56th Pennsylvania, the Tar Heels blasted a volley at the 76th New York. The Rebel projectiles slashed the flank and front of the New York regiment. Colonel Connally pressed his 55th North Carolina forward. Then, in parade-like fashion, he wheeled his line to the right. Once the regiment performed this maneuver, Connally seized the outfit's battle flag and dashed ahead of his men, defiantly waving the colors as he did so. Union musketry, instinctively concentrating on the Rebel color guard, wounded Connally in his left arm and right hip. Major Belo rushed to his aid and "asked him if he was badly wounded. Colonel Connally replied: 'Yes, but do not pay any attention to me; take the colors and keep ahead of the Mississippians.'"[8]

The maneuver, deftly performed by the 55th North Carolina, placed the regiment perpendicular to the 76th New York's right flank. The Rebels, recalled William Mantanye, "kept advancing up on us and outnumbered us so much as to out flank us on both right and left and poured a tremendous cross fire into us. I

7 E. D. Haviland Letter to his Mother, August 11, 1863, Paul Meuse Collection; Cook, "A Day at Gettysburg;" Uberto Burnham to his mother, July 31, 1863, Burnham Papers.

8 *OR* pt. 1, p. 285; Clark, ed., *North Carolina Regiments,* Vol. 3, p. 297; 55th NC, *GDN,* p. 9. Connally was too badly injured to be transported back to Virginia. He was captured and his left arm amputated.

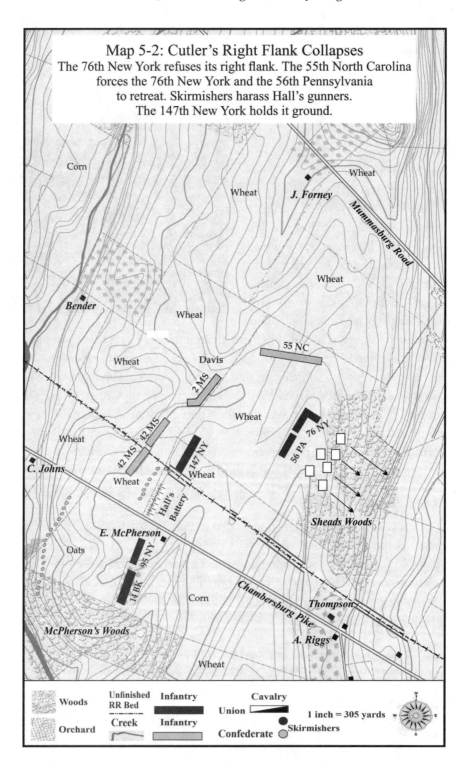

Map 5-2: Cutler's Right Flank Collapses
The 76th New York refuses its right flank. The 55th North Carolina
forces the 76th New York and the 56th Pennsylvania
to retreat. Skirmishers harass Hall's gunners.
The 147th New York holds it ground.

never saw men fall so fast." The wicked crossfire ravaged the two Federal regiments.[9]

C. A. Watkins also provided his impressions of the scene:

> The 76th New York being in advance of the Corps, of course were on the extreme right, and subject to a cross fire from the enemy, who had succeeded in flanking us. Our gallant boys now returned their fire with interest as the enemy arose from their cover in a wheat field and charged upon us, supposing we were raw militia, they advanced their line steadily firing as they came. Our officers and men were falling upon every side and it was evident that they meant to surround us by their superior numbers ... as we were completely flanked.[10]

To check the flanking threat posed by the Tar Heels, Major Grover ordered his right wing to change front to rear. His New Yorkers expertly completed this difficult maneuver despite the galling fire. About this time, Rebel musketry killed Grover's horse, so he commanded "on foot, cheering on his men." Both sides loaded and pulled triggers with demonic fury. The 76th New York's line now took the shape of an inverted L, part of it facing north and the rest facing west.

Soon after giving the order, a Rebel bullet struck Grover near the heart. He lived long enough to hand his watch and badges of rank to a friend, requesting that they be given to his wife. Captain John Cook assumed command despite having received a slight wound. Several other officers were hit including Captain Story, who had only minutes earlier escaped death when the artillery round passed between his legs. Story's luck expired when a Southern projectile smashed into his thigh, shattering his femur into three pieces. The captain's comrades would eventually carry him to the home of Mrs. William Culp, where surgeons were only able to remove one piece of the destroyed bone. After the battle, Story's wife and sister hustled to Gettysburg to be with him and remained at his side until he died on August 6.[11]

The situation was becoming extremely critical for Cutler's two regiments. For nearly half an hour, these Union infantrymen, originally totaling 627 officers and

---

9 Wm. Mantanye, "Camp Correspondence—76th New York N.Y.S.V.," 76th New York Newspaper Clippings File, New York State Military Museum.

10 C. A. Watkins letter, in 76th New York Newspaper Clippings File, New York State Military Museum.

11 OR pt. 1, p. 285; Hassler, *Crisis at the Crossroads*, p. 43; *New York at Gettysburg*, p. 616; Smith, *76th New York*, pp. 353, 357, 371- 372; Mantanye, "Camp Correspondence."

On the morning of July 1, the 76th New York and the 56th Pennsylvania retreated into these woods on Seminary Ridge. *Author*

---

men, fought against an advantageously positioned and numerically superior enemy (640 officers and men in the 55th North Carolina and a portion of the 492 officers and men of the 2nd Mississippi). Determined to hold their ground, the boys in blue stood fast even as their casualty count mounted rapidly. Sergeant Moses M. Whitney of the 76th New York proudly recalled that his regiment held their line "with a spirit and bravery never excelled." General Wadsworth eventually realized that if he did not withdraw the regiments to form a new line to the rear, his exposed troops might be annihilated. The division commander ordered Cutler to withdraw the 76th New York, 56th Pennsylvania, and the 147th New York to the wooded portion of Seminary Ridge north of Cashtown Pike. Thereafter, Wadsworth rode south to evaluate the deployment and performance of the recently arrived Iron Brigade, which had just engaged the enemy in McPherson's Woods.[12]

---

12 OR pt. 1, pp. 245, 282-285; *New York at Gettysburg*, p. 616; Hofmann, *PWP;* Coddington, *The Gettysburg Campaign*, p. 270; James S. Montgomery, *The Shaping of a Battle* (New York, 1959), p. 51; *Retreat from Gettysburg*, p. 277; Stine, *History of the Army of the Potomac*, p. 462; Whitney, "The 76th New York"; Cutler's Brigade Field Returns, July 1, 1863, RG 393, Part 2, NARA. The woodlot covering Seminary Ridge north of Cashtown Pike was known as Sheads Woods. See Chapter 6 for further details on the withdrawal of Cutler's regiments.

A minor controversy developed concerning Wadsworth's retreat order. Lieutenant Colonel John Kress, one of Wadsworth's aides, had watched the Iron Brigade deploy near McPherson's Woods before rejoining Wadsworth somewhere behind Cutler's brigade. Kress would later write that once he arrived there, "a crowd of wounded men and stragglers rushed across the little valley to Seminary Ridge." During Kress's absence, Maj. Clinton Hanks Meneely, another of the general's aides, had warned Wadsworth that Cutler's troops could not hold their position. Almost immediately, Kress claimed he witnessed the 7th Indiana, 147th and 76th New York, and 56th Pennsylvania break, "vigorously followed by the 2nd and 42nd Mississippi." Even though Maj. Gen. Abner Doubleday had informed Kress that Wadsworth ordered the retreat of Cutler's men, the staff officer remained skeptical. "I am sure that he [Wadsworth] did not give any orders to retreat," Kress adamantly insisted. "Certainly I did not hear or know of any, and I was very near him during the time when the order would have been given. . . . He and the staff officers labored faithfully to keep the brigade on the line first formed, but it was overwhelmed," he continued, "doubled up and crowded to the rear by a sudden and fierce attack on its right flank by a portion of Davis' Mississippi brigade. Hence, the order to retreat came from the enemy, and not from General Wadsworth."[13]

Kress was mistaken in his belief that Wadsworth had not issued a retreat order. Doubleday, Cutler, and Captain Cook of the 76th New York acknowledged in their official reports that Wadsworth ordered the withdrawal. Captain Timothy Edwards Ellsworth, also a member of Wadsworth's staff, admitted that he delivered the order to the 147th New York. In his postwar account, Kress placed the 7th Indiana on the battlefield. His memory failed him. The Hoosier regiment had been assigned guard duty that morning and had not participated in the morning fight west of town. Perhaps Kress failed to recall the delivery of the retreat orders. More likely, though, Wadsworth issued the directives to withdraw before Kress reunited with the general.[14]

Not surprisingly, reports vary as to the orderliness of the retreat. The 76th New York's Captain Cook claimed in his official report that his men performed the retrograde movement "in good order and the line reformed on the railroad track near the Seminary." Later, in a letter to Abner Doubleday, Cook explained that the

13 Kress, "Tales of the War."

14 OR pt. 1, pp. 282, 285; New York at Gettysburg, p. 1005. Hofmann confirmed that Wadsworth gave the retreat order. Hofmann, Remarks on the Battle of Gettysburg, p. 5.

76th New York and the 56th Pennsylvania retreated first to the crest of Seminary Ridge and thereafter fell back behind a small wooded area on the eastern slope of the ridge, where they reorganized their depleted ranks.

Several authors, including Warren Hassler, Edwin Coddington, and J. H. Stine, share in the belief that the retreat was orderly. However, Glenn Tucker's book *High Tide at Gettysburg* claimed the two regiments retired at a run across fields to the northern extension of Seminary Ridge where, after a brief pause, they continued all the way to the outskirts of town. Tucker probably based his interpretation on the report of Lt. Col. Rufus Dawes of the 6th Wisconsin (Iron Brigade), as well as the writings produced by General Doubleday. Dawes, for example, recalled seeing Cutler's regiments being destroyed during a disorderly retreat, while Doubleday wrote the regiments withdrew to the suburbs of Gettysburg. Undoubtedly, there was some level of confusion during the retreat, but only a complete lack of cohesiveness would have forced the troops to retire all the way back to the outskirts of town.

An 1865 letter written by the Acting Assistant Adjutant General John A. Kellogg to John B. Bachelder vindicated the two Union regiments. "General Cutler," explained Kellogg, "received an order to fall back to the town and barricade the streets, and the order to fall back in line of battle was given; before crossing the flat from the Seminary ridge to the town, however, this order was countermanded." To the credit of the 56th Pennsylvania and 76th New York, they reformed their ranks on the portion of Seminary Ridge north of the railroad cut and, despite heavy casualties, fought effectively later that same afternoon.[15]

Although the time between the first enemy volley and the retreat was only 20 to 30 minutes, Cutler's two Union regiments suffered heavily. During the three days of the battle, the 76th New York, which entered the fight with 375 officers and men, lost two officers and 30 men killed, 16 officers and 116 men wounded, and 70 men captured or missing. Sergeant Whitney estimated his 76th New York lost 169 officers and men during the brief bloody morning contest, the majority of which represented men struck by Rebel fire. Franklin Pratt wrote to his parents to inform

---

15 *OR* pt. 1, p. 285; Tucker, *High Tide at Gettysburg*, p. 114; Bandy, eds., *The Gettysburg Papers*, pp. 217-218; Doubleday, *Chancellorsville and Gettysburg*, p. 132; Stine, *History of the Army of the Potomac*, p. 462; Hassler, *Crisis at the Crossroads*, p. 45; Coddington, *The Gettysburg Campaign*, p. 270; Kellogg to Bachelder, November 1, 1865, Bachelder Papers Typescript; Colonel J. E. Cook to Doubleday, January 3, 1887, Abner Doubleday Papers, New York Historical Society. Cook claimed the 76th New York lost half of its force on the middle ridge and that only nine officers survived.

them that of the 30 men in his company who entered the fight that morning, only six answered roll call after the battle, meaning the rest had been killed, wounded, captured, or were missing. Cutler reported the losses of the 56th Pennsylvania as six officers wounded (one mortally), eight men killed, and 64 rank and file wounded. Thus, of the 252 officers and men who had marched to Gettysburg, 78 were casualties before 11:00 a.m. The headquarter guard, stationed on the right of the 76th New York, lost 12 out of 18 men.[16]

The withdrawal of the 76th New York and 56th Pennsylvania, though militarily sound and coming none too soon, caused more problems for the Union army. The retreat exposed and endangered Hall's 2nd Maine battery and the 147th New York.

16 OR pt. 1, pp. 282-283; *New York at Gettysburg*, p. 616; Busey and Martin, *Regimental Strengths at Gettysburg*, p. 24; Franklin F. Pratt to his Parents, July 4, 1863, Robert L. Brake Collection; Whitney, "The 76th New York." Discrepancies concerning losses are frequently found among sources. The morning of July 2, 12 officers and 81 rank and file of the 56th Pennsylvania answered roll call. In the 76th New York, only eight officers and 80 men reported for duty. Cutler's Brigade Field Returns, July 2, 1863, RG 393, Part 2, NARA.

The railroad cut, looking west. This is where the 147th New York crossed the cut. *Author*

This is a view of the railroad cut on the westernmost ridge. Note the gradual slope of the hill on the right of the cut. The left flank of the 147th New York's line was near the closest telephone pole. *Author*

CHAPTER SIX

The Stand of the 147th New York

The 147th New York under Lt. Col. Francis Miller crossed the railroad cut around 10:30 a.m., about the same time Brig. Gen. Lysander Cutler and Col. J. William Hofmann spotted the 55th North Carolina. Once across the cut, Miller ordered his men to change front to the west and the regiment advanced through a wheatfield up the gentle slope of the western ridge. At this time, Capt. James Hall's 2nd Maine battery, on the left of the New Yorkers, was firing at enemy artillery on Herr's Ridge and a portion of the 42nd Mississippi threatening his guns. The 56th Pennsylvania and the 76th New York, off the right and rear of the 147th New York, had just become engaged with the 55th North Carolina and part of the 2nd Mississippi. Colonel Edward Fowler's 14th Brooklyn and the 95th New York, posted near the McPherson's Woods and buildings, sparred with Brig. Gen. James J. Archer's skirmishers. Brigadier General Solomon Meredith's Iron Brigade, which had just reached the Codori house on Emmitsburg Pike, prepared to cut across the fields toward the rising sounds of battle.

The men of the 147th New York spotted the enemy before reaching the crest of the western ridge. A late crop of wheat partially obscured portions of the 42nd and 2nd Mississippi regiments advancing along the opposite slope. According to Pvt. Francis Pease, the Rebels were "not more than 30 or 40 rods [165-220 yards] off and their colors flying." John Bartlett remembered that "when the enemy opened fire on us we were about on a line with where the battery caissons stood." The Confederate musketry was heavy. Lieutenant J. Volney Pierce vividly described the situation:

While we were advancing in the wheatfield the battle opened on our right, and the bullets from the enemy were flying thick and fast as we marched rapidly towards our opponents. The wheat heads fell with rapid noddings, as the bullets from the Confederate line commenced their harvest of death. Men dropped dead, and the wounded men went to the rear before they had emptied their muskets; Corp. Fred. Rife and his file closer, Hiram Stowell, dropped dead, one upon the other. We continued to advance in the nodding wheat of death until our left touched on the railroad cut, supporting Hall's Battery.[1]

The 147th New York continued toward the crest of the ridge. Bursts of Confederate musketry staggered the New Yorkers, but they rallied to force back the Rebels and reach a position just below the crest. Hall's battery, which was 20 to 30 yards in advance of the 147th New York, now had infantry support on its right. Lieutenant Colonel Miller ordered his regiment to lie down and return fire.[2]

"The line of the 147th New York was lying in a field at and below the ridge, a wheatfield, ready for harvest," declared Capt. James Coey. "The fire of the enemy, the zipping of their bullets, cut the grain, completely covering the men, who would reach over the ridge, take deliberate aim, fire and then slide back under their canopy or covering of straw; reload and continue their firing. Those of the regiment wounded here were wounded in the head or upper part of the body, consequently more fatal."[3]

For numerous reasons, the 147th New York could not be seen by nearby units. First, the regiment was not in a direct line with any other Yankee outfit. Its position was slightly behind and to the right of Hall's guns, but ahead and to the left of the 76th New York and 56th Pennsylvania. The New Yorkers fought from a prone position, masked by the tall wheat surrounding them. Thick powder smoke

---

1 *Maine at Gettysburg, Report of Maine Commissioners Prepared by the Executive Committee* (Portland), 1898, p. 17; *New York at Gettysburg*, p. 991; Snyder, *Oswego County, New York in the Civil War*, p. 63; John Bartlett Letter; *Addresses Delivered Before the Historical Society of Pennsylvania Upon the Occasion of the Presentation of a Portrait of Major General John F. Reynolds* (Philadelphia, 1880), p. 23; Coe to Hofmann, July 12, 1888, John William Hofmann Papers, Society Small Collection.

2 John Bartlett Letter; Coe to Bachelder, December 28, 1888, Bachelder Papers Typescript; Allfort, "Memory of the First Engagement," Henry Harrison Lyman Collection.

3 Coey, "Cutler's Brigade." Four days after the fight, Burns E. Parkhurst provided his parents with a description of the ferocity of the conflict: "The first thing I knew the bullets were whistling around my head in all directions. One went through the top of my hat; another went through my blouse; a piece of shell struck the seam of my pants and ripped them about a foot. But that was all. It did not hurt me. But in about two seconds after a bullet hit me in the leg . . . but it is not a very bad wound." Burns E. Parkhurst, "Dear Parents," *Mexico Independent*, July 23, 1863.

Taken from the crest of the ridge held by the 147th New York, this photograph reveals the gradual slope of the height. *Author*

This photo was taken from the middle ridge, just north of the railroad cut. The westernmost ridge, where the 147th New York staged its heroic defense, is in the center of the picture. Note how gradually the ridge slopes. A person did not have to be on the crest to see someone on the opposite side. *Author*

Lieutenant Colonel Francis Miller

Courtesy of Allan Zellnock

reduced visibility. In the fury of combat, the Union troops on the 147th New York's flanks paid attention to the enemy—not to the Oswego boys. Finally, in a postwar correspondence, Surgeon Algernon Coe and Colonel Hofmann agreed that a fence lined with bushes separated the 147th's battle line and partially blocked the regiment from view. The regiment's battle front had formed in a visibly isolated location.[4]

Depending on which account you read, a wheat-covered interval between 30 to 80 yards separated the Union and Confederate infantry. Adjutant Henry H. Lyman described the fighting as short range and destructive. The Mississippians in the 42nd and a portion of the 2nd regiment kept up a steady and effective fire against the New Yorkers. Their Rebel yells intensified the alarming nature of the combat. The Mississippians made gradual advances, but the Federal line held firm. The crash of musketry, the roar of cannon fire, and the Rebel screams melded into an indistinguishable din that drowned out every order. Private Pease wrote to his family six days later that "the balls whistled round our heads like hail." Many men around him fell, including Franklin Halsey, who was shot through the head as he stood next to Pease. Lieutenant Volney Pierce saw Capt. Delos Gary fall to one knee after taking a bullet in the head. The ferocity of the moment gripped the Oswego boys. Captain Nathaniel Wright, fighting on Pierce's right, pounded the ground and encouraged his command to give the Confederates "hell."[5]

4 Coe to Hofmann, July 12, 1888, John William Hofmann Papers, Society Small Collection.

5 John Bartlett Letter; Whitney, "The 76th New York;" "A Chaplain at Gettysburg," p. 148; *New York at Gettysburg*, pp. 991, 992, 1001-1002; Love, "Mississippi at Gettysburg," p. 30; Bandy., eds., *The Gettysburg Papers*, p. 243; Snyder, *Oswego County, New York in the Civil War*, p. 63; Allfort, "Memory of the First Engagement," Henry Harrison Lyman Collection.

This photograph, taken from the left flank position of the 147th New York, gives a good indication of how much support Hall's Battery received. The guns in the right center background are where Hall's left section was located. Fowler's men were positioned beyond the statue and straight back to McPherson's Woods in the background. *Author*

This view shows the line held by the 76th New York and the 56th Pennsylvania, as seen from the line held by the 147th New York. *Author*

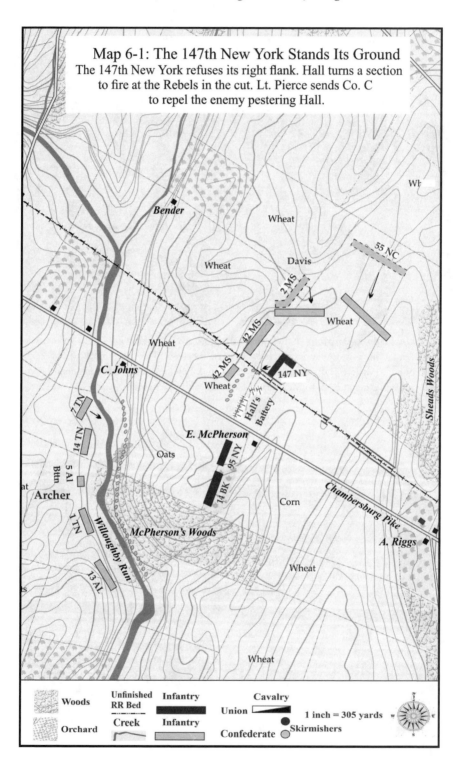

Map 6-1: The 147th New York Stands Its Ground
The 147th New York refuses its right flank. Hall turns a section
to fire at the Rebels in the cut. Lt. Pierce sends Co. C
to repel the enemy pestering Hall.

Confederate accounts confirm the savagery of the firefight. Mississippian Samuel Hankins watched as Union officers rode up and down the Federal line. "After we had advanced through the wheat, across the valley, and up the slope to within good shot of their line," remembered Hankins, "they jumped to their feet and opened fire on us. We continued advancing and firing." Captain Leander G. Woollard of the 42nd Mississippi recalled that he was leading his men across Willoughby Run and up the slope when he spotted a regiment of "blue bellies" less than 100 yards away. The officer ordered his men to lie down. A Union volley ripped overhead but managed to only wound a few of his men. Subsequent Federal musketry, however, riddled the Confederate line. Casualties mounted as Woollard and a lieutenant stood behind the line threatening to use their swords on any soldiers who considered fleeing. In the frightful caldron of fire and frenzy, Woollard noted that the Mississippians demonstrated an anxious tendency to surge forward. The relentless pressure from the 42nd Mississippi and part of the 2nd Mississippi threatened the 147th New York's line. Finally, after 15 or 20 minutes of vicious fighting, Lt. Col. Miller received Brig. Gen. James Wadsworth's order to withdraw.[6]

Tracing the origin and path of the communication that Miller received from Wadsworth offers an interesting commentary on how Civil War commanders issued battlefield orders. Wadsworth positioned himself during the fighting somewhere behind Cutler's brigade, possibly on Seminary Ridge between Cashtown Pike and the railroad cut. When the Rebel advance made the positions of the Union regiments north of the railroad grade untenable, Wadsworth grew concerned. He directed Capt. Timothy Ellsworth, one of his aides, to find and inform Maj. Gen. John Reynolds that unless reinforcements arrived soon, he would have to withdraw his force. Ellsworth found Capt. Robert W. Mitchell of Reynolds's staff standing beside the slain general just outside the east edge of McPherson's Woods. Ellsworth initially believed that Reynolds had merely fallen from his horse, but a closer examination revealed the general's dying gasps. Ellsworth promptly spurred his mount back to Wadsworth and informed the division commander of Reynolds's demise. Wadsworth took the initiative to send another courier to Cutler with instructions to withdraw his men from their

---

6 Samuel Hankins, "Simple Story of a Soldier—VII, VIII," *Confederate Veteran* (1913), Vol. 21, p. 113; Roger Long, "A Mississippian in the Railroad Cut," *The Gettysburg Magazine*, Issue Number 4 (January 1991), pp. 22-23.

advanced positions. Cutler, in turn, forwarded one of his aides to retrieve the 147th New York.[7]

Before Lt. Col. Miller could give the command to his New Yorkers to retreat, a Rebel bullet ripped through the scalp on the top of his head. Miller's frightened horse carried him away from the scene. Major George Harney, who assumed command after Miller's injury, knew nothing about the retreat order, so he maintained the regiment's advanced position. The 76th New York and the 56th Pennsylvania, meanwhile, pulled back to Seminary Ridge, and in doing so exposed the 147th New York's northern (right) flank.[8]

With the two Union regiments in retreat, the 2nd Mississippi and the 55th North Carolina increased the pressure against the 147th New York's naked flank. Concurrently, fire along the left side of the regiment's line slackened. Major Harney withdrew those right companies lying north of the fence separating the regiment so they could align along the south side of the barrier to meet the new threat. For a second time in the battle, an acting Union regimental commander ordered a difficult maneuver to meet a Confederate flanking maneuver. A deadly Southern crossfire, however, ripped through the inverted L-shaped Union line. "The boys on the right were falling like autumn leaves; the air was full of lead," recalled Lieutenant Pierce.[9]

The Confederate fire on the Union left front slackened for two reasons. First, the Confederate line shifted left, undoubtedly influenced by the retreat of the 56th Pennsylvania and 76th New York and by the 147th New York's change to the L-shaped formation. Second, the 42nd Mississippi concentrated more attention against Hall's 2nd Maine guns. Using the railroad cut and other terrain features as cover, Confederate skirmishers began picking off Hall's cannoneers and horses. Other Mississippians formed a "heavy straggling skirmish line" between the pike and the railroad cut, further threatening the Maine artillerymen. In an effort to counter the skirmishers, Hall ordered his right section under Lt. William Ulmer to change direction. Ulmer turned his guns northward to fire double loads of canister at the pesky skirmishers. The blasts did little to sway the Mississippi skirmishers, who continued to fire as they advanced. One group of Rebels in particular,

---

7 T. E. Ellsworth to H. H. Lyman, September 3, 1888, Henry Harrison Lyman Collection. Part of this letter appears in *New York at Gettysburg*, p. 1005.

8 Francis Miller's pension file documents the nature of his wound on the top of his head. Francis Miller, Proof of Disability Document, Pension File, NARA.

9 *New York at Gettysburg*, pp. 991, 992, 1001.

The left flank of the 147th New York held this area. The 42nd Mississippi was aligned along the tree line (which was not present in 1863). *Author*

bunched in a fence corner a short distance beyond the cut, caused especial havoc within the Maine battery.

Lieutenant Pierce, operating on the left of the 147th New York, wondered about the dwindling fire on his front and advanced his Company C to the crest of the ridge to investigate. When he spotted the increasing danger to Hall's exposed gunners, he ordered "left, oblique, fire" and Companies C and G responded with several volleys. The combination of canister fire and musketry dropped a number of the Rebel skirmishers and drove the balance down the hill.[10]

While Pierce's force helped drive back the Mississippians, Major Harney held a conference with the surviving officers near him to determine what to do: follow the 56th Pennsylvania and the 76th New York, leaving Hall's battery to face certain capture, or maintain the regiment's present line despite being outnumbered and outflanked? Perhaps there was some important reason not readily apparent to him

---

10 *New York at Gettysburg*, pp. 991, 1001-1002; *Maine at Gettysburg*, pp. 17-18; Stine, *History of the Army of the Potomac*, pp. 461-462; H. H. Lyman to Bachelder, December 12, 1888, Henry Harrison Lyman Collection.

(Left) Major George Harney
Author's Collection

(Below) Lieutenant J. Volney Pierce
Courtesy of William Howard

why the embattled 147th New York should remain where it stood. The fluid swirl of events relieved Major Harney from his command burden.

First, Hall decided it was time to get out before he lost all of his guns. The captain based his decision on the proximity of the Rebels and on his observation of the retreat of Cutler's right wing. Undoubtedly, the thick smoke caused by the innumerable cannon and musketry discharges obscured the prone 147th New York. John Bartlett, a member of the Oswego regiment, later admitted that the dense sulfuric clouds blocked Hall's guns from his view. It seems reasonable to conclude that the same smoke may have obscured the prone New Yorkers from Hall's vision. The captain directed Lieutenant Ulmer to retire his section 250-300 yards so his guns could enfilade the railroad cut. Hall, meanwhile, continued firing his other four pieces. Before Ulmer could ready his section to cover the battery's retreat, however, gunfire from Rebel skirmishers from the 2nd Mississippi and 55th North Carolina convinced the lieutenant to abandon his position. Ulmer saved his section even though one gun had to be dragged away by hand after all its horses had been shot.

Hall, too, sized up the situation and decided to withdraw his remaining guns. The captain went down to the limbers to order his drivers to reverse up the slope. Under cover of smoke, the cannoneers dragged their pieces down the incline to

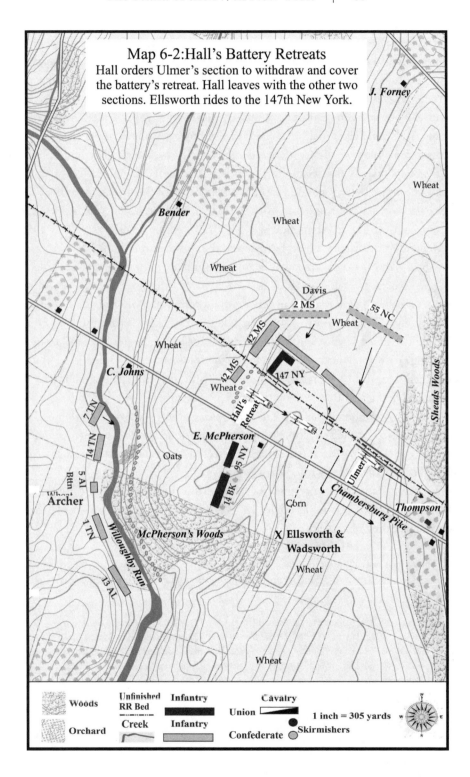

Map 6-2: Hall's Battery Retreats

Hall orders Ulmer's section to withdraw and cover the battery's retreat. Hall leaves with the other two sections. Ellsworth rides to the 147th New York.

meet the vehicles. Once they hitched the cannon to the limbers, Hall directed the drivers to cut across the field to Cashtown (Chambersburg) Pike and head for Seminary Ridge. Only one gun at a time could exit the field through a small gap in the wooden fence paralleling the road. Although the choke point delayed the drivers, all but one gun made it to safety. The artillerymen abandoned the last piece because of extensive casualties to cannoneers and horses alike. According to one account, Hall claimed the Confederates shot the horses of the last limber, while another version has him claiming the Rebels bayoneted them. In fact, the only reason the entire battery avoided capture was because of the proximity of the 147th New York on its right and the 14th Brooklyn and the 95th New York on its extreme left. If these regiments had withdrawn while Hall was still in place, Confederate skirmishers would have seized the unsupported guns.[11]

The 147th New York, meanwhile, three regiments to one, continued its heroic struggle against overwhelming odds. The 55th North Carolina pressed on and crossed the south side of the rail fence, driving the right wing of the Union line back. "Fierce flamed the fire around the altar of the Union from the guns of the One hundred and forty-seventh New York," recalled Volney Pierce. "The smoke of carnage rose as an incense, and wrapped the folds of the flag defended within its shortened lines. Not a man flinched; none left the field except the wounded; the untouched living and the dead remained."[12]

The Confederate infantry matched the valor of the gallant New Yorkers. When the 55th North Carolina's colors dropped to the ground and the regiment started to lose its cohesion, a Tar Heel officer corrected the unit's alignment as if the maneuver was being performed on a parade ground.[13]

General Wadsworth and Asst. Adj. Gen. Timothy E. Ellsworth observed the 147th New York's mortal struggle. In 1888, Ellsworth explained to Henry H. Lyman what they observed that July 1 morning:

> About the time that the First Brigade [Iron Brigade]—in the woods —had its success there, and not long afterwards, the fight there having lulled, riding back towards the rear with

---

11 Coey, "Cutler's Brigade;" *New York at Gettysburg*, pp. 992, 1005; Stine, *History of the Army of the Potomac*, p. 462; *Maine at Gettysburg*, p. 18; *OR* pt. 1, pp. 359-360; John Bartlett Letter; Colonel John B. Bachelder, "Hall's Maine and Calef's U. S. Batteries at Gettysburg," *Grand Army Scout and Soldiers Mail*, December 26, 1885; Hall to Bachelder, December 29, 1869, Bachelder Papers Typescript.

12 *New York at Gettysburg*, p. 992.

13 *New York at Gettysburg*, p. 992.

General Wadsworth, the position of your regiment was observed by him, apparently the only command remaining on that third ridge and seemingly under heavy fire. He asked me what that regiment was doing up there; said he had given orders some time ago for those troops to be withdrawn, and directed me to go and withdraw them unless there was some special occasion, which was not apparent to him, for their remaining.[14]

Ellsworth did as ordered, riding along the depression between the middle and western ridges until he reached the center of the 147th New York's line. Then he rode "directly up the hill," waving his hat as he approached the New Yorkers. When Ellsworth confronted Harney, he asked the major why the regiment remained on the western ridge. Harney explained that he had not received the retreat directive. Ellsworth repeated the order to withdraw; the aide later admitted that he retired "as rapidly as I conveniently could."[15]

According to Capt. James Coey, "Major Harney then gave orders, to be communicated along the line, for the men to divest themselves of everything but the rifle and cartridge box. Thus went our rations, and until July 4, only two crackers from a passing regiment sustained us."[16]

For half an hour the 147th New York endured a brutal combat baptism with supreme courage. Despite mounting casualties and the fact that troops on both sides had retreated, the New Yorkers stood their ground and fought gallantly against superior odds. When Harney received Ellsworth's order to retire, the ground to the rear and on the left of the regiment lay open. The rapid Confederate advance from the west and north, however, threatened to cut off the regiment. Mississippians from the 42nd regiment closed in on the ground Hall had evacuated; others filtered through the western end of the railroad cut. Captain Woollard of the 42nd Mississippi wrote that when his men saw the 2nd Mississippi surge ahead on the left, his own men charged with an enthusiastic Rebel yell. From the north, part of the 2nd Mississippi and the entire 55th North Carolina overlapped the depleted ranks of the New Yorkers. Finally, Harney gave the order, "in retreat, double-quick, run." As the regiment rose to retreat, several bullets struck and

14 Parkhurst, "At Gettysburg," *New York at Gettysburg*, p. 1005.

15 *New York at Gettysburg*, p. 1005; Coey, "Cutler's Brigade;" Parkhurst, "At Gettysburg."

16 Coey, "Cutler's Brigade." Lieutenant Lyman also remembered losing his rations: "From the morning of the first till 5:00 p.m. of the 4th of July we received or had nothing to eat, except small issues of fresh beef which was eaten without salt." Lyman to Bachelder, no date, Bachelder Papers Typescript.

instantly killed Color Sgt. John Hinchcliff. His falling body wrapped itself in the tattered flag as his blood drenched the standard.[17]

"On the first break to the rear, the colors, not appearing," explained Captain Coey, "Serg't William A. Wybourn, a brave Irish lad, hastened to the line, unrolled the color-bearer from the enveloping folds of the flag, tearing it from its shattered staff, rolling it up in his race to the rear, he was struck by the enemy's fire and went to the earth." Lieutenant J. Volney Pierce, continued Coey, "hastened to him to recover the flag." Pierce recalled trying to "remove the colors, but he [Wybourn] held to them with true Irish grit. I commanded him to let go, and to my surprise he answered, 'Hold on, I will be up in a minute,' rolled over and staggered to his feet and carried them all through the fight, and was commissioned for his courage."[18]

The regiment split into two distinct parts during its retreat to reach Seminary Ridge. According to Amos Allfort, it was "every man for himself." The men on the left of the line descended into the railroad cut in an attempt to reach safety. Once inside, they received fire from members of the 42nd Mississippi. The bullets chased the Yankees as they climbed the southern edge of the embankment and raced along the meadow between the cut and Cashtown Pike. The survivors crossed the pike, passed through a small peach orchard, and finally came to a halt near the Seminary buildings.[19]

Some who chose the railroad cut as a means of escape were not as lucky. "We got no orders to retreat until the Rebs got up very close. We was then ordered to retreat, which we did at a fast rate," explained Pvt. Francis Pease in a letter to his parents on July 7. He continued:

> We left awful sight of dead and wounded on the field as we retreated. We got into an old railroad ravine, and was going along as fast as we could, but not very, for the road was so crowded. Besides, there was a good many wounded men that had hobbled along and got into the ravine. The Rebel balls whistled over the ravine like hail. Soon the Rebels came up each side of the bank in large numbers, and we had to throw down our arms and surrender ourselves to them as their prisoners.[20]

---

17 *New York at Gettysburg*, pp. 992, 994, 1001-1002; Lyman to Bachelder, no date, Bachelder Papers Typescript; Coey, "Cutler's Brigade"; Long, "A Mississippian in the Railroad Cut," p. 24.

18 Coey, "Cutler's Brigade"; *New York at Gettysburg*, p. 993.

19 *New York at Gettysburg*, p.993; Amos Allfort, "Memory of the First Engagement," Henry Harrison Lyman Collection.

20 Snyder, *Oswego County, New York in the Civil War*, p. 63.

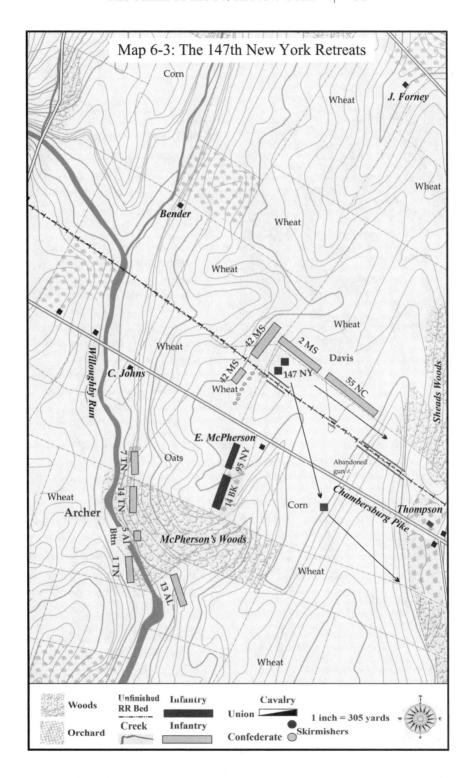

Map 6-3: The 147th New York Retreats

Corn

Wheat

J. Forney

Wheat

Bender

Wheat

Wheat

Wheat

42 MS

2 MS

Davis

42 MS

147 NY

55 NC

Willoughby Run

C. Johns

Wheat

Wheat

Sheads Woods

E. McPherson

Oats

95 NY

7 TN

14 BK

Abandoned gun

Chambersburg Pike

Wheat

14 TN

Corn

Thompson

Archer

5 AL

McPherson's Woods

Bttn 1 TN

13 AL

Wheat

Wheat

Woods | Unfinished RR Bed | Infantry | Cavalry
Orchard | Creek | Infantry | Union
| | | Confederate | Skirmishers

1 inch = 305 yards

147th New York Monument

Steven Floyd

The New Yorkers on the right of the line kept north of the railroad cut as they retired toward Seminary Ridge. James Coey left a vivid description of their experience:

Fresh from lying down, with the enemy winded by their quick thrust forward, we made progress to the rear. As soon as our guns were loaded the line halted, faced about, the volley given, then the march continued, men falling at every step. Many of the enemy, in their excitement and haste to capture us, failed to draw their ramrods after loading their guns, shooting them at us. . . . The enemy was now so near, even their camp hatchets were hurled among us, with vile and opprobrious taunts as bitter as their fire, calling on us to surrender.[21]

Major Harney's encouragement and coolness under fire helped prevent a mass capture. Eventually, the regiment reunited on Seminary Ridge north of the eastern railroad cut.

The previously untested men of the 147th New York had made a magnificent stand along the western ridge. St. Clair A. Mulholland, a Union officer in the Irish Brigade and an author after the war, later declared that the "147th New York was the first regiment to make the great record at Gettysburg."[22] Warren Hassler described the performance of the New Yorkers as "the highlight of the first day's battle." T. C. Harris of the 2nd Mississippi would admit the soldiers of the 147th

21 Coey, "Cutler's Brigade."

22 St. Clair A. Mulholland, *Percentage Losses at Gettysburg Greatest in History* (Gettysburg, 1911), p. 1.

"were hard fighters and retired only at the point of bayonet after most of them were killed."[23]

The cost had been dear. Out of 430 officers and men that entered the fray, 207 fell. Cutler reported that two officers and 42 men had been killed, while 10 officers and 153 men had been wounded. A number were taken prisoner, and others simply reported as missing. Despite the heavy losses, the regiment would fight again later that same afternoon. By evening, only 79 men responded when roll was called. The regiment sustained the overwhelming majority of its losses in the ferocious fight on the first morning of the three-day battle.[24]

The sacrifice of the 147th New York had not been in vain. By holding its position, the regiment allowed Hall to save five of his guns. The unit also delayed the Confederate advance, which enabled the 56th Pennsylvania and 76th New York to regroup. Most importantly, the Oswego boys provided precious time so help could be sent to support Cutler's collapsing right flank. Along with the 76th New York and 56th Pennsylvania, they had inflicted substantial casualties upon Joe Davis's Rebel brigade. Confederate officer losses were particularly high. The 55th North Carolina lost Col. John Connally and Lt. Col. M. T. Smith. In the 42nd Mississippi, both Lt. Col. Hillary Moseley and Maj. William Feeney fell wounded. The 2nd Mississippi's losses included Col. John M. Stone. The heavy proportion of officer casualties, the exhaustion caused by the long march to the battlefield, the sweltering heat, and the anxiety of combat all contributed to the disorganized state of the Confederate troops.

Nonetheless, the victorious Rebels ignored their crumbling cohesiveness and other issues to dash after the three retreating regiments.[25]

23 St. Clair A. Mulholland, *Percentage Losses at Gettysburg Greatest in History* (Gettysburg, 1911), p. 1; Hassler, *Crisis at the Crossroads*, p. 47; T. C. Harris, "The Second Mississippi at Gettysburg," *Confederate Veteran* (1917), Vol. 25, p. 527.

24 OR pt. 1, p. 282; Hassler, *Crisis at the Crossroads*, pp. 47, 143; Coey, "Cutler's Brigade"; *New York at Gettysburg*, p. 993. On the morning of July 2, only 10 officers and 79 men from the 147th New York answered roll call. Cutler's Brigade Field Return, July 2, 1863, RG 393, Part 2, NARA.

25 OR pt. 2, pp. 648-650; *New York at Gettysburg*, pp. 1002, 1006; Vanderslice, *Gettysburg: Then and Now*, pp. 119, 303-304.

A Desperate Stand: The 147th New York Infantry at Gettysburg, by Mark Maritato. *Courtesy of Mark Maritato*

CHAPTER SEVEN

Fowler's Demi-Brigade and the Fight at the Middle Railroad Cut

Colonel Edward Fowler received the order to place the 14th Brooklyn and the 95th New York on the left of Capt. James Hall's 2nd Maine battery about 10:00 a.m.

While the rest of Brig. Gen. Lysander Cutler's brigade deployed farther north, Colonel Fowler marched his newly created demi-brigade up the eastern slope of the western ridge. The 14th Brooklyn formed on the left and Col. George Biddle's 95th New York held the right. The new Union deployment held a line stretching between the McPherson's Woods and the McPherson home, outbuildings, and garden.

Within a short time they spotted Brig. Gen. James J. Archer's Confederate skirmishers directly ahead and in the woods to their left front. As the main Southern battle line prepared to cross Willoughby Run, a ripple of musketry erupted along both lines. Confederate projectiles whistled along the ridge as Colonel Fowler's men vigorously returned fire. Colonel George Biddle was wounded early in the contest, so Maj. Edward Pye assumed command of the 95th New York. Casualties mounted as the fighting steadily escalated. In a clear display of the severity of the musketry, a pair of bullets struck the head of Fowler's horse in rapid succession. A spent ball also smacked against Fowler's thigh, breaking

Colonel Edward Fowler's demi-brigade formed near here, facing west. McPherson's Woods are on the left. *Author*

Fowler's initial July 1 position would have extended toward Chambersburg Pike. McPherson's Barn is to the right. The building to the left of the picture, on the opposite side of Chambersburg Pike, no longer exists. Hall's 2nd Maine Battery served in that vicinity. *Author*

(Right) Colonel Edward Brush Fowler
Author's Collection

(Below) Colonel Solomon Meredith
Courtesy of Craig Johnson

through the skin and causing a severe bruise. Another round struck the mount of the 14th Brooklyn's adjutant in the head.[1]

The fire from Fowler's two regiments discomfited Archer's men. As casualties mounted, the Rebels who had crossed Willoughby Run shifted to their right to seek safety in McPherson's Woods. As a result, the Confederate musketry striking Fowler's line slackened. The refuge sought by the Confederates proved short-lived. As Archer's main line splashed across Willoughby Run to enter McPherson's Woods, Col. Solomon Meredith's Iron Brigade reached the battlefield. Its leading regiment, the 2nd Wisconsin, penetrated the woodland from

---

1 OR pt. 1, p. 286; Tevis and Marquis, *The History of the Fighting Fourteenth*, pp. 82, 83, 132-133; Swinton, *Twelve Decisive Battles*, p. 329; Hoke, *The Great Invasion*, pp. 267-268; *New York at Gettysburg*, pp. 733, 736. Fowler hinted that Biddle remained on the field during the morning fight and did not retire until the afternoon. See Tevis and Marquis, *The History of the Fighting Fourteenth*, p. 134. Major Edward Pye's official report does not clearly detail when he took command. Apparently, Biddle did remain on the battlefield but turned over command of the regiment to Pye.

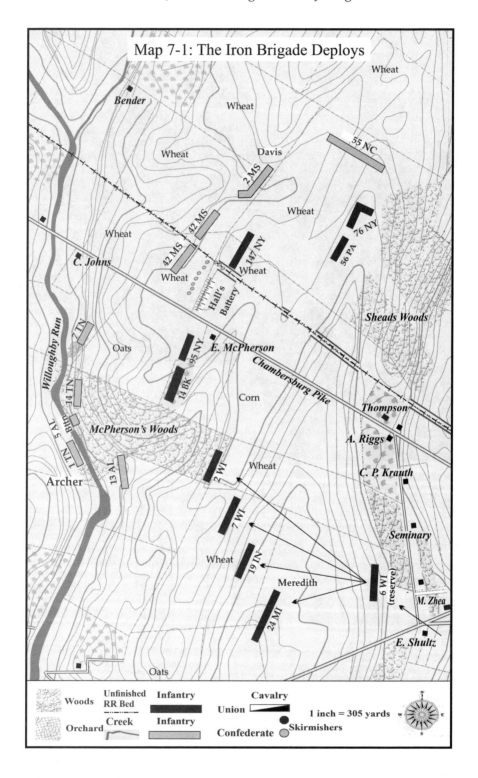

Map 7-1: The Iron Brigade Deploys

the opposite direction, followed en echelon by the 7th Wisconsin, 19th Indiana, and 24th Michigan. Fowler's men heard an explosion of musketry in the timber to their left rear—a clear indication the Westerners had arrived. The veteran Iron Brigade reinforcements overwhelmed Archer's surprised men, drove them back across Willoughby Run, and captured many, including General Archer.[2]

Shortly after the arrival of the Meredith's brigade, Fowler noticed a Rebel battle line north of the pike advancing east past his flank. He also witnessed Hall's last gun fire and its crew retreat. Fortunately for the Union cause, Brig. Gen. Joseph Davis exercised little control over his advancing men. Evidently paying little or no attention to his right, Davis allowed a large portion of his brigade to pursue Hall's cannoneers and the three retiring Union regiments north of Chambersburg Pike. Had Davis swung his brigade against Fowler's right flank, the Confederate brigadier could have endangered not only the remainder of Cutler's brigade but the Iron Brigade as well. A concerted effort on Davis's part may have forced the Federals to yield McPherson's Woods, one of the key terrain features of the first day's fight.[3]

Scattered shots from the north began striking the right and rear of Fowler's line, prompting the colonel to react to the new threat. While still under sputtering fire from Archer's retiring men and from Southern cannon perched on Herr's Ridge, Fowler directed his two regiments to face to the rear. About this time, the 147th New York's valiant stand ended with its retreat toward Seminary Ridge. As the Oswego boys hustled to safety, Fowler calmly marched his two regiments down the east slope of the western ridge. The colonel moved his command past the rear of the McPherson house and halted once his regiments aligned with the advance of Davis's Confederates. Once there, Fowler ordered the 14th Brooklyn and 95th New York to change front forward on the right. To complete this difficult maneuver, the right company of Fowler's command (the one nearest the woods) pivoted to face Chambersburg Pike. The rest of the demi-brigade, meanwhile, continued marching toward the seminary. When the first company completed its maneuver, the next company followed suit. Eventually, the line of the 14th Brooklyn and the 95th New York paralleled Chambersburg Pike, which placed it

---

2 Tevis and Marquis, *The History of the Fighting Fourteenth*, pp. 83, 132; Bandy and Freeland, *The Gettysburg Papers*, p. 176; OR pt. 1, p. 286; Philip Cheek and Mair Pointon, *History of the Sauk County Riflemen* (Gaithersburg, 1984), p. 73.

3 Freeman, *Lee's Lieutenants*, Vol. 3, p. 80; Coddington, *The Gettysburg Campaign*, p. 271.

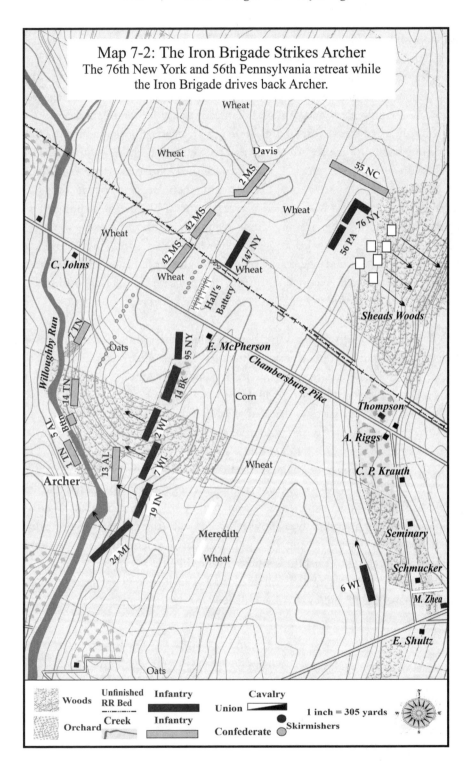

Map 7-2: The Iron Brigade Strikes Archer
The 76th New York and 56th Pennsylvania retreat while
the Iron Brigade drives back Archer.

The men of the 14th Brooklyn, with their left flank near the barn, charged across this field to attack Joe Davis's Brigade located in and around the railroad cut. *Author*

perpendicular to the Rebel troops north of the road. The two regiments coolly advanced to a position near the pike and lay down for several minutes.[4]

Reinforcements joined Fowler's contingent. Maj. Gen. Abner Doubleday, who had arrived on the battlefield as the Iron Brigade rushed into action, assumed overall command of the Union forces after Maj. Gen. John F. Reynolds was killed around 10:45 a.m. Doubleday had prudently withheld part of the Iron Brigade as a reserve. This force consisted of the 6th Wisconsin under Lt. Col. Rufus Dawes, bolstered by 100 men of the Iron Brigade guard. All told, the reinforced regiment numbered approximately 450 veteran fighters. When Doubleday spotted the crisis north of Chambersburg Pike, he decided to commit his reserve.

Doubleday dispatched the Westerners at a double-quick toward the turnpike to shore up the collapsing Federal right flank. As the 6th Wisconsin's column approached the pike, Dawes changed the front of his regiment so that it faced the flank of the Rebel force. The Wisconsin troops now occupied the low ground between the eastern and middle ridges. Dawes's horse was wounded while riding toward the turnpike, so the lieutenant colonel fought the rest of the battle on foot.

4 Tevis and Marquis, *The History of the Fighting Fourteenth*, pp. 83, 133; *New York at Gettysburg*, p. 995; *OR* pt. 1, p. 286.

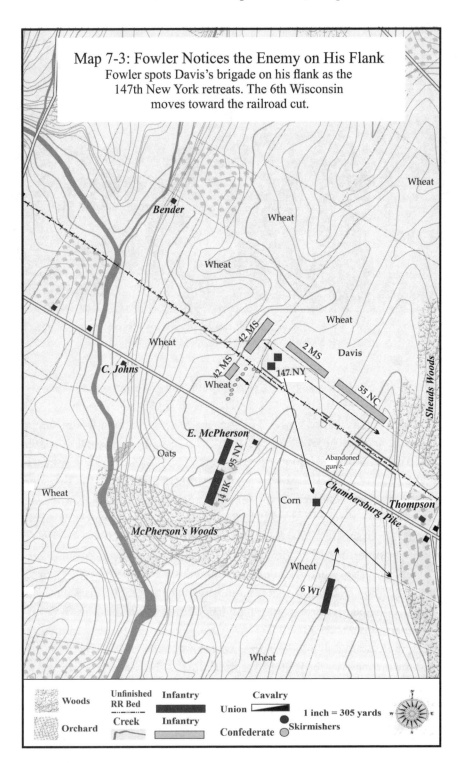

Map 7-3: Fowler Notices the Enemy on His Flank
Fowler spots Davis's brigade on his flank as the
147th New York retreats. The 6th Wisconsin
moves toward the railroad cut.

95th New York Monument

Steven Floyd

In a stroke of good fortune, the 6th Wisconsin and Fowler's demi-brigade reached Chambersburg Pike about the same time.[5]

One of the great controversies concerning the first day's fight was whether the 6th Wisconsin single-handedly charged and captured the Southerners posted in the railroad cut north of the turnpike. Many 6th Wisconsin veterans, including Dawes, adamantly maintained the Westerners spearheaded that assault. A number of the Wisconsin fellows not only insisted they charged alone, but swore they had led the march to Gettysburg. In his memoirs, Dawes claimed he never saw the 14th Brooklyn. He also suggested that the 14th Brooklyn and the 95th New York combined had fewer men than the 6th Wisconsin. C. W. Okey of the 6th Wisconsin noted his regiment halted briefly, "waiting for the 14th Brooklyn to form on our left, which . . . they failed to do." Another Wisconsin veteran, Lloyd G. Harris, wrote angrily that the 95th New York never joined the flank of his regiment and never participated in the charge.[6]

5 *OR* pt. 1, pp. 245, 246, 287-288; Dawes, *Service with the Sixth Wisconsin*, pp. 165-167; Coddington, *The Gettysburg Campaign*, p. 271; Bandy, ed., *The Gettysburg Papers*, p. 217; Cheek and Pointon, *History of the Sauk County Riflemen*, p. 74.

6 Dawes, *Service with the Sixth Wisconsin*, p. 167, 345-347; Rufus Dawes, "Align on the Colors," *Milwaukee Sunday Telegraph*, April 27, 1890; Lance Herdegen and William Beaudot, *In the Bloody Railroad Cut* (Dayton, 1990), pp. 182-189, 287-299. Herdegen and Beaudot offer an excellent account of the 6th Wisconsin on July 1, 1863; C. W. Okey, "After That Flag," *Milwaukee Sunday Telegraph*, April 29, 1883. The 6th Wisconsin did not outnumber the 14th Brooklyn and 95th New York. Fowler's demi-brigade entered the battle with a combined 600 men.

Lieutenant Colonel Rufus Dawes

Courtesy of Craig Johnson

The passionate accounts by 6th Wisconsin veterans proclaiming their unsupported accomplishments must be analyzed with care. Rufus Dawes, in his many accounts of the charge, made slight but noteworthy changes in his renditions of the fight. For instance, in an 1868 letter to Gettysburg historian John Bachelder, Dawes acknowledged that the 14th Brooklyn accompanied the charge, en echelon. More importantly, Dawes affirmed in his official report that after crossing the fence, the 95th New York and 14th Brooklyn joined him. Without using any sources outside the regiment, the claims by 6th Wisconsin members suggesting they carried the attack alone can be easily dismissed. Philip Cheek and Mair Pointon, in their Company A history of the 6th Wisconsin, acknowledged that "as soon as the 14th Brooklyn and 95th New York Regiments joined us on the left, the line went forward with great spirit." In almost all of his accounts, Rufus Dawes indicated that he and Maj. Pye agreed to charge the railroad cut together. Even Maj. Alfred H. Belo of the 55th North Carolina wrote after the war that the 6th Wisconsin was "at the same time joined by the 95th New York and 14th Brooklyn."[7]

Sources written by members of Cutler's brigade affirmed the joint nature of the charge. Over the years, Colonel Fowler consistently claimed the 6th Wisconsin joined his command. In a July 6, 1863, newspaper article, Fowler stated his demi-brigade was "joined by the 6th Wisconsin Regiment (who fought most gallantly)." Three days later in his official report, Fowler noted that after his command changed front to face Davis's Brigade, "the 6th Wisconsin Regiment gallantly advanced to our assistance." On July 28, 1863, Fowler penned his

---

7 David and Aubrey Ladd, ed., *The Bachelder Papers*, 3 Vols. (Savas Beatie, 2021), Vol. 1, pp. 323-324; Cheek and Pointon, *History of the Sauk County Riflemen,* p. 74; Belo, "The Battle of Gettysburg," p. 165; OR pt. 1, p. 276.

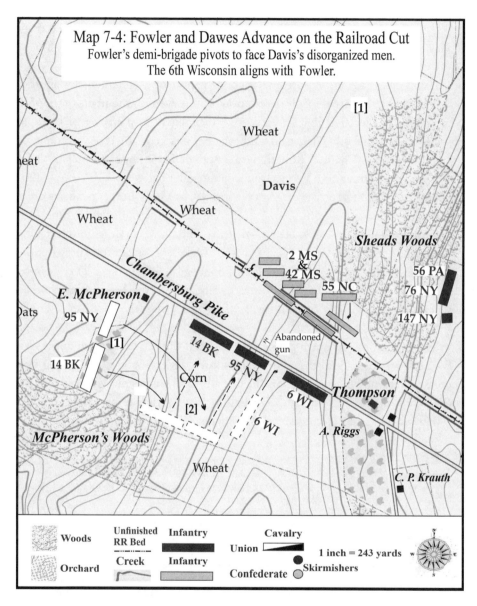

Map 7-4: Fowler and Dawes Advance on the Railroad Cut
Fowler's demi-brigade pivots to face Davis's disorganized men.
The 6th Wisconsin aligns with Fowler.

recollections of the battle while in camp near Warrenton Junction. "The 6th Wisconsin," he insisted, "advanced bravely to our assistance." Fowler's diary extracts are almost identical to his July 28 account. The colonel wrote these statements shortly after the battle while the events remained fresh in his mind. The only other account to surface concerning Fowler's recollections of the event was a letter he wrote on August 30, 1883, to J. William Hofmann, colonel of the 56th Pennsylvania. Fowler's account remained unchanged: "I immediately moved my two regiments to the rear to uncover McPhersons house and barn, changed front to face north, was joined on our right by the 6th Wis. and charged." Fowler's story never wavered throughout his accounts.[8]

Major Pye's sketchy report and a confirmation of a statement by another officer of the brigade are the only descriptions of this event by members of the 95th New York. Pye declared that Fowler's two regiments "formed line of battle in connection with the 6th Wisconsin, and together charged." In 1886, a veteran of the 95th New York named Robert Bard responded to a letter from J. William Hofmann. The former 56th Pennsylvania commander had sent Bard a copy of his January 13, 1886, article concerning the first day at Gettysburg. In his account, Hofmann maintained the 6th Wisconsin connected to the right flank of the 14th Brooklyn and 95th New York. He also gave the 95th New York credit for retaking Hall's abandoned gun. Bard replied that the article was so carefully prepared he could offer Hofmann no additional facts nor suggest any changes. There can be little doubt that Fowler's demi-brigade and the 6th Wisconsin charged simultaneously. The only question was when and where the two forces linked together.[9]

As Davis's Brigade north of the pike pursued the retreating 76th and 147th New York regiments and the 56th Pennsylvania, its cohesion as a fighting unit decreased. At one point, Maj. John Blair of the 2nd Mississippi could not find a single other regimental officer. According to Blair, "All the men were jumbled together without regard to regiment or company." The whereabouts of Davis and

---

8 Fowler, "The Fourteenth Regiment;" Tevis and Marquis, *The History of the Fighting Fourteenth*, p. 133; Fowler Extract; *OR* pt. 1, pp. 286-287; Fowler to Hofmann, August 30, 1888, J. William Hofmann Papers, Society Small Collection.

9 Hofmann, *PWP;* Robert Bard to Hofmann, February 21, 1886, J. William Hofmann Papers, Society Small Collection. The 6th Wisconsin advanced toward the railroad cut in the swale between the eastern and middle ridges. Members of the Western regiment could not see the 14th Brooklyn, which attacked the railroad bed from the low ground between the middle and western ridges. Essentially, the middle ridge served as a visual barrier that prevented the two regiments from seeing one another. Dawes stated he observed the 95th New York on his left. However, he declared he was "ignorant of the fact" that the 14th Brooklyn was "farther to the left." Dawes also admitted, "I did not know he [Fowler] was on the field until the charge was over." Fowler knew of the presence of the 6th Wisconsin because part of his demi-brigade, the 95th New York, connected to the left flank of Dawes's men. This is verified by Fowler's claim that he ordered all three regiments to charge the cut. Because soldiers in the 6th Wisconsin could not see the 14th Brooklyn, any statements they made suggesting the chasseurs lagged behind during the charge on the railroad cut should be considered with caution. Dawes, *Service with the Sixth Wisconsin*, p. 167; *OR* pt. 1, pp. 286-288.

The railroad cut, looking east. The bridge indicates the location of the middle ridge. The 6th Wisconsin charged the portion of the cut on the opposite side of the bridge. The foreground is the portion of the cut captured by Fowler's men. *Author*

Col. H. R. Miller of the 42nd Mississippi cannot be determined from official reports or reminiscences. They may have watched the rapidly unfolding events from a location northwest of the cut.

When Blair and the 55th North Carolina's Major Belo reached the vicinity of the middle ridge, they noticed the three Federal regiments forming along the turnpike. Belo suggested to Blair that they charge the Union troops before the Yankees completed their formation. As Davis's Brigade wheeled to the right, Union infantry along Chambersburg Pike rested their muskets on the fence rails and delivered a withering fire. Despite the enfilade, the Rebels completed the maneuver. Many Confederates dropped into the railroad cut to escape the Union volleys. Part of the 55th North Carolina extended beyond the deep portion of the cut and fired at the Union infantry from the embankment. A brief, though brisk, fire fight erupted.

The Federal musketry was particularly effective. When the Union regiments first opened on Davis's Brigade, the color guard of the 2nd Mississippi stood a short distance south and east of the railroad cut. In less than five minutes, Union gunfire killed or wounded the entire color guard. More than a dozen bullets riddled the Rebel banner while other projectiles cracked and splintered the flag staff.

Although many of Davis's men returned fire, the depth of the cut in some places prevented the Confederates sequestered there from supporting their comrades posted along the embankment. Davis finally realized his exhausted troops were in a critical position. In addition to the threat from the south, W. B. Murphy of the 2nd Mississippi later recalled seeing Cutler and his staff along the ridge line to the east. Soon thereafter, remnants of the 76th and 147th New York Regiments and the 56th Pennsylvania appeared at the edge of wooded Seminary Ridge. A gun from Calef's battery unlimbered on Chambersburg Pike, where it crossed Seminary Ridge, so as to enfilade the massed Confederates. With Union troops on two sides, Davis prudently ordered a retreat. The Mississippians and North Carolinians received word to retire via the railroad cut while a portion of the 55th North Carolina fought a delaying action.[10]

Rebel musketry slackened when the Confederate retreat began. Without conferring, both Fowler and Dawes decided to charge. Fowler would later claim he sent a messenger to Dawes with an order to attack, but Dawes never acknowledged receiving it. The historian of the 14th Brooklyn explained what happened next:

> At the Colonel's command they [the demi-brigade] rushed forward with a cheer. There was an ascent of about three feet at the pike. As the troops, charging with dash and spirit, reached this little eminence, they were met with a murderous hail of musket balls. The balls came so thick and fast that the whirring noise they made sounded like the steady rhythm of machinery. For just an instant, as the full force of this terrible fire broke along their front, the line wavered. But it was only for an instant, and then, with another cheer, louder and more determined, the men rushed on.[11]

Two sturdy fences had to be scaled in order to cross the turnpike. A storm of Southern lead struck numerous Yankees in all three regiments as they climbed the obstructions. The Rebel fire intensified once the Federals crossed the fences. According to Fowler, the enemy showered "bullets at us like hail, and our brave

---

10 *New York at Gettysburg*, p. 1006; Belo, "The Battle of Gettysburg," p. 165; 55th NC, *GDN*, p. 9; Dawes, *Service with the Sixth Wisconsin*, pp. 167, 345-347; *OR* pt. 2, p. 649; Tevis and Marquis, *The History of the Fighting Fourteenth*, p. 83; Clark, ed., *North Carolina Regiments,* Vol. 3, p. 298; Cheek and Pointon, *History of the Sauk County Riflemen*, p. 74; Murphy to Dearborn, June 29, 1900, Papers of E. S. Bragg, Vertical File 4-9d, GNMP. Calef claimed he used one of his guns to enfilade the railroad cut. Bachelder substantiated the claim in a newspaper article. Calef, "Gettysburg Notes," p. 49; *OR* pt. 1, p. 1031; Bachelder, "Hall's Maine and Calef's U. S. Batteries at Gettysburg."

11 Dawes, *Service with the Sixth Wisconsin*, p. 167; Tevis and Marquis, *The History of the Fighting Fourteenth*, pp. 83-84, 133; *OR* pt. 1, p. 286.

boys were dropping at every step." The Union demi-brigade recaptured the gun Hall's cannoneers had earlier abandoned. As the troops paused to reform, they answered Southern musketry with volleys of their own. Fowler recalled a tendency on the part of the men to halt at this time. The troops were caught in the fury of the moment and anxious to pay back Confederate bullets with Yankee lead. Casualties mounted along the lines of the exposed Union force.[12]

The advanced Union position was in a precarious state. The 6th Wisconsin's colors fell several times, but on each occasion another member of the color guard hoisted the emblems. Dawes repeatedly urged his men to align on the colors. As he later recalled, it was the only instruction that could keep his rapidly dwindling force cohesive. Dawes then noticed for the first time that the 95th New York supported his left flank. Believing Maj. Pye to be in charge, Dawes described what he did next:

> I ran quickly to him and hurriedly said: 'We must charge. . .' Pye said, 'we are with you,' and swinging his sword, shouted 'forward! forward! charge!' I ran to the rear of my colors shouting 'forward! forward! charge! align on the colors! align on the colors! . . . The musketry crashed with an unbroken roar before us.[13]

In 1893, a remarkable newspaper article appeared in the *Rockland County Messenger*. Apparently, Silas G. Mackey, a veteran of the 95th New York, had invited Rufus Dawes to the upcoming New York Day celebration at Gettysburg. Dawes wrote Mackey, promising he would make the trip, if possible. On June 1, 1893, the *Messenger* published the entire letter written by Dawes. In his response to Mackey, Dawes acknowledged: "The real leader of the 95th on that memorable day was my intimate and congenial friend then Major Edward Pye. Colonel Biddle was a brave man and he was there, but Pye with uplifted sword ran ahead of his men to start our charge." This obscure letter refutes any and all claims that the 6th Wisconsin charged the railroad cut alone.[14]

---

12 Tevis and Marquis, *The History of the Fighting Fourteenth*, pp. 83-84; OR pt. 1, p. 276; Dawes, *Service with the Sixth Wisconsin*, pp. 167-168.

13 Dawes, "Align on the Colors." Dawes, *Service with the Sixth Wisconsin*, p. 168.

14 "With Reference to the 95th," *Rockland County Messenger*, June 1, 1893. Credit goes to Lance Ingmire for discovering this article. Unfortunately, Major Pye only submitted a brief report covering the 95th New York's participation in the battle: "The left wing of your brigade," he wrote, "comprising the Fourteenth New York State Militia and the Ninety-fifth New York Volunteers, under the command of Colonel Fowler, seeing the right wing of the brigade give way, retired a short distance, and then formed line of battle in connection with the Sixth Wisconsin Volunteers, and together charged upon and took as prisoners a large number of the

Major Edward Pye

*Courtesy of Civil War Library and Museum,
Philadelphia, PA*

Colonel Fowler also realized the stationary Union line would be doomed if it did not advance. The Brooklyn colonel "commanded, urged and shouted to advance, which after some little hesitation was done." The Union line, probably a bit scrambled, surged toward the enemy. The 6th Wisconsin's line assumed the shape of a V, with the color guard at the apex leading the way.

Scores of blue-clad soldiers fell under a horrendous fire. The thinning Federal line pressed on, and after great sacrifice reached the edge of the railroad cut. The 6th Wisconsin may have reached the cut slightly ahead of Fowler's two regiments, but the reason was not superior valor. The distance between the pike and the unfinished railroad diminished as the two thoroughfares approached Gettysburg. The Badger troops arrived first because they had less ground to traverse.[15]

Fowler's men gave a tremendous cheer when they reached the cut. Fowler sent his adjutant to Dawes with the suggestion that the 6th Wisconsin "flank the enemies' position by advancing . . . [its] right wing." Although Dawes denied

---

enemy." Several important details can be gleaned from his concise account. First, Pye acknowledged that Fowler commanded the 14th Brooklyn and 95th New York. It is doubtful whether Pye would have advanced without Fowler's approval. Second, Pye stated the three regiments, together, formed a line, and <u>together</u> charged and took prisoners. Finally, Pye failed to mention any conversation with Dawes. It does not mean the discussion did not take place. It does raise the question, however, whether Pye would have suggested a charge without consulting with Fowler. If Pye had survived the war, the controversy might have been prevented. Unfortunately, he suffered a severe wound at Cold Harbor on June 3, 1864, during Lt. Gen. Ulysses S. Grant's Overland Campaign and died soon thereafter. *OR* pt. 1, p. 287; "Death of Colonel Pye," *Peeksville Messenger*, June 23, 1864.

15 Bandy, ed., *The Gettysburg Papers*, pp. 219, 220; Tevis and Marquis, *The History of the Fighting Fourteenth*, p. 133; Dawes, *Service with the Sixth Wisconsin*, pp. 167-169; Kellogg to Bachelder, November 1, 1865, Bachelder Papers Typescript; Murphy to Dearborn, June 29, 1900, Papers of E. S. Bragg, Vertical File 4-9d, GNMP; Dawes, "Align on the Colors."

Gettysburg, by Allen C. Redwood. The 14th Brooklyn's veteran association commissioned Allen Redwood, a Confederate veteran and artist, to produce this painting that depicted the Fighting Fourteenth in action at the Railroad Cut, July 1, 1863. *Courtesy of the New York State Military Museum, New York State Division of Military Affairs*

receiving the directive, his adjutant anticipated the order by posting 20 men perpendicular to the cut, capping its eastern end. The maneuver allowed this small group to enfilade the trapped Southerners in and above the railroad grade. A brief firefight took place, and pockets of hand-to-hand combat erupted. Many of the Rebels realized the folly of remaining in place and continuing the uneven conflict, so they availed themselves of any means to avoid death or capture. "The enemy's line extended beyond ours on our left," recorded Fowler, "and that part not immediately confronted by our line were escaping by passing westerly through the cut." Along Fowler's immediate front, Rebels dropped their muskets. To Fowler's right, the confrontation between the 6th Wisconsin and the Rebels holding the railroad bed persisted. When Rufus Dawes spotted an enemy officer, he demanded the surrender of the Confederates in the cut. The trapped Rebels had no choice but to comply.[16]

16 Tevis and Marquis, *The History of the Fighting Fourteenth,* pp. 84, 133-134; Dawes, *Service with the Sixth Wisconsin,* pp. 168-169; *OR* pt. 1, p. 287; Fowler Extract.

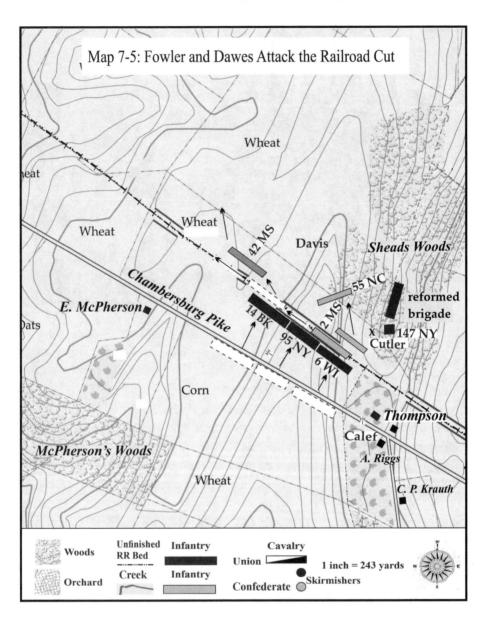

Map 7-5: Fowler and Dawes Attack the Railroad Cut

Woods | Unfinished RR Bed | Infantry
Orchard | Creek | Infantry
Union Cavalry | Confederate Cavalry
Skirmishers | 1 inch = 243 yards

While many surrendered, other more fortunate Confederates escaped through the west end of the cut or scrambled out and ran through the fields to the north. Dawes recalled years later, "The coolness, self-possession, and discipline which held back our men from pouring in a general volley saved a hundred lives of the

14th Brooklyn Monument

Steven Floyd

enemy, and as my mind goes back to the fearful excitement of the moment, I marvel at it." He added, "The fighting around the rebel colors had not ceased when this surrender took place."[17]

17 Dawes, *Service with the Sixth Wisconsin*, p. 169.

The authors of many Gettysburg histories credit Dawes's 6th Wisconsin with single-handedly capturing a large portion of Davis's Brigade. Their conclusions misinterpret what really occurred. Dawes wrote in his official report that he captured seven officers, 225 men, and the 2nd Mississippi's battle flag. The 6th Wisconsin undoubtedly collected that bounty of prisoners. It must be noted, however, that the 14th Brooklyn and 95th New York funneled their prisoners through the cut to the east, where the 6th Wisconsin corralled the captured Rebels. Dawes's men had considerable help bagging this sizeable lot of prisoners.[18]

The cost of blunting the Confederate attack and saving the Federal line came at an expensive price. Dawes claimed the 6th Wisconsin lost seven out of 12 company commanders. Overall, the regiment suffered around 220 casualties. Of these, about 180 men fell between Chambersburg Pike and the railroad cut. Casualties for the 14th Brooklyn during the entire battle included 13 killed, 105 wounded, and 99 missing out of 357 officers and men engaged. Many Red Legs listed as missing became prisoners later in the day when the regiment retreated through Gettysburg. But the morning conflict accounted for the vast majority of the Brooklyn lads killed and wounded during the battle. Rebel musketry from Davis's men stationed in and above the railroad bed thinned approximately 100 chasseurs from the ranks of the 14th Brooklyn. In the three days of fighting at Gettysburg, the 95th New York had seven men killed, 62 wounded, and 46 missing out of 239 soldiers engaged. Like the 14th Brooklyn, most of these casualties occurred during the attack on the railroad cut.[19]

What had Cutler's brigade accomplished? The brigade had rushed forward without benefit of skirmishers or reconnaissance to blunt the Confederate advance led by two of Maj. Gen. Henry Heth's brigades. On the left, Fowler's demi-brigade

---

18 OR pt. 1, p. 276; Bandy and Freeland, *The Gettysburg Papers*, p. 221; Tevis and Marquis, *The History of the Fighting Fourteenth*, p. 134. Dawes collected approximately seven officers and 225 men from the entire Confederate brigade. Murphy, in a letter to Dr. F. A. Dearborn, claimed only Major Blair and 87 men of the 2nd Mississippi were captured. Murphy to Dearborn, June 29, 1900, Papers of E. S. Bragg, Vertical File 4-9d, GNMP. For a detailed look at the 6th Wisconsin's attack on the railroad cut, see Herdegen and Beaudot, *Into the Bloody Railroad Cut*, pp. 190-210.

19 Dawes had split the Iron Brigade Guard into two parts, which accounts for the 12 companies. The seven commander casualties included: two officers from Company K; lieutenants from Companies A, C, and H; and both lieutenants leading the two brigade guard units. Dawes, *Service with the Sixth Wisconsin*, pp. 168, 354; Bandy, ed., *The Gettysburg Papers*, p. 225; 14th Brooklyn Battlefield Monument; Tevis and Marquis, *The History of the Fighting Fourteenth*, p. 100; Vanderslice, *Gettysburg: Then and Now*, pp. 112, 303-304; Busey and Martin, *Regimental Strengths at Gettysburg*, p. 24; Cutler's Brigade Field Return, RG 393, Part 2, NARA.

diverted General Archer's attention, which allowed the Iron Brigade to smash an unsuspecting foe. On the right, the stand of the 147th New York enabled Hall's battery to retreat with the temporary loss of but one gun. The charge on the railroad cut by the 14th Brooklyn and 95th New York, in conjunction with the 6th Wisconsin, stopped Davis's surging Rebel brigade in its tracks. Cutler's men inflicted so much damage that Davis's Mississippians and North Carolinians were of little use for the rest of the day. On July 1, Davis's outfit lost nearly 500 killed and wounded and more than 200 prisoners out of 1,707 men engaged. Davis's organization, like Cutler's command, was reduced to a mere skeleton of its former self. Most importantly, Cutler's men helped hold the vital third ridge and McPherson's Woods. From these positions, the Federal 1st Corps stymied Confederate advances until late in the afternoon, thereby providing the time necessary for Maj. Gen. George Gordon Meade to concentrate the balance of the Army of the Potomac at Gettysburg. The seeds of the Union victory were sown during the desperate morning fight with the blood of Cutler's brigade.[20]

---

20 Vanderslice, *Gettysburg: Then and Now*, pp. 119, 303-304. The three regiments of Davis's Brigade present on July 1 reported a total loss of 695 killed and wounded for all three days of the battle. On July 3, Davis's Brigade participated in Pickett's/Longstreet's Charge. Vanderslice estimated Davis's Brigade lost 200 men during the July 3 assault.

Chapter Eight

A Typical Casualty

The morning combat, which lasted a little more than an hour, inflicted devastating losses within General Cutler's regiments. The savage clash cost the brigade more than 600 killed, wounded, or missing/captured.

Sterile statistics, however, inadequately portray the brutality of Civil War combat. Measuring losses in mathematical form for armies, corps, divisions, brigades, or regiments detaches readers from the grim horror of war's cruelty. Only by examining what took place at the individual level can the stark reality of 19th Century combat be fully realized, especially when considering the pain and suffering inflicted by lead and iron projectiles. One effective way to understand the immediate and long-term implications of Civil War combat is to follow the ordeal of a particular soldier wounded in battle. The military service of Pvt. John J. Jochum offers a good example.

On August 20, 1862, John Jochum left his trade as a sign painter to enlist as a replacement in the 14th New York State Militia (14th Brooklyn). The 25-year-old recruit had no outstanding physical characteristics. His black hair, brown or hazel eyes, dark complexion, and five foot, nine and one-half inch height were typical of thousands of other soldiers. Jochum mustered into service a day later as a private in Company B of the 14th Brooklyn.[1]

---

1 Most of the information found in this chapter came from John Jochum's Compiled Service Record and his Pension File located in the NARA.

Private Jochum had served less than three weeks when he was assigned to the first of two non-combat positions. On September 8, 1862, the new recruit replaced John H. Fisher as the regiment's hospital steward.[2] In this capacity, Jochum cared for 2nd Bull Run casualties, so he quickly recognized the destructive capabilities of soft lead bullets and artillery projectiles. It must have been unnerving to be so familiar with battle's inevitable aftermath prior to entering a fight. When Fisher returned to duty February 16, 1863, Jochum rejoined his company. His stay with the regiment was short-lived. In April 1863, the private was detailed to the Quartermaster Department of the 30th New York. Within a month he returned to the 14th Brooklyn.[3]

During the Chancellorsville Campaign in late April and early May of 1863, the Union 1st Corps (to which Jochum's regiment was attached), saw limited action. In June 1863, Jochum traveled north with his regiment in pursuit of the invading Confederate army. Like so many others, he probably suffered severely from the forced marches and oppressive heat. On the morning of July 1, the former sign painter trudged with his regimental comrades to Gettysburg. During the attack against the railroad cut, a bullet or shell fragment struck the private behind the right ear, fracturing the occipital and right parietal bones of his skull and knocking him unconscious. He regained his senses only to experience a brief bout of blindness. After Jochum recovered his sight, he applied an ersatz bandage to his wound before staggering to the division hospital in Gettysburg. Within a few hours, large-scale Confederate assaults from west and north of town broke the Union lines and forced a general retreat to Cemetery Hill. The Rebels captured the town and laid claim to the wounded soldiers in the Federal hospitals there.

Civil War hospitals, such as the one Jochum entered on July 1, were woefully inadequate by modern standards. Advances in medicine had not kept pace with military technological improvements. Physicians had little if any knowledge about germs and their relationship to infection. Operating procedures were primitive, and the high number of casualties required that surgeries be performed as quickly as possible. A Union soldier named Charles Johnson described the examining techniques of a surgeon who had treated his wounded captain. The officer had been shot in the head with a musket ball that had entered his brain through the upper part of the occipital bone. The surgeon began his assessment by thrusting his

2 Fisher had been captured soon after the Battle of Brawner's Farm, on either August 28 or 29, 1862.

3 The 30th New York was a two-year regiment; it mustered out of service in late May 1863.

John Jochum

The Buffalo Sunday Morning News

unwashed index finger into the wound. He completed his work by using a filthy bullet probe to extract the ball. It is not surprising that head wounds, with the potential for brain damage, were among the most fatal of Civil War injuries. The mortality rate of wounds involving penetration or perforation of the skull was about 80%. John Jochum somehow defied the odds and survived both his wound and the hospital.[4]

Fortunately for the New Yorker, Jochum's term as a prisoner of war lasted but a short time. On July 5, when the Confederates retreated from Gettysburg, they left behind the seriously wounded Union captives. Jochum's long ordeal to recovery was only beginning. Soon after the battle, he traveled with other wounded Yankees to Littlestown, Pennsylvania.[5] From there, he had brief stays at a Baltimore hospital, Satterlie Hospital in Philadelphia, and Central Park Hospital in New York. Finally, medical authorities admitted him to New York's Ladies Home Hospital.

Unfortunately, Private Jochum's wound failed to heal properly. November and December passed with the private still hospitalized. His condition remained unchanged throughout the winter months of 1863 and into 1864. On May 22, 1864, authorities transferred Jochum to the 5th New York Veteran Volunteer

4 Dr. Gordon W. Jones, "Surgery in the Civil War," *Civil War Times Illustrated, Vol. 2, No. 2.* (May 1963), p. 7. Charles Johnson, "The Regimental Hospital," pp. 769 and 794 in Henry Steele Commager, ed., *The Blue and the Gray, Vol. 2* (New York, 1950).

5 Jochum claimed he walked to Littlestown. John Jochum, "His Brain Laid Bare," *The Buffalo Sunday Morning News*, April 23, 1893. This article is reproduced in Appendix 8.

Infantry by order of Maj. Gen. George Gordon Meade.[6] Jochum never joined the regiment. On July 6, a surgeon reported that the private had had several large pieces of skull bone removed and that the injury had not healed. The doctor's dire prediction was that more bone would have to be extracted.

Jochum finally received his "Certificate of Disability for Discharge" on July 25, 1864—one year and 24 days after being wounded. Alex. B. Mott, Surgeon-in-Charge, deemed Jochum incapable of further service, including the Invalid Corps, because of extensive exfoliation of the occipital bone. The doctor expected that fragments of the chasseur's skull bone would continue to break loose. The surgeon rated Jochum's degree of disability as one-fourth.

A soldier's medical discharge required a great deal of paperwork. On July 29, Dr. Charles Rowland filled out the "Examining Surgeon's Certificate." Rowland performed the exam to ascertain the existence and/or extent of disability for pension purposes. Rowland believed that Jochum's wound was much more debilitating than Dr. Mott had concluded, and that the head injury left him three-quarters disabled. According to Rowland,

> The above named applicant's disability consists in a severe wound, by a piece of shell fracturing the skull, back of the right ear, from which a number of pieces of bone have been extracted leaving quite an indentation, and still discharging, causing at times severe pain, vertigo with impaired memory. . . . He is a moral man, and will eventually recover, but at present unable to work.

John Jochum returned to Brooklyn by July 30, the same day he appeared before the Clerk of the City Court of Brooklyn to file a "Declaration for Army Invalid Pension." Jochum appointed Walter Griffith as his lawful attorney to handle his case.

Bureaucratic red tape and foul-ups rapidly ensued. On November 5, 1864, Jochum received a form letter from the Adjutant General's Office in Washington, D.C., claiming no evidence existed on file of his enrollment in Company B, 14th Brooklyn. The bureaucrat did note that his name appeared on the muster roll for July and August 1863. The regimental clerk listed Jochum as "Absent sick, wounded in action July 1, 1863."

---

6 Around this time, the 14th Brooklyn's term of service expired. Recruits like Jochum, who had enlisted for three years in 1862, were transferred to the 5th New York Veteran Volunteers, which was organized in New York City in October 1863. John Jochum Compiled Service Record, NARA.

There was no recourse for the disabled private but to write a letter to Joseph H. Barrett, Commissioner of Pensions, in compliance with the form sent by the Pension Office. After reviewing the story of his wound on July 1, his capture, and his transfer from hospital to hospital, Jochum turned to his physical condition. At Ladies Home Hospital, surgeons had performed several operations during which they had removed substantial portions of his fractured skull, the largest measuring 3 1/2" by 2 1/2". His wound, he added, "is still open and other pieces of the skull exfoliating. There are three openings which discharge rendering it necessary that the dressings be changed at least twice a day." Jochum concluded by stating that his physicians had recommended one additional operation. James L. Farley, a former surgeon of the 14th Brooklyn, endorsed Jochum's letter to the pension commissioner.

Jochum's correspondence failed to convince Commissioner Barrett, so the bureaucrat sent a letter to Satterlie Hospital seeking information concerning Jochum. The acting surgeon-in-charge completed a form letter on January 28, 1865. He acknowledged that John Jochum had been admitted in July of 1863 with a gunshot wound to the head, and that he had transferred to New York on July 24, 1863. The surgeon even indicated at the bottom of the form which bed Jochum occupied during his stay at Satterlie. And then nothing else happened. The case remained in bureaucratic limbo.

Jochum, meanwhile, suffered constantly from his combat wound. More than a year had passed since he sought financial relief from the pension commissioner. On August 6, 1866, Jochum appeared before the Clerk of the City Court of Brooklyn. The former soldier, pension number 38570, was understandably dissatisfied with the paltry $6.00 per month pension he currently received. He believed his debilitating condition entitled him to an increased pension of $15.00 per month, as provided by the first section of the June 6, 1866, Supplementary Pension Act. Jochum divulged that his bones had suffered, and that his wound forced him to remain bedridden for considerable periods of time. Government officials failed to adjust Jochum's pension.

In order to receive a pension, an individual had to tolerate biennial, annual, or semi-annual examinations. On September 12, 1873, 10 years, two months, and 11 days after being severely wounded at Gettysburg, John underwent such a physical. Dr. Leighton examined Jochum in Brooklyn. The physician reported that Jochum's disability should remain three-fourths—$6.00 per month. The doctor also noted that the patient's wound contained an open ulceration. Indeed, the injury had never healed.

On February 3, 1875, Jochum attempted yet again to increase his $6.00 monthly pension. Surgeon Atwood and two colleagues examined Jochum. They described on the "Examining Surgeon's Certificate of an Applicant for Increase of Pension" form what they observed. Jochum, now 37 years old, had a depressed area in the skull two inches wide by 3/4 inch deep—the deformity marked the location where the occipital bone had loosened and flaked away over the years. The wound was still discharging infection—a familiar nuisance. In addition, Jochum suffered from "dizziness and flashes of fire across the eyes to such an extent as to prevent the regular pursuit of any occupation." After the thorough examination, the surgeons concurred John Jochum's pension should be increased to $18.00 per month.

Jochum's pension battle continued. Although his monthly allowance had been raised, he sought back pay entitled to him by law. The pension commissioner rejected the claim. On July 8, 1879, 16 years and seven days after being wounded, Jochum wrote another letter to the pension office. His communication displayed remarkable restraint and solid reasoning. Jochum made no attempt to deceive the government. Instead, he relied on objectivity and logic to achieve a favorable resolution. "I beg leave respectfully to state that my disability has not been progressive," he began,

> and that it was not greater in 1875 than in 1872 or 1873 as alleged, but that the apparent increase of disability is caused by the fact that it was not until after my application for increase had been filed that a thorough examination of my wound was made and the true extent of my disability ascertained. Previous to that time the function of the examining surgeons being only to decide as to the continuance or reduction of pension, a mere glance at my wound was deemed sufficient to entitle me to a continuance . . . in cases where a similar injury exists in either of the limbs the increased pension was allowed to commence at the time when the law went into effect although the disability was merely local, while in my case where the injury exists in a more vital region and affects the whole system I am deprived of the increase for nearly three years. It seems hard that I should not receive the full benefit of the law by reason of the inadvertence of the surgeon.

The last examination papers on file concerning Jochum's case are dated November 26, 1886, and January 5, 1887. Now 49 years old, Jochum attempted once more to obtain another pension increase. According to the records, by this time he was suffering from vertigo, disordered vision, headaches, limited visual field, luminous flickering, and twitching muscles in the extremities. The surgeon noted that the carious [bone decaying] disease had crossed to the left side of the head. Furthermore, two fistulous openings still discharged. Based on Jochum's condition, the doctor rated his disability as third grade—the equivalent of the loss of a hand or a foot.

From the moment a Confederate projectile shattered his skull on July 1, 1863, until the day his son found him dead in bed on January 16, 1894, John Jochum carried war's permanent badge. His ordeal failed to generate a delightful memoir. Instead, he spent more than 20 years battling pain, impaired health, and a bureaucratic pension office that had denied him reasonable compensation. Surprisingly, Jochum's moral character and mental toughness withstood the torture of the years.[7]

On July 1, 1863, he lived when odds declared he should die. During the subsequent decades, he understood intimately the lingering cruelty of Civil War combat.

7 Preliminary reports suggested that Jochum died of heart disease. "John Jochum's Death," *The Brooklyn Daily Eagle*, January 16, 1894.

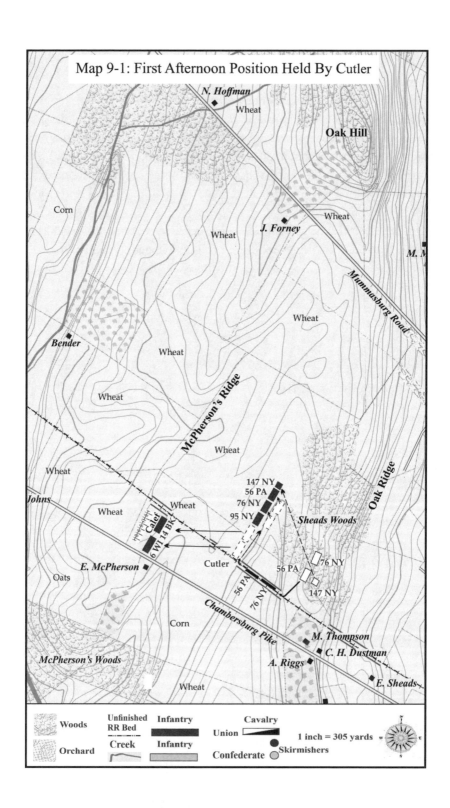

Map 9-1: First Afternoon Position Held By Cutler

N. Hoffman

Wheat

Oak Hill

Corn

Wheat

J. Forney

Wheat

M. M

Mummasburg Road

Wheat

Bender

Wheat

Wheat

McPherson's Ridge

Wheat

Wheat

147 NY
56 PA
76 NY
95 NY

Sheads Woods

Oak Ridge

Johns

Wheat

Wheat

Calef
6 WI 14 BK

76 NY

56 PA

147 NY

E. McPherson

Cutler

56 PA
76 NY

Oats

Corn

Chambersburg Pike

M. Thompson
C. H. Dustman

McPherson's Woods

A. Riggs

E. Sheads

Wheat

Woods	Unfinished RR Bed	Infantry	Cavalry			
	Creek	Infantry	Union		1 inch = 305 yards	
Orchard			Confederate	Skirmishers		

CHAPTER NINE

The Afternoon Fight

The fierce storm of combat that marked the early and mid-morning hours of July 1 abated suddenly with the repulse of the brigades led by Brig. Gens. James J. Archer and Joseph Davis. Only the occasional discharges of artillery cloaked the groans and cries of the wounded Union and Confederate soldiers blanketing the fields west of town. Despite their initial successes, the Federal forces could neither relax nor savor their victory. Major General Henry Heth's entire division had gathered along Herr's Ridge; another division under Maj. Gen. William Pender rested nearby in support. Yankee cavalry videttes had also announced the approach of strong Confederate forces coming down from the north, which further imperiled the Union position.

To help meet the threat of Heth and Pender, Brig. Gen. James Wadsworth ordered Brig. Gen. Lysander Cutler to reform his command and advance to the middle ridge, where the 56th Pennsylvania and 76th New York had fought. In response, Cutler regrouped the three regiments occupying Seminary Ridge north of the eastern cut. Those members of the 147th New York who had retreated across Chambersburg Pike toward the Seminary used this interval to refill their canteens before rejoining their comrades. Cutler's reformed command advanced about 1:00 p.m. The 147th New York numbered approximately 75 officers and men, the 76th New York about 141, and the 56th Pennsylvania roughly 174.

Two of Cutler's reformed regiments took a circuitous route to reach the middle ridge. Prior to moving, the 56th Pennsylvania on the left and the 76th New York on the right occupied the copse of trees north of the eastern railroad cut.

Cutler could have sent the two outfits directly west to the middle ridge. He may have been worried that passing through the timber would disrupt their battle lines, or that Confederate artillery fire would target the regiments once they exited the woods. To prevent either from coming to pass, he moved the pair of regiments in column along the unfinished railroad for a short distance. Then Cutler turned the units to the right, where they could take advantage of the low ground between the middle ridge and the northern extension of Seminary Ridge. The two units redeployed into a battle line before marching to the crest of the middle ridge.

Apparently, the 147th New York did not follow this route. Major George Harney, in postwar correspondence with Col. J. William Hofmann, stated that "the 56th and 76th marched on to the ground and the 147th followed and took position on the right of the 56th." Lieutenant Henry H. Lyman confirmed the positioning of the 147th New York in a letter in which he mentioned that his regiment "took post on right of the Brigade, which again advanced." As these three regiments formed along the middle ridge, Col. Edward Fowler's demi-brigade, reinforced with the 6th Wisconsin, realigned with Cutler. Thus, Cutler's formation from south to north was the 6th Wisconsin, the 14th Brooklyn, the 95th New York, the 76th New York, the 56th Pennsylvania, and the 147th New York. Cutler's line waited in a prone position.[1]

Once in position, some of Cutler's men tried to help their comrades who had been wounded during the morning engagement. One soldier asked Hofmann's permission to move ahead of the battle line so he could carry off an injured friend. Captain John Cook acknowledged that his men "brought off many of our dead and wounded." George Harney remembered giving an injured 76th New York soldier a drink of water. Four members of the 14th Brooklyn offered to retrieve Cpl. George W. Forrester, who lay on the field wounded. After receiving permission, they took

---

1   OR pt. 1, p. 282; Pierce to Bachelder, November 1, 1882, Bachelder Papers Typescript; *New York at Gettysburg*, p. 1002; George Harney to Colonel Hofmann, August 16, 1865, Bachelder Papers Typescript; Lieutenant H. H. Lyman to Bachelder, undated, Bachelder Papers Typescript; *New York at Gettysburg*, p. 993. The movements during the afternoon phase of the battle are difficult to determine. I relied heavily upon Cutler's report in the OR as a framework and tried to flesh this out with regimental and other first-hand accounts. The Harney letter was extremely helpful. The time of 1:00 p.m. for the advance is used for several reasons. Cutler reported that the enemy [Robert Rodes's infantry division, Ewell's Second Corps] formed on his right one-half to three-quarters of an hour after taking the new position. Cutler claims to have changed position again and received no support until 2:00 p.m. The march to the middle ridge, the one-half to three-quarters of an hour time before the enemy appeared, and a brief interlude prior to Brig. Gen. Henry Baxter's arrival, place the advance at about 1:00 p.m.

On the afternoon of July 1, 1863, Cutler's brigade changed front to face Rodes's Division approaching from the north of Oak Hill in the left background (note the Peace Memorial, which is visible on its slope). Part of Cutler's brigade later took cover in the woods partially seen to the right. *Author*

along a piece of tent canvas to serve as a litter. After rolling the injured Forrester onto the fabric, each man lifted a corner and the rescue party hurried back to its lines. Unfortunately, a Confederate shell exploded in their midst, mortally wounding Forrester and injuring three of his would-be rescuers. One of the chasseurs had his leg blown off, "and his scream of agony," recalled an eyewitness, "was heard even above the vast, pulsating roar of the battle." The Good Samaritan died during his transport to a field hospital.[2]

Wadsworth, meanwhile, decided to give his line a bit more punch by ordering Lt. John Calef's horse artillery to the position formerly held by Capt. James Hall's 2nd Maine Battery. Once that was underway, the division commander sent the 6th Wisconsin forward to support the guns. A short time later Wadsworth dispatched the 14th Brooklyn as an additional reinforcement. Colonel Charles Wainwright, commander of the 1st Corps Artillery, deployed Capt. Gilbert H. Reynolds's

2 George Harney to Colonel Hofmann, August 16, 1865, Bachelder Papers Typescript; Tevis and Marquis, *The History of the Fighting Fourteenth*, pp. 84-85. Forrester died on July 2.

Battery L, 1st New York Light Artillery to bolster this group. Not long after the 14th Brooklyn took its new position, Fowler noticed an ominous sight developing off Cutler's right flank: four batteries of artillery were moving out of the woods and deploying on Oak Hill. The guns comprised Lt. Col. Thomas Carter's artillery battalion, which was attached to Maj. Gen. Robert Rodes's Division. They were perfectly positioned to rake the Federal line. Fowler also spied large bodies of Southern infantry forming along the edge of the woods on Oak Hill. Colonels Charles Wainwright and Edward Fowler both sent word of the Southern threat to Cutler. Wadsworth, relying on Cutler's judgment, gave him discretionary orders to form as the brigadier judged best.[3]

It is difficult to discern how Cutler handled this threat. Many sources imply Cutler immediately fell back to the woods, formed a line along the northern extension of Seminary Ridge, and faced west. This seems unlikely for several reasons. First, the move east to the woods would have left the entire flank of the 1st Corps wide open. The Iron Brigade was deployed in McPherson's Woods south of Chambersburg Pike, and Col. Roy Stone's brigade of Pennsylvania Bucktails occupied the ground around the McPherson buildings. Cutler was too experienced to expose those Federals to the Rebel force posted along Oak Hill. Second, Cutler and a number of his men acknowledged that at least part of the brigade took up a position facing north. In his official report, Cutler stated, "with the balance of the brigade present [I] changed front to the right, and endeavored to hold the enemy in check as best I could, having no support on either my right or my left until 2 o'clock."[4]

After the war, Col. J. William Hofmann wrote in the *Philadelphia Weekly Press* that the brigade moved to "the North edge of the woods on Seminary Ridge, where a zig-zag fence bounded on the hither side a field of wheat." J. A. Kellogg, in a letter to battlefield historian John Bachelder, mentioned that when Cutler was "attacked [on our] front and on our right flank, Brigadier General Cutler changed the front of his Brigade under fire and opened on the enemy." There was no mention of falling back to the woods. Lieutenant Henry H. Lyman wrote that Cutler "retreated by the right, halted in Oak Woods on the Hill, made a slight breastwork of rail-fence, [and]

---

3 OR pt. 1, pp. 266, 282, 356; Tevis and Marquis *The History of the Fighting Fourteenth*, p. 134; Allan Nevins, ed., A *Diary of Battle, The Personal Journals of Colonel Charles S. Wainwright, 1861-1865* (New York, 1962), p. 234.

4 The 14th Brooklyn was still detached at this time. Most historians who write on this portion of the battle do not provide details on Cutler's maneuver, or in some instances when or how he formed his line.

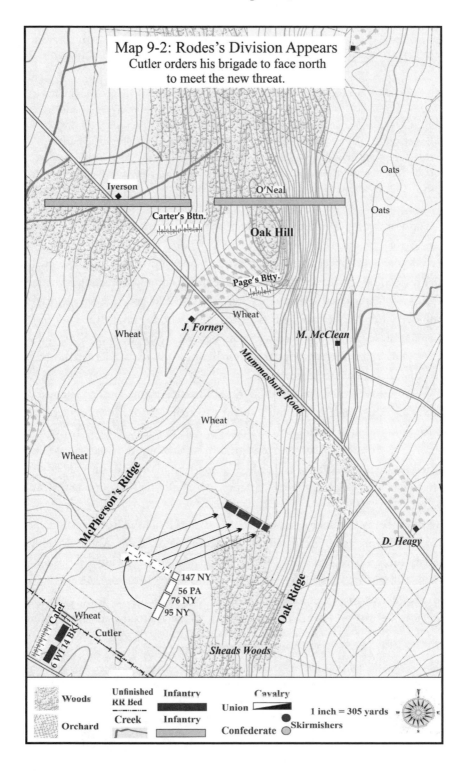

Map 9-2: Rodes's Division Appears
Cutler orders his brigade to face north
to meet the new threat.

bales of hay." General Rodes, whose Confederate division had arrived from the north and threatened Cutler's position, substantiated this view in his official report:

> Carter's battalion was ordered forward, and soon opened fire upon the enemy, who at this moment, as far as I could see, had no troops facing me at all…before my dispositions were made, the enemy began to show large bodies of men in front of the town [11th Corps] … almost at the same time a portion of the force opposed to General Hill changed position so as to occupy the woods on the summit of the same ridge I occupied. . . . Either these last troops or others which had hitherto been unobserved behind the same body of woods, soon made their appearance directly opposite my center.[5]

It appears that Cutler first ordered his brigade to form a line facing northward. Once in that position, only the 147th New York and the 56th Pennsylvania received adequate protection from the fence line and timber. Soon thereafter, Cutler refused his left flank to take advantage of the natural protection provided by the wooded Seminary Ridge. Such a maneuver would account for reports that mentioned the brigade moved back to the woods along the ridge. This interpretation would also explain why members of the 147th New York and 56th Pennsylvania claimed that they faced north while the remainder of the brigade stated that their final facing was to the west.[6]

While Cutler's men held this inverted L-shaped line, other changes were underway on the right flank of the 1st Corps. General Wadsworth recalled Calef's and Reynolds's batteries, the 6th Wisconsin, and the 14th Brooklyn from their exposed positions. During this retrograde movement, Lt. Col. Rufus Dawes shuffled his men through the unfinished railroad cut in order to provide cover for his regiment. Once again, the two infantry regiments fell into line with Cutler's brigade.

The other major transformation involved Brig. Gen. John Robinson's division. When the enemy threat on Oak Hill appeared, Maj. Gen. Abner Doubleday ordered Robinson to send one of his brigades to bolster Cutler's right flank. Robinson dispatched the 11th Pennsylvania and 97th New York. Moments later, the remainder of Brig. Gen. Henry Baxter's brigade followed the two regiments. Baxter's men crossed Chambersburg Pike and the railroad bed and continued

---

5 *OR* pt. 1, p. 282; Hofmann, *PWP;* Hofmann, *Remarks on the Battle of Gettysburg*, p. 6; Kellogg to Bachelder, November 1, 1865, Bachelder Papers Typescript; Lieutenant H. H. Lyman to Bachelder, undated, Bachelder Papers Typescript; *OR* pt. 2, p. 552.

6 *OR* pt. 1, pp. 285-286; Tevis and Marquis, *The History of the Fighting Fourteenth*, p. 134.

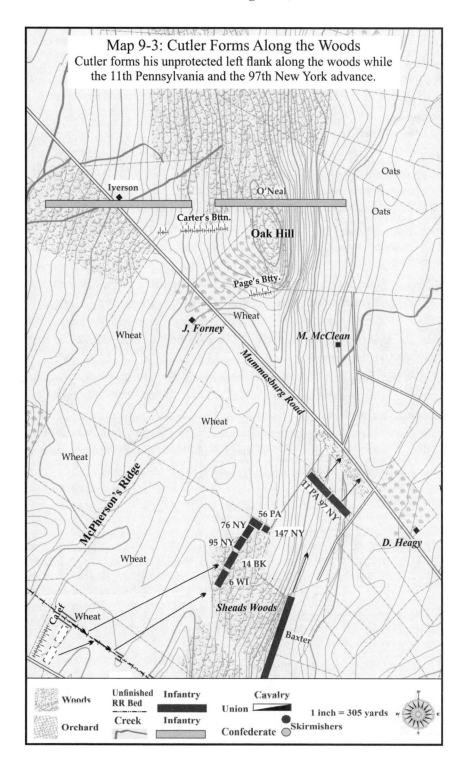

Map 9-3: Cutler Forms Along the Woods
Cutler forms his unprotected left flank along the woods while
the 11th Pennsylvania and the 97th New York advance.

Oats

Iverson

O'Neal

Carter's Bttn.

Oats

Oak Hill

Page's Btty.

Wheat

Wheat

J, Forney

M. McClean

Wheat

Wheat

Mummasburg Road

Wheat

McPherson's Ridge

11 PA 97 NY

Wheat

56 PA

76 NY

147 NY

95 NY

D. Heagy

Wheat

14 BK

6 WI

Sheads Woods

Baxter

Cref

Wheat

Woods	Unfinished RR Bed	Infantry	Cavalry	
	Creek	Infantry	Union	
Orchard			Confederate	Skirmishers

Infantry — Union

Infantry — Confederate

Skirmishers

1 inch = 305 yards

moving behind Cutler's men, keeping to the east side of the ridge. The woods and the ridge line sheltered Baxter's men from view. The 11th Pennsylvania formed near Cutler's northern flank while the 97th New York extended its line toward the east. Both of Baxter's regiments faced north. With skirmishers in front, the regiments moved toward Mummasburg Road. A portion of this force may have slightly overlapped the part of Cutler's line that also faced to the north. The remainder of Baxter's regiments soon arrived to reinforce their comrades.[7]

General Rodes, "finding that the enemy was rash enough to come out from the woods to attack me," decided to launch his assault first. He formed Col. Edward A. O'Neal's Alabama brigade on his left, Brig. Gen. Alfred Iverson's North Carolina brigade in the middle, and Brig. Gen. Junius Daniel's North Carolina brigade on his right. A fourth brigade under Brig. Gen. Stephen Ramseur served as a reserve. Fences, woods, brush, and uneven terrain disrupted O'Neal's advance, as did musketry from Baxter's brigade, which struck the Alabama brigade in front. At the same time, cannonading and gunfire from 11th Corps troops (the 45th New York and Capt. Hubert Dilger's and Lt. William Wheeler's batteries) pestered O'Neal's left flank. Caught in a Yankee crossfire, O'Neal's Brigade faltered and fell back.[8]

In a July 11th letter home, Capt. Hershel Pierce of the 76th New York claimed he participated in O'Neal's repulse. Pierce acknowledged that officers usually had little time to pay attention to individual enemy soldiers, but this fight was an exception. The color bearer of the 26th Alabama, he explained, flaunted "his defiant flag in the faces of our men about the time that Carpenter was shot. Both causes operated so strongly upon me that I could not resist any longer but unslung my carbine from my shoulder. I shot him dead in his tracks and felt the better for doing it."[9]

---

7 Tevis and Marquis, *The History of the Fighting Fourteenth*, pp. 134-135; Dawes, *Service with the Sixth Wisconsin*, pp. 174-175; OR pt. 1, pp. 248, 266, 276, 307; Lieutenant Colonel Benjamin F. Cook, *History of the 12th Massachusetts* (Boston, 1882), pp. 100-101; L. B. Paul, Jr., *Paul's Brigade at Gettysburg* (1966), no pg. numbers; Isaac Hall, *History of the 97th Regiment New York Volunteers in the War for the Union* (Utica, 1890), pp. 134-135; John D. Vautier, *History of the 88th Pennsylvania Volunteers* (Philadelphia, 1894), pp. 122-123.

8 OR pt. 2, p. 553; Paul, *Paul's Brigade at Gettysburg*, no page #s; Vautier, *History of the 88th Pennsylvania Volunteers*, p. 134; OR pt. 1, p. 307.

9 Captain Hershel W. Pierce to his Brother, July 11, 1863, Dick Bridgeman Collection. During the battle, the 76th New York lost two men with the last name Carpenter. Adj. Hubert Carpenter was wounded, and Cpl. Benjamin Carpenter was killed. It is uncertain which Carpenter Pierce was referencing in his letter. Travis W. Busey and John W. Busey, *Union Casualties at Gettysburg, A Comprehensive Record*, 3 vols, (McFarland, 2011), vol. 1, p. 492.

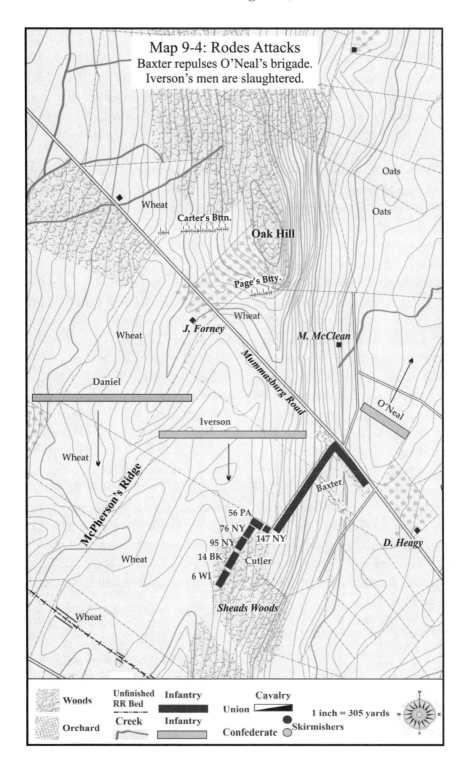

Map 9-4: Rodes Attacks
Baxter repulses O'Neal's brigade.
Iverson's men are slaughtered.

Oats

Wheat

Oats

Carter's Bttn.

Oak Hill

Page's Btty.

Wheat

Wheat

J. Forney

M. McClean

Mummasburg Road

Daniel

O'Neal

Iverson

Wheat

McPherson's Ridge

Baxter

56 PA

76 NY

95 NY   147 NY

D. Heagy

14 BK   Cutler

Wheat

6 WI

Sheads Woods

Wheat

Woods

Unfinished
RR Bed

Infantry

Cavalry

Union

Creek

Infantry

1 inch = 305 yards

Orchard

Confederate

Skirmishers

O'Neal's repulse was immediately followed by one of the most avoidable slaughters of the war. As the Alabamians retreated back to Oak Hill, Iverson's Brigade followed an oblique, southeast path toward the patch of timber held by Cutler's men. A thin cloud of skirmishers normally preceded a battle line to shield it from unseen dangers, but in this instance the North Carolina brigade forged ahead without a protective screen. Complicating matters, Iverson remained in the rear and did not advance with his brigade.

When Baxter spotted this advance, he changed his front to left to conceal most of his brigade behind a stone wall running along the crest of the ridge. Some of Brig. Gen. Gabriel Paul's regiments may have plugged a small gap between Baxter and Cutler at the same time. Iverson's line halted briefly to allow Carter's artillery to shell the Federal position in the woods. Cutler's infantry who had a clear field of fire opened at long range on Iverson's vulnerable right flank.

The North Carolina outfit continued its advance until its left flank was within 80 to 100 yards of Baxter's hidden men. As a unit, Baxter's infantry rose and fired a volley into the unsuspecting foe. The fire drove the surviving North Carolinians back a short distance to a small gully, leaving behind distinct rows of dead and wounded Tar Heels. The small arms fire was so intense that one member of the 23rd North Carolina was found with five bullets through his head.

Cutler seized this opportunity by pushing his men out of the woods, forming on Iverson's flank, and opening fire. Captain John Cook, now in command of the 76th New York, recalled that Cutler's men advanced at a right oblique, obtained a good position, and helped silence the enemy's musketry. Cook also reported that his regiment shot down the colors of one Rebel outfit. This crossfire, made possible by Cutler's instinctive move, crushed the effectiveness of Iverson's embattled command. When a portion of Baxter's brigade charged Iverson's depleted force, some of Cutler's men joined them. During this part of the fighting, Major Harney of the 147th New York sustained a wound to his hand. In less than 30 minutes, the combined efforts of Baxter, Paul, and Cutler repulsed Iverson's command, which lost three stands of colors and about 500 men killed, wounded, or captured.[10]

10 Vautier, *History of the 88th Pennsylvania Volunteers*, p. 135; *OR* pt. 2, pp. 554, 579; *OR* pt. 1, pp. 282, 286; Lieutenant H. H. Lyman to Bachelder, undated, Bachelder Papers Typescript; Stine, *History of the Army of the Potomac*, pp. 472-473; Vanderslice, *Gettysburg: Then and Now*, pp. 83-84; *New York at Gettysburg*, pp. 616, 736; Hassler, *Crisis at the Crossroads*, p. 92; Clark, ed., *North Carolina Regiments*, Vol. 2, pp. 235, 237.

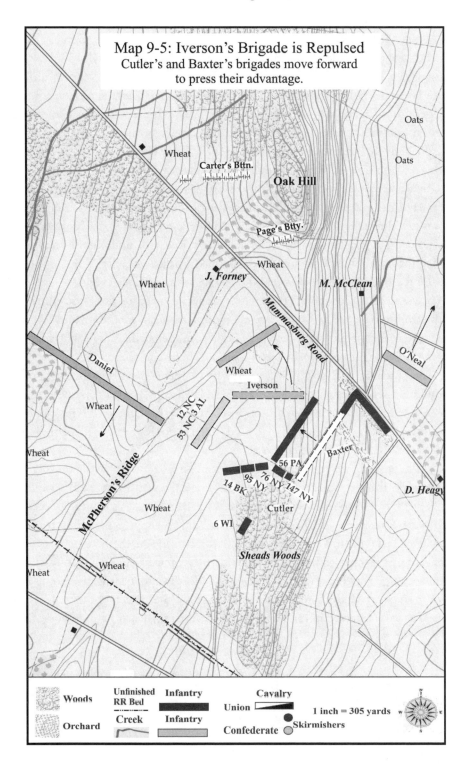

Map 9-5: Iverson's Brigade is Repulsed
Cutler's and Baxter's brigades move forward
to press their advantage.

While the Federal regiments annihilated Iverson's Brigade, Daniel's large North Carolina brigade moved past Iverson's right flank. Daniel's 53rd North Carolina, the 3rd Alabama (detached from O'Neal), and the 12th North Carolina (from Iverson's right flank) now threatened Cutler's left flank. Cutler once more changed front, this time by pulling his brigade back to the wooded ridge to reform on Robinson's left flank. "Old Graybeard's" regiments continued the fight from that position in conjunction with Roy Stone's Pennsylvania Bucktails, catching Daniel's North Carolinians in another vicious crossfire.

Reinforcements from Robinson's division soon arrived to relieve Cutler's men, who had but few rounds left in their cartridge boxes. Cutler withdrew his troops east through the woods. The fatigued brigade spent the next 20 minutes to one hour resting under the brow of Seminary Ridge behind Robinson's men, waiting for ammunition Cutler had requisitioned. Shells from a Rebel battery north of Mummasburg Road burst among the resting men, injuring several.[11]

It was now approaching 4:00 p.m. Confederate pressure along the entire 1st Corps front intensified. From the west, divisions under Henry Heth and William Pender renewed attacks with fresh brigades. From the north, Maj. Gen. Oliver O. Howard's 11th Corps gradually yielded ground before an onslaught delivered by Lt. Gen. Richard S. Ewell's Second Corps. Cutler's men, still awaiting their ammunition, caught sight of the retreating 11th Corps troops. Colonel Fowler passed this distressing information on to Cutler and Lt. Col. John Kress, one of Wadsworth's aides. The retreat by Howard's men exposed the right flank of the 1st Corps and threatened its line of retreat.

Cutler was still awaiting ammunition when Kress returned with an order for him to send three regiments to support Lt. James Stewart's Battery B, 4th U. S. Artillery. "Old Graybeard" dispatched the 14th Brooklyn, 147th New York, and 76th New York south of the eastern railroad cut to support the left section of Stewart's guns; the 6th Wisconsin from the Iron Brigade guarded the right section. Bolstered by this makeshift line of Union infantry, Stewart's gunners repulsed two or three charges by Brig. Gen. Alfred Scales's North Carolina brigade. About this time, the rest of Cutler's regiments (and possibly the detached portion of the brigade as well) received its long-awaited resupply of small arms ammunition. The

---

11 Vanderslice, *Gettysburg: Then and Now*, p. 84; *OR* pt. 1, p. 282; Lieutenant H. H. Lyman to Bachelder, undated, Bachelder Papers Typescript; Tevis and Marquis, *The History of the Fighting Fourteenth*, p. 135; Smith, *76th New York*, p. 240; Hofmann, *PWP*; Kress, in "Tales of War," noted that Cutler's men were down to 3 or 4 cartridges apiece.

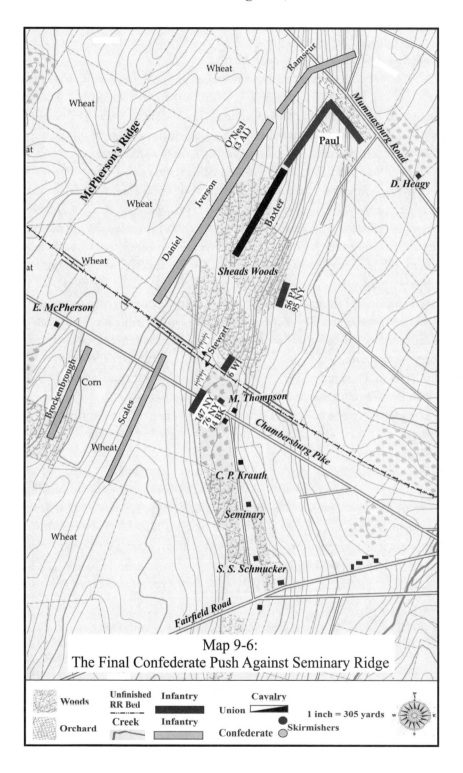

Map 9-6:
The Final Confederate Push Against Seminary Ridge

strategic position, however, continued to deteriorate as the Confederate vise tightened around the 1st Corps position.[12]

With all hope lost of holding out any longer, and with both flanks of the corps crumbling and turned, Wadsworth gave Cutler the order to retreat. The stout resistance by Stewart's battery and Cutler's brigade allowed many of Baxter's and Paul's men to slip away and avoid capture. Cutler formed his men on the railroad embankment and marched them in orderly fashion toward town.

During the retreat, Cutler's horse was killed from beneath him. The intrepid officer mounted another and continued monitoring the withdrawal of his unit. His command, he would later write, "marched with perfect steadiness and no excitement." Cutler's men, recalled Kress, were "in plain view of the advancing enemy, who soon halted his line of battle evidently expecting that Cutler's brigade would form line and oppose his approach." In other words, Cutler's calm retreat in column inadvertently prevented Southern soldiers north of Chambersburg Pike from advancing and firing at Federal troops leaving their defensive positions near the Lutheran Seminary. The Rebels instead slowed their pursuit by dispatching skirmishers. Because of this, and also because the butternut troops preferred artillery horses rather than humans for targets, Cutler's brigade reached town without too much additional trouble. While all of this was transpiring, men from the 14th Brooklyn helped drag away one of Stewart's guns.[13]

The smooth retreat ended in Gettysburg. Retreating soldiers from both the 1st Corps and 11th Corps flooded the streets from different directions. The town's deceivingly intricate road patterns only added to the growing confusion. Wounded soldiers further impeded progress. Confederate artillery made matters worse by opening on the massed mobs of blue. When a Rebel shell struck a building, a portion of the structure tumbled into the road. The debris nearly killed Colonel Fowler and his adjutant. Fortunately for them, their horses shied away from the explosion, which allowed the officers to escape with merely a light dusting of brick fragments and pulverized mortar.

---

12 Lieutenant H. H. Lyman to Bachelder, undated, Bachelder Papers Typescript; Kellogg to Bachelder, November 1, 1865, Bachelder Papers Typescript; Tevis and Marquis, *The History of the Fighting Fourteenth*, pp. 85, 135; OR pt. 1, pp. 282-283. Fowler misidentified Wadsworth's aide as "Krep."

13 Tevis and Marquis, *The History of the Fighting Fourteenth*, pp. 86, 135-136; OR pt. 1, p. 283; Hofmann, *PWP;* Smith, *76th New York*, p. 240; Hassler, *Crisis at the Crossroads*, p. 123; Kress, "Tales of War."

The Confederate artillery fire stopped when friendly infantry entered Gettysburg from two directions. The proximity of Southern troops added enemy musketry to the chaotic retreat. Cutler had another horse killed in the town, and Captain Cook of the 76th New York later reported that he lost eight to 10 men in the streets from falling bricks and Rebel small arms fire. Fowler momentarily contemplated dispersing his men and ordering the colors taken from the staff, but he just as quickly changed his mind. He also considered forming his troops into a battle line to confront the rapidly advancing Southerners but reconsidered when he realized that a halt of any duration would result in the encirclement and capture of his entire regiment. Fowler continued directing his men toward the rallying point southeast of Gettysburg.[14]

The retreating blue mass streamed south along Baltimore Pike toward the foot of the northern slope of Cemetery Hill. Cutler's survivors spilled over the crest, finally reaching temporary sanctuary. Earlier in the day, Maj. Gen. Oliver O. Howard had placed a portion of his corps on Cemetery Hill to serve as a rallying force in case the tide of battle turned against the Federals. Cutler's men spent a brief period of time reorganizing behind this 11th Corps group in the vicinity of the lower drive of the city cemetery.

During this respite, Maj. Gen. Winfield S. Hancock arrived. By special orders from Maj. Gen. George Gordon Meade, Hancock assumed command of the Union troops milling about the knoll. He instructed Doubleday to deploy part of Wadsworth's division along the western slope of Culp's Hill. According to one of Hancock's staff officers, Doubleday objected because his men were exhausted and nearly out of ammunition. Hancock overruled him. Fortunately, the 7th Indiana, which had been on guard detail, rejoined Cutler's brigade at this time. Doubleday directed Wadsworth to send the 437-man Indiana regiment as a vanguard to occupy Culp's Hill. Not long thereafter, the remnants of the Iron Brigade reinforced the 7th Indiana.

The rest of Cutler's depleted brigade bivouacked in the meadow opposite the cemetery entrance. The 14th Brooklyn camped near the McKnight property. The 147th New York rested that evening near a small barn and house on the northeast side of Baltimore Pike. During this interlude, another spent projectile struck Colonel Fowler. He was reclining on the grass when a ball caromed off a nearby fence and slammed into the hand supporting his head. Although the colonel saw

14 Hofmann, *Remarks on the Battle of Gettysburg*, p. 7; Tevis and Marquis, *The History of the Fighting Fourteenth*, p. 136; Hofmann, *PWP; OR* pt. 1, p. 286.

stars and suffered with a headache for the rest of the night, he had once again escaped serious injury.[15]

Cutler's gallant men, engaged from 10:00 a.m. until after 4:00 p.m., settled down for a well-deserved rest. That morning "Old Graybeard's" five regiments (nearly 1,600 men) had deployed along the ridges west of Gettysburg. That evening, less than 500 went into bivouac on Cemetery Hill; the rest had been killed, wounded, captured, or were missing. Cutler was justifiably proud of his command. Its skillful maneuvers and determined fighting had helped repulse or stall Confederate brigades led by Archer, Davis, Iverson, Daniel, and Scales. Cutler's was the first Union infantry to engage the enemy at Gettysburg and one of the last Yankee outfits to leave the July 1 battlefield. Although the brigade sustained high casualties, Cutler's men had also inflicted a great many. Few outfits achieved as much glory at Gettysburg as did Lysander Cutler's men on July 1, 1863.[16]

The overnight rest atop Cemetery Hill refreshed Cutler's exhausted command. The brigade's strong group of regimental leaders—Fowler, Pye, Hofmann, Cook, and Harney—spent the night hours collecting stragglers and consolidating their units. Although diminished by the day's fierce battle west of Gettysburg, these veteran regiments quickly regained their combat effectiveness.

The extent of their rapid recovery would be tested the next two days by the ferocious fighting on a hill east of their nocturnal bivouac.

---

15 Hofmann, *Remarks on the Battle of Gettysburg*, p. 7; Coddington, *The Gettysburg Campaign*, p. 297; Hofmann, *PWP;* Pearson, *James S. Wadsworth of Geneseo*, pp. 223-225; Lieutenant H. H. Lyman to Bachelder, undated, Bachelder Papers Typescript; *OR* pt. 1, pp. 252, 283; Doubleday, *Chancellorsville and Gettysburg*, pp. 150-152; Lt. Col. Charles Morgan Report, no date, Bachelder Papers Typescript. Doubleday's accounts do not mention any hesitation on his part about sending Wadsworth's men to Culp's Hill.

16 Cutler's Brigade Field Returns, July 2, 1863, RG 393, Part 2, NARA. Cutler's men probably had very little to do with the repulse of O'Neal's Brigade.

CHAPTER TEN

Action on Culp's Hill

Colonel Ira Grover's 7th Indiana, part of Lysander Cutler's brigade, spent the morning and early afternoon hours of July 1 guarding the 1st Corps's cattle herd and ammunition train. When the Hoosiers stopped for lunch along Emmitsburg Road, probably in the early afternoon, they heard the faint, distant thunder of cannon to the north. Soon thereafter, a galloping courier reined in his horse to inform Grover that General Reynolds had been killed and that Rebel forces were overpowering the outnumbered Union troops. The colonel expected another regiment to relieve the 7th Indiana from its guard duty, but the Vermont regiment assigned to do so failed to appear. Acting on his own initiative, Colonel Grover ordered his men to form ranks and started them for Gettysburg.[1]

The 7th Indiana reached Cemetery Hill around 5:00 p.m. by way of Baltimore Pike. Some Hoosiers maintained they saw the remnants of the 1st and 11th Corps fighting their way through the town toward the safety of the hill. The 7th's Orville Thomson saw large clusters of battle-grimed soldiers milling around the high ground in an apparent attempt to reorganize. One of the first high-ranking officers

---

1 Jerry M. Easley, ed., *1863 Civil War Diary, James M. Hart, 7th Indiana Volunteer Infantry* (n.p., n.d.). Many of the diary pages are unnumbered. This item is located at the United States Army Military History Institute, formerly the War College Library, in Carlisle, Pennsylvania. Paul Truitt, "The Seventh Indiana Fighters," *National Tribune*, Nov. 11, 1925; Thomson, *Narrative of the Service of the Seventh Indiana Infantry*, pp. 161-162.

the Hoosiers came across was their division commander. "We found General Wadsworth sitting on a stone fence by the roadside, his head bowed in grief, the most dejected woe-begone person . . . a live picture of despair," began Thomson. "The General greeted us warmly, adding, 'I am glad you were not with us this afternoon;' and, in response to a remark of General Cutler, 'If the Seventh had been with us we could have held our position,' said, 'Yes, and all would now be dead or prisoners.'"[2]

While the other regiments of the brigade rested, the 7th Indiana formed a battle line to serve as a rallying point upon which broken units could reform. Subsequent to the 7th Indiana's arrival, Maj. Gen. Winfield S. Hancock ordered Maj. Gen. Abner Doubleday to occupy Culp's Hill, which, in turn, resulted in Brig. Gen. James Wadsworth ordering his only fresh regiment—the 7th Indiana—to move to the crest of the wooded height with instructions to hold it at all cost. The remains of the Iron Brigade followed and aligned on Grover's left. The 6th Wisconsin rested next to the Hoosiers. All of the units began constructing breastworks once they arrived on the hill. Together with other units, the 7th Indiana now protected the extreme right flank of Meade's army. Holding the position was imperative to preserve the integrity of the Union position.[3]

Union control of Culp's Hill had not yet been solidified as darkness settled over the July 1 battlefield. If the Rebels had seized the height late that afternoon or during the night, they could have menaced the rear of the Federal army assembling on Cemetery Hill and Cemetery Ridge and potentially cut off a primary withdrawal route along Baltimore Pike. In all probability, Confederate occupation of Culp's Hill would have forced the Army of the Potomac to abandon the excellent defensive terrain now in its possession.

Lieutenant Henry Lyman confirmed the importance of Culp's Hill in a postwar letter to J. William Hofmann:

It has always seemed strange to me that writers upon this Great Battle have not recognized this point. Volumes have been written upon the matter of Round Top and its great

---

2 Thomson, *Narrative of the Service of the Seventh Indiana Infantry*, pp. 162-163.

3 Truitt, "The Seventh Indiana Fighters;" Dawes, *Service with the Sixth Wisconsin*, pp. 179-180; Stine, *History of the Army of the Potomac*, p. 492; Coddington, *The Gettysburg Campaign*, p. 712n. Somewhere along their march, the 7th Indiana apparently changed its route from Emmitsburg Road to Baltimore Pike. Thomson, *Narrative of the Service of the Seventh Indiana Infantry*, pp. 162-163; J. N. Hubbard, "Gettysburg: Wadsworth's Division on Culp's Hill," *National Tribune*, March 15, 1915.

importance in maintaining the line. The possession of Culps Hill by the enemy would have caused disaster and compelled retreat much quicker than the loss of Round Top.[4]

The hill upon which the Hoosier's of the 7th Indiana found themselves was rocky and heavily wooded. Orville Thomson described Culp's Hill as "somewhat on the order of our Ohio river hills—its sides pretty heavily timbered, and strewn with rocks varying in size from a chicken-coop to a pioneer's cabin." The top of the hill was roughly L-shaped. Part of the "L" faced north, while the other section faced east. The Iron Brigade, supported by a portion of the 7th Indiana, held the northern segment of the "L." The remainder of the 7th Indiana covered the east-facing leg. The 7th Indiana's Company B deployed near the base of the eastern edge of the elevation as an advanced outpost. The isolated Indiana soldiers patrolled a sector of ground east of the lines later occupied by the 12th Corps on July 2 and 3. Not long after its deployment, Company B consolidated its picket line only a few yards to the right of the main line of battle.[5]

This repositioning of Company B's outposts took place concurrently with a Rebel reconnaissance. Lieutenant General Richard S. Ewell, commander of the Confederate Second Corps, decided earlier that evening that an attack on Cemetery Hill from the town was impossible. From his vantage point, Ewell judged the best way to eventually drive the Federals off Cemetery Hill was to occupy Culp's Hill, which he described in his official report as "a wooded hill to my left, on a line with and commanding Cemetery Hill." Ewell directed Maj. Gen. Edward Johnson to place his 6,433-man division opposite the peak. Once in place, he launched a reconnaissance party from the 42nd Virginia, a regiment in Brig. Gen. John M. Jones's Brigade, with instructions to explore Culp's Hill so as to determine whether the Yankees held the elevation.

The Virginians set off on their intelligence mission around 10:00 p.m. The Southern scouts approached the summit without the slightest resistance. For a while, it seemed as though the key to the Union rear was within the Confederacy's grasp. However, the 7th Indiana picket post on the extreme right of the line, consisting of Sgt. William Hussey and Pvts. A. J. Harshberger and W. S. Odell, detected the enemy advance. Although unable to see much of anything, the three

4 Henry Lyman to John William Hofmann, March 21, 1885, Henry Harrison Lyman Collection.

5 "At Gettysburg, How a Proposed Night Attack by the Enemy Was Foiled," *National Tribune*, February 11, 1886, 3une, *History of the Army of the Potomac*, pp. 492-493; Thomson, *Narrative of the Service of the Seventh Indiana Infantry*, p. 163.

Hoosiers distinctly heard the rustle of brush and the snapping of twigs. The trio moved cautiously toward the noise and hid behind some huge boulders. The Indiana soldiers allowed a Rebel officer to pass, after which Sergeant Hussey leaped from his concealed position and grabbed the unsuspecting Virginian. Harshberger and Odell simultaneously fired pointblank in the direction of the other members of the reconnaissance party. The firing brought the remainder of Company B to the aid of their Indiana comrades. Surprised by this rapid show of force, the Rebels fled toward their own lines. Culp's Hill remained safely in Union control.[6]

The performance of the 7th Indiana's Company B played a vital role in the defense of Culp's Hill. If the Confederate scouts had brushed aside the thin Union skirmish line and determined a major portion of the hill remained unoccupied, there was every indication Ewell would have tried to secure at least a foothold there before daybreak on July 2. Around midnight, Ewell sent a message to Johnson asking him "to take possession of this hill, if he had not already done so." When Johnson replied that his reconnaissance party had been repulsed, Ewell dismissed further efforts to occupy the hill that night. One of the many Confederate opportunities to win the Battle of Gettysburg had been squandered. A Confederate division occupying Culp's Hill would have overlooked the rear of the Union army, threatening Federal reserve artillery batteries, ammunition trains, and a major route of withdrawal along Baltimore Pike. Meade would have had two alternatives: abandon his present position, or assault the Rebels entrenched atop Culp's Hill. Neither option would have appealed to the newly appointed Army of the Potomac commander.[7]

While Company B repulsed the Confederate scouting party, Union troops occupying Culp's Hill continued erecting breastworks by felling trees and arranging them into formidable barriers. According to Thomson of the 7th Indiana, it was the first time his regiment had performed "work of that character." He and his comrades, he added, attended to the construction with "unusual alacrity."[8]

About 3:00 a.m. on July 2, the Union forces occupying Culp's Hill arose to prepare for action; the Rebel scouting party had aroused suspicion. Action that morning was limited to intermittent skirmish fire. Around 7:00 a.m., Cutler's

---

6 OR pt. 2, pp. 445-446, 504; Tucker, *High Tide at Gettysburg*, pp. 195-196; Stine, *History of the Army of the Potomac*, p. 493; "At Gettysburg;" Thomson, *Narrative of the Service of the Seventh Indiana Infantry*, pp. 164-166. Thomson identified the Confederates as members of the 42nd Virginia.

7 OR pt. 2, p. 446; "At Gettysburg."

8 Thomson, *Narrative of the Service of the Seventh Indiana Infantry*, p. 163.

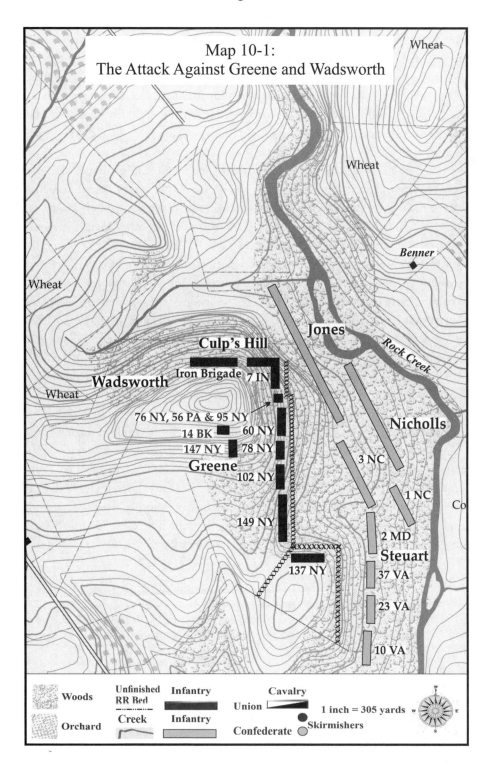

Map 10-1:
The Attack Against Greene and Wadsworth

brigade left its bivouac on Cemetery Hill and headed for Culp's Hill. The brigade's morning field return provided a grim reminder of just how desperate the fighting had been on July 1. The 56th Pennsylvania, for example, was down to 12 officers and 81 men. It was no better in the other regiments: 76th New York (eight officers and 80 men); 95th New York (11 officers and 95 men); 147th New York (10 officers and 79 men); and 14th (Brooklyn) New York State Militia (22 officers and 96 men).

Once he had the bulk of his brigade on Culp's Hill, Cutler aligned the 76th New York, 56th Pennsylvania, and 95th New York to the right of the 7th Indiana's eastern-facing line. Contrary to usual interpretations, all three regiments faced east. The right end of Cutler's force connected to the left of Brig. Gen. George S. Greene's 12 Corps' brigade, which also faced east. The 147th New York and the 14th Brooklyn held a second line as a reserve. The remainder of the 12th Corps extended Greene's line south. Food was scarce, so the men relied on any rations remaining in their haversacks. Fortunately, the shade of the oak trees protected the men from the sun. To pass the time, explained the 14th Brooklyn's historian, "The men quietly busied themselves brushing up and cleaning their guns." They also strengthened their rifle pits and breastworks. When skirmish fire intensified, the 14th Brooklyn moved to the threatened area in case it was needed there. The tattered remnants of Cutler's brigade were ready to fight once more.[9]

Around 4:00 p.m., Lt. Gen. James Longstreet launched a rolling, two-division en echelon assault against the Union left flank on the southern side of the field. Part of Lt. Gen. A. P. Hill's Corps, which was aligned on Longstreet's left, entered the attack a couple hours later when the fighting reached that front. The Rebel offensive crumbled the advanced and ill-placed Federal 3rd Corps under Maj. Gen. Dan Sickles. The collapse imperiled the Army of the Potomac's entire left flank. General Meade reinforced his embattled wing with the Maj. Gen. George Sykes's 5th Corps, part of Hancock's 2nd Corps, and the majority of Maj. Gen. Henry

---

9 Dawes, *Service with the Sixth Wisconsin*, p. 180; Easley, ed., *James Hart Diary*, p. 8; OR pt. 1, p. 283; Lieutenant H. H. Lyman to Bachelder, no date, Bachelder Papers Typescript; Lyman Diary; Tevis and Marquis, *The History of the Fighting Fourteenth*, pp. 90, 137; Hubbard, "Gettysburg;" D. J. Dickson, "At Culp's Hill," *National Tribune,* April 15, 1915. This article and the one by Hubbard were crucial in understanding Cutler's alignment on July 2 and 3. Cutler's Brigade Field Returns, July 2, 1863, RG 393, Part 2, NARA. Many sources have Wadsworth's entire division facing north or northwest, which is not entirely correct, as noted in the main text. See for example, Tucker, *High Tide at Gettysburg*, p. 301; Bates, *The Battle of Gettysburg*, pp. 81, 100-101, 139; Vanderslice, *Gettysburg Then and Now*, p. 136; Coddington, *The Gettysburg Campaign*, map facing p. 333, 342, 431; Doubleday, *Chancellorsville and Gettysburg*, p. 160.

Slocum's 12th Corps. When Slocum's troops left Culp's Hill about 6:30 p.m., only Greene's brigade and Wadsworth's depleted division remained to confront any Confederate troops who might try to capture the rocky wooded heights. Slocum directed Greene to extend his men southward to occupy as much of the evacuated line as possible. Greene dutifully slid Col. David Ireland's 137th New York into trenches previously held by some of the men in Brig. Gen. Thomas Kane's 2nd Brigade of Brig. Gen. John Geary's 2nd Division.

The long-expected Southern assault against Culp's Hill began about 7:00 p.m. Major General Johnson's Rebel skirmishers drove back their Union counterparts as they moved up hill. Johnson deployed three assaulting brigades as follows: Brig. Gen. George Steuart on the left; Col. Nicholls's Brigade, led by Col. J. M. Williams, in the center; and Brig. Gen. John M. Jones on the right. The Southerners presented a magnificent battle front of 17 veteran regiments arranged in three deep lines. The panorama of the Confederate advance in the muted evening light must have been a spectacular sight.[10]

Greene realized quickly that his 1,424 officers and men would have trouble holding the entire 12th Corps position, so he asked Wadsworth and Maj. Gen. Oliver O. Howard for help. Jones's Brigade, comprised of the 21st, 25th, 42nd, 44th, 48th, and 50th Virginia regiments, meanwhile, hammered Cutler's men as well as Greene's 60th New York. Nicholls's Louisiana Brigade hit Greene's 78th, 102nd, and 149th New York regiments. Steuart's Brigade, containing the 2nd Maryland, 1st and 3rd North Carolina, and 10th, 23rd, and 37th Virginia regiments, struck Greene's final regiment, the 137th New York, which held the part of the line recently evacuated by Kane's brigade. Protected by stout breastworks, Greene's and Cutler's soldiers held Jones and Nicholls at bay. "They [Jones's Brigade] kept coming on firing as they came until they came close enough for us to reply to them," recalled a member of the 7th Indiana. He continued:

> The battle raged until 10 o'clock that night when they withdrew, leaving their dead on the field. A terrible sight met our eyes the next morning. The dead Confederates lay in heaps,

---

10 Busey Martinand , *Regimental Strengths at Gettysburg*, p. 151; Richard Eddy, *History of the 60th Regiment, New York State Volunteers* (Philadelphia, 1864), pp. 260-262; *Retreat from Gettysburg*, p. 317; *In Memoriam, George Sears Greene* (Albany, 1909), pp. 42-46; OR pt. 1, p. 856. Johnson's Division included a fourth brigade under Brig. Gen. James Walker, which spent the day protecting the army's left flank. This task, more properly performed by cavalry, kept the veterans out of the attack on Culp's Hill.

and in all conceivable positions on the rocks and up to our temporary works. The trees were shot to splinters.[11]

Colonel J. William Hofmann of the 56th Pennsylvania agreed. "The enemy were moving up the hill in large force. Instantly the crest of the works was lighted up, as it were, by a long flash of tongued lightning, as the regiments took their place in the woods," he began in his vivid description of the horrific event. "One flash following another," he continued,

and each increasing in vividness as the daylight disappeared, its disappearance accelerated by the clouds of smoke, which at first hung among the foliage above, but soon seemed to roll down and obscure everything in front of the works — everything but the flashes of the enemy, who advanced, covered in a measure by the very abruptness of the face of the hill, and some…taking shelter from tree to tree and rock to rock.[12]

Some of Jones's force managed to advance within 20 yards of the Union breastworks, but they never seriously threatened to overwhelm the Federals. General Greene recalled four separate charges. Lieutenant Colonel John Kress, one of General Wadsworth's aides, took note of the courage displayed by the division leader:

[He] exposed himself in a very reckless manner, in order to encourage the men; amid the hottest of the firing he took a seat on a rock immediately in rear of and above our line of battle; the bullets pattered against the rock continually. No persuasion of his officers could induce him to quit the place until the enemy ceased the attack.

In another act of bravery, Cpl. Patrick Burns of the 56th Pennsylvania encouraged his regiment by waving the colors over the works. This was not the silken emblem normally carried by the regiment; that flag was in Philadelphia being lettered. Instead, Burns hoisted a dark blue bunting camp flag decorated with "56th Regt. P.V." in white muslin and a red disc representing the 1st Corps badge in the center. His inspiring efforts were cut short when a bullet pierced his hand as buckshot struck his shoulder. The losses demonstrate that fighting along the front held by Cutler and the 60th New York raged fiercely: Colonel Hofmann's 56th

11 Hubbard, "Gettysburg."

12 Hofmann, *PWP*.

56th Pennsylvania Flag

Courtesy of the Massachusetts Commandery
Military Order of the Loyal Legion and the USAMHI

Pennsylvania lost two killed and 10 wounded out of 93 engaged despite fighting from behind formidable breastworks.[13]

The situation off to the south was critical: part of Steuart's Brigade occupied a portion of the 12th Corps's vacated works and overlapped Greene's right flank. Several regiments from Wadsworth's division and others from Howard's 11th Corps (including the 6th Wisconsin, 147th New York, 14th Brooklyn, 157th New York, 45th New York, 82nd Illinois, and 61st Ohio) reinforced Greene's line.[14]

13 Busey and Martin, *Regimental Strengths at Gettysburg*, p. 96; *Retreat from Gettysburg*, p. 317; *In Memoriam, Greene*, pp. 45-47; Tevis and Marquis, *The History of the Fighting Fourteenth*, pp. 91-92, 138; Lyman Diary; Coddington, *The Gettysburg Campaign*, p. 431; *OR pt. 1*, p. 856; Bates, *History of the Pennsylvania Volunteers, Vol. 2*, p. 221; Hubbard, "Gettysburg;" Healy Diary; Hofmann, *PWP*; Richard Sauers, *Advance the Colors, Volume 1* (Harrisburg, 1987), p. 156. The most thorough study of the fighting on Culp's Hill is Harry Pfanz's *Gettysburg: Culp's Hill and Cemetery Hill* (Chapel Hill, 1993).

14 Lieutenant H. H. Lyman to Bachelder, undated, Bachelder Papers Typescript. Although there is some indication the 147th New York accompanied the 6th Wisconsin and the 14th Brooklyn to Greene's threatened right, it seems more likely the New Yorkers supported the

To fully understand the maneuvers of the Union infantry, it is necessary to determine the location of Steuart's men. Steuart's mixed command splashed across Rock Creek before advancing up the wooded hillside. When he realized his brigade had drifted too far to the left, Steuart ordered it to oblique to the right. This maneuver placed his two right regiments, the 3rd North Carolina and the 2nd Maryland, in a vicious crossfire between the 137th and 149th New York. Although staggered by the Federal musketry, Steuart's men pressed on. A spirited charge by the 23rd Virginia forced the 137th New York to retire to a position perpendicular to its former alignment. The Virginians, together with the 2nd Maryland, 37th Virginia, and 10th Virginia, scrambled into the vacated works. The 3rd North Carolina inexplicably remained in its exposed position despite being nearly out of ammunition. Steuart's Rebel brigade, less its two North Carolina regiments, formed a battle line between the captured breastwork and a stone wall nearly paralleling it. From this position, Steuart's men enfiladed the 149th New York.[15]

Steuart, meanwhile, worried that his men might be firing at friendly forces. As a result, the Rebel musketry was intermittently discontinued. Steuart finally ordered Colonel Warren to shift his 10th Virginia, which had been on the extreme left of the brigade and arranged perpendicular to the wall, to a front aligned with the barrier and facing northeast. Warren then slid his 10th Virginia by its left flank along the stone fence until it reached the rear of the 137th New York. Once in position, Warren ordered his regiment to open fire on the right flank of the exposed New Yorkers, which forced a portion of the Federal regiment to fall back.[16]

Darkness settled over the tree- and rock-studded hill as Col. Edward Fowler and Lt. Col. Rufus Dawes advanced their men to the support of Colonel Ireland's 137th New York. Thick woods and waning sunlight made it difficult to see beyond a short distance. Dawes met Greene at the crest of Culp's Hill. The brigadier directed Dawes to form his men so as to occupy the breastworks a few rods down the slope. Apparently, Greene meant for Dawes to align on the right of the 137th New York's second line. Dawes had his men rush down the crest so that when his

---

right flank of the 60th New York. In one letter to John Bachelder, Lyman claimed the 147th was to the right of the 60th New York. In another, on December 12, 1888, Lyman placed the 147th New York to the left of the 149th New York, near "a big low rock extending to an oak tree in an angle of the woods, and we occupied from the tree to a stump." Lyman to Bachelder, Henry Harrison Lyman Collection; Pfanz, *Culp's Hill and Cemetery Hill*, p. 213.

15 *OR* pt. 2, pp. 509-511; W. W. Goldsborough, *The Maryland Line in the Confederate Army* (Darnestown, 1983), pp. 103-105.

16 Goldsborough, *The Maryland Line in the Confederate Army*, pp. 103-105; *OR* pt. 1, pp. 866-867.

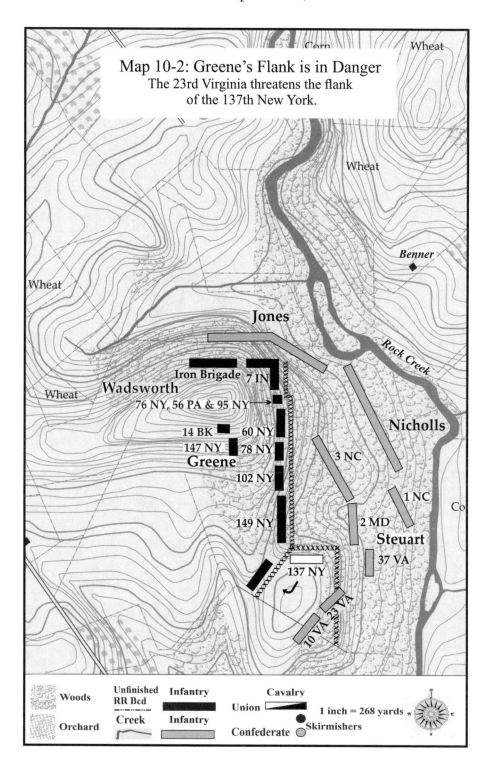

Map 10-2: Greene's Flank is in Danger
The 23rd Virginia threatens the flank
of the 137th New York.

Corn

Wheat

Wheat

Benner

Wheat

Jones

Rock Creek

Iron Brigade   7 IN

Wadsworth

76 NY, 56 PA & 95 NY →

Wheat

Nicholls

14 BK   60 NY

147 NY   78 NY

Greene

3 NC

1 NC

102 NY

Co

149 NY

2 MD

Steuart

37 VA

137 NY

10 VA 23 VA

Woods

Orchard

Unfinished
RR Bcd

Creek

Infantry

Infantry

Cavalry

Union

Confederate

Skirmishers

1 inch = 268 yards

N
W   E
S

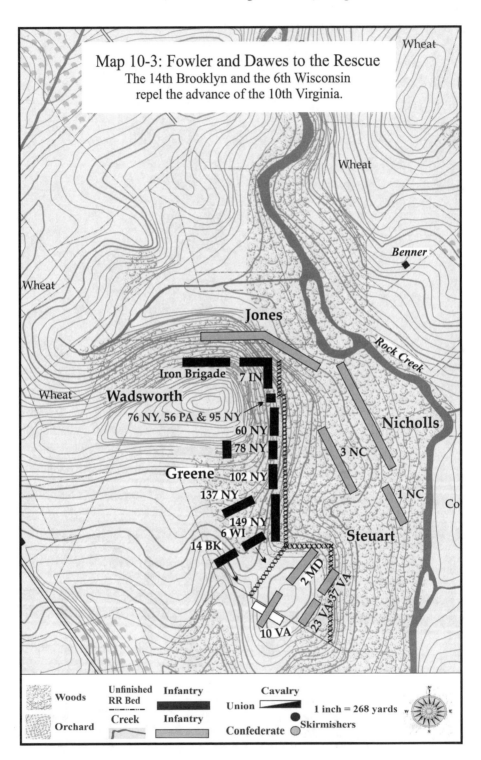

Map 10-3: Fowler and Dawes to the Rescue
The 14th Brooklyn and the 6th Wisconsin
repel the advance of the 10th Virginia.

line "came in relief against the sky on the top of the hill," there would be little chance the Rebels could deliver an effective volley. Before the 6th Wisconsin began this move, however, the 14th Brooklyn, on Dawes's right, started down the slope.[17]

Lieutenant John J. Cantine, one of General Greene's aides, met Fowler so that he could lead the 14th Brooklyn toward the right of the Union line. After the group advanced a short distance, an unidentified soldier demanded that Cantine and Fowler surrender. Simultaneously, a few shots rang out from a nearby patch of timber. Fowler rushed back to his regiment and deployed it to face the woods. By this time, Colonel Warren's 10th Virginia had achieved its flanking position and fired into the side and rear of the 137th and 149th New York regiments. Then a few scattered shots to the left and rear of the Confederate regiment alerted Warren of impending danger. These shots may have been the ones fired at Cantine and Fowler. Colonel Warren realigned his men perpendicular to the wall to face in the direction from which the musketry had been heard.

While the 10th Virginia was shifting its front, darkness and large rocks and trees slowed Fowler's advance. Fowler detected strange voices ahead in the gloom. A sudden and unexpected volley of musketry slashed through the 14th Brooklyn's ranks. Unable to ascertain whether it was enemy or friendly fire, Fowler maneuvered his men to face the unseen foe. Once realigned, he asked for volunteers to scout ahead. John Cox and one other Red Leg offered their services. The men slithered along the ground toward the unknown force. The balance of the 14th Brooklyn remained in line as bullets zipped and buzzed past. This was, confessed Fowler four days later, "the most trying position the Regiment had yet been in — the night was intensely dark, and the bullets were whistling around us like hail." It took remarkable courage for the chasseurs to stand fast in the deepening darkness and receive volleys—friendly or otherwise—without being able to respond.

A wounded John Cox returned a short time later to declare that the troops firing at Fowler's men belonged to the 10th Virginia. That was enough to convince Fowler, who ordered his regiment to fire a volley and follow it with a charge. This attack coincided almost perfectly with the 6th Wisconsin's rush down the slope of Culp's Hill. For the second day in a row, the 6th Wisconsin and the 14th Brooklyn participated in an unplanned, simultaneous assault against a startled foe. Dawes's

17 Dawes to Bachelder, March 18, 1868, Bachelder Papers Typescript; Tevis and Marquis, *The History of the Fighting Fourteenth*, pp. 91-92, 138-139.; Dawes, *Service with the Sixth Wisconsin*, pp. 181-182. The 11th Corps units were apparently distributed as reinforcements along Greene's line. See Pfanz, *Culp's Hill and Cemetery Hill*, pp. 213-215.

men, unaware the enemy held the line they were approaching, likewise received a volley. The 10th Virginia, however, was no match for two crack Federal regiments. In his report, General Steuart claimed the 10th Virginia repulsed a bayonet charge before withdrawing in an orderly fashion on his orders. It is much more likely that the sudden attack by two veteran outfits forced the Virginians into a disorderly departure. The Confederates took a new position behind the vacated 1st Division breastworks.[18]

The 6th Wisconsin lost two men killed in the skirmish and remained in the recaptured entrenchments. Fowler, meanwhile, marched his chasseurs up the slope to relieve a regiment said to be out of ammunition. When Fowler located the command, he found it supported by two lines of battle. When no further instructions arrived, Fowler moved his men back to the top of the hill. Once there, a staff officer directed him to return back down the slope to relieve Ireland's 137th New York. Although a few members of the 14th Brooklyn incurred wounds in the Culp's Hill action, not a man was killed.[19]

Once again, Cutler's brigade played an important role in holding back a numerically superior Confederate force. The 7th Indiana, 56th Pennsylvania, and 76th and 95th New York regiments each helped to repulse Jones's Virginia brigade.

---

18 Truitt, "The 7th Indiana Fighters;" Dawes, *Service with the Sixth Wisconsin*, p. 182; Tevis and Marquis, *The History of the Fighting Fourteenth*, pp. 92-95, 138; OR pt. 2, p. 510. The shots that alerted the 10th Virginia may have been errant discharges from the 71st Pennsylvania. Earlier that evening, the regiment was sent to Culp's Hill to reinforce the position and for a short time formed to the right of the 14th Brooklyn. Due to darkness and confusion, the 71st Pennsylvania never participated in the attack against the 10th Virginia. Pfanz, *Culp's Hill and Cemetery Hill*, p. 222; Fowler, "The Fourteenth Regiment." The compilers of the 14th Brooklyn regimental history claimed two men volunteered to scout ahead. One was John Cox. They identified the other soldier as "McQuire" and stated he was wounded during this encounter. No one by the name of McQuire exists on the regimental roll. There is a James McGuire in the regiment, but he was not wounded at Gettysburg. The only chasseur wounded on July 2 or 3 with a name similar to McQuire was William Magonigle (also spelled as McGonnigle), who suffered a slight wound to the head. Seth Low's dedication speech in *New York at Gettysburg*, Vol. 2, p. 689, also mentioned that two men performed the scout; one was wounded, and the other returned with the news that the regiment faced the 10th Virginia. Fowler twice referred to the incident in his writings. Each time he suggested that he dispatched a single volunteer. In one account, he named John Cox as the scout who conducted the reconnaissance. Tevis and Marquis, *History of the Fighting Fourteenth*, p. 138; Fowler to Bachelder, October 2, 1889, Bachelder Papers Typescript. It seems reasonable to send more than one man to conduct such a vital mission. If two men went out, Fowler's recollections may have been skewed by the fact that only one of the men returned with the desired information.

19 Tevis and Marquis, *The History of the Fighting Fourteenth*, pp. 94, 138; Dawes, *Service with the Sixth Wisconsin*, p. 182; OR pt. 1, p. 867.

Lieutenant Henry H. Lyman

*Courtesy of the Oswego County
Historical Society*

The 147th New York reinforced the Union line somewhere between the 60th and 149th New York regiments to help blunt the attack by Nicholls's Louisiana brigade. The greatest service of the evening, however, was performed by the 14th Brooklyn and the 6th Wisconsin. If Warren's 10th Virginia had routed the outflanked 137th New York, the entire Union position on Culp's Hill might have been taken in reverse. A successful attack by the 10th Virginia would have provided General Steuart with the opportunity to march up the hill and topple each entrenched regiment out of its position. The gallant charge by the 14th Brooklyn and stalwart advance by the 6th Wisconsin thwarted the chance.

The fighting on Culp's Hill ended around 10:00 p.m. The Confederates held the bottom of the hill throughout the night. They also received substantial reinforcements—four brigades led by Brig. Gens. Junius Daniel, James A. Walker, William Smith, and Col. Edward A. O'Neal, These new arrivals went into position in support of Johnson's left flank. The Confederates planned to swing this reinforced left wing early the next morning obliquely against the lines held by Greene during the evening of July 2.

The Federals also received support that night. Major General Henry Slocum's 12th Corps troops, sent to reinforce the embattled Union left flank, returned to Culp's Hill. Once there, they prepared not only to defend the height but to launch an attack of their own. The brigades under Brig. Gen. Thomas Kane and Col. Charles Candy of John Geary's division recovered most of their positions to the right of Greene's men. As the 12th Corps soldiers settled into the entrenchments, the 6th Wisconsin and 14th Brooklyn retired to their respective commands. Colonel Archibald McDougall's brigade extended Geary's line to face the enemy's left flank. Colonel Silas Colgrove's brigade formed a line perpendicular to

McDougall's deployment, extending to Rock Creek and confronting the Confederate left flank.[20]

At 4:30 a.m. on July 3, Union 12th Corps artillery opened on the Rebel lines for 15 minutes. General Geary intended to launch his division against the Southerners clinging to the base of Culp's Hill once the bombardment stopped. Before Geary's men could move, General Johnson launched his own offensive. This assault failed, but the Confederate regiments continued raking the Union line with heavy musketry fire. Occasionally, a Rebel regiment pushed up the hill, only to be blasted back by the entrenched Federals. The heavy fighting lasted throughout the morning.

While the rest of Cutler's brigade fought from behind breastworks, the 147th New York and the 14th Brooklyn rushed once more to aid Greene's embattled command. Fowler's men barely had time to prepare breakfast before they entered the trenches. During the prolonged combat, the Union troops fought in shifts. When a regiment on the firing line exhausted its ammunition, it fell back to allow a fresh unit to take its place. After being relieved, the men replenished their ammunition and cleaned their fouled muskets. At one point, Lt. Henry Lyman and Sidney Cook dashed out of the breastworks "through a storm of bullets" in search of the ammunition wagons. The intrepid soldiers returned to their regiment carrying a box of cartridges in a blanket. The 147th New York was relieved four times in this manner; the 14th Brooklyn constantly cycled in and out of the breastworks.

The soldiers in these two regiments fought well despite their exhausted condition. The Oswego and Brooklyn lads had gone three days with their only nourishment being a couple of crackers and a few sips of water. They had enjoyed but little sleep during the past two nights, and two days of marching and fighting had left them mentally and physically drained. Clouds of thick sulfurous smoke choked their lungs and irritated their eyes. Nonetheless, they fought with dogged determination. The Southerners, protected by trees and rocks, kept up an incessant fire, but because of the strength of the breastworks, only a few of Fowler's men sustained injuries. According to Henry Lyman of the 147th New York, only one man was killed along his line. The intense Rebel musketry shattered the staff of the 14th Brooklyn's state colors and riddled both of their flags. A fellow in the 147th

20 Coddington, *The Gettysburg Campaign*, pp. 467-475; Dawes, *Service with the Sixth Wisconsin*, p. 182; Tevis and Marquis, *The History of the Fighting Fourteenth*, p. 138; Eddy, *History of the 60th New York*, p. 263.

New York reported that every officer and man in his regiment fired more than 300 cartridges during the morning fight. The inferno on the wooded rocky slopes did not end until about 11:00 a.m., when the Confederates abandoned their attempts to take Culp's Hill.[21]

Fowler's regiment and the 147th New York remained in support of Greene's brigade much of the day. In the early afternoon, approximately 150 Rebel cannon on Seminary Ridge suddenly erupted, sending their lethal missiles toward Cemetery Ridge. Union artillery answered, and the ground on Culp's Hill trembled from the thunderous discharges. The Southern artillery fire was not particularly accurate. Many of the guns routinely overshot their mark, so errant shells often landed amongst the Union troops operating in the rear and on Culp's Hill. The 147th New York was "shelled like blazes," noted Henry Lyman in his diary. Several of Fowler's men sustained wounds during the barrage. Eventually, the prolonged cannonade subsided, followed by the sound of infantry combat off to the west and southwest. When the fighting finally ended about 4:30 p.m., cheers erupted up and down the Federal lines proclaiming a Union victory. Longstreet's failed assault against the center of Meade's army, known popularly as "Pickett's Charge," ended the Battle of Gettysburg.[22]

In spite of the repulse of the Confederate assault against Cemetery Ridge, Union commanders believed General Lee might renew hostilities. Colonel J. William Hofmann was ordered to lead the 7th Indiana, the 56th Pennsylvania, and the 95th and 76th New York regiments to Cemetery Hill, where they would support the line held by the 11th Corps. The 14th Brooklyn and 147th New York occupied the pits vacated by their sister regiments. Hofmann's group returned to Culp's Hill a short time later. Cutler's troops finally received rations—beef for their stomachs and ammunition for their cartridge boxes. The fatigued soldiers rested as best they could that night as a heavy rain drenched their exhausted bodies.[23]

The morning of July 4 revealed the effectiveness of the Union musketry during the two previous days on Culp's Hill. "The woodlands looked like a cyclone of hail

21 Coddington, *The Gettysburg Campaign*, pp. 469-475; Tevis and Marquis, *The History of the Fighting Fourteenth*, pp. 96-99, 138-139; Lyman Diary; Lieutenant H. H. Lyman to Bachelder, undated, Bachelder Papers Typescript; Cooke to Lyman, December 23, 1897, Henry Harrison Lyman Collection; Unidentified newspaper article, Bachelder Papers Typescript. Ramon Cardona spliced the 14th Brooklyn's splintered state flag staff together.

22 Tevis and Marquis, *The History of the Fighting Fourteenth*, p. 139; Lyman Diary.

23 Hofmann, *PWP*; Tevis and Marquis, *The History of the Fighting Fourteenth*, p. 139; Lieutenant H. H. Lyman to Bachelder, no date, Bachelder Papers Typescript; Lyman Diary.

had swept over them," recalled the historian of the 14th Brooklyn. "The ground was a network of shorn limbs; the bark had been literally shot from the trees." Human destruction was everywhere. "[F]or fully 100 feet in front the Confederate dead lay piled so thick that it was difficult to pick a way through the bodies." A member of the 7th Indiana agreed, recalling the enemy dead covered the ground in some places four and five bodies deep. Richard Eddy, who wrote a history of the 60th New York in 1864, counted 391 Rebel dead in front of his brigade. The waves of bullets fired by Federal troops from behind the stout breastworks had shattered the valiant efforts of the veteran Southern infantry.[24]

That morning, a detail from Cutler's brigade—the 56th Pennsylvania and the 7th Indiana under Colonel Hofmann—moved to explore part of the town. General Wadsworth, who accompanied the expedition, hoped to retrieve any wounded who may have been left there. As the group passed through the center of town on the way back to Culp's Hill, a Rebel sharpshooter on Seminary Ridge fired. The round hit a member of the 7th Indiana. The unlucky fellow was the last casualty suffered by Cutler's brigade during the Battle of Gettysburg.[25]

---

24 Tevis and Marquis, *The History of the Fighting Fourteenth*, p. 98; Truitt, "The 7th Indiana Fighters;" Eddy, *History of the 60th New York*, p. 264.

25 Hofmann, *PWP*. The identify and fate of the member of the 7th Indiana is unknown.

The Cost of Valor

Three days after the battle, Col. Edward Fowler of the 84th New York (14th Brooklyn) wrote a letter to his hometown newspaper detailing the action at Gettysburg. The regiment, he concluded,

> has suffered fearfully, the color bearer and all the color guard but one, were killed or wounded. The colors are completely perforated —the staff of the State color being shot in half. Hardly an officer or man that is left but has received a scratch of some kind, but all are ready to renew the conflict.[1]

The 14th Brooklyn's Headquarters Record posted the regiment's losses as 20 killed and mortally wounded, 104 wounded, and 100 missing. The rest of Cutler's brigade suffered similar losses.[2]

The chart on the following page vividly outlines the losses Lysander Cutler's command sustained at Gettysburg. The "present" figures come from Cutler's field return dated July 1, 1863. The casualty totals were primarily obtained from the *Official Records*. However, the Roll of Honor found in *New York at Gettysburg* was used to amend the *Official Records* numbers. (The Roll of Honor often indicated higher killed and mortally wounded totals.) It should be noted that a large number

---

1 Fowler, "The Fourteenth Regiment," Headquarters Record, 14th Brooklyn, 1863.

2 Ibid..

of the wounded later died from their injuries, and many of those listed in the "captured or missing" column had been killed.[3]

Casualty Chart for Cutler's Brigade at Gettysburg					
Regiment	Present	KIA/MW*	WIA**	Captured/ Missing	Total Casualties
7th IN	437	2	5	3	10
76th NY	375	32	132	70	234
14th BR	357	13	105	99	217
95th NY	239	7	62	46	115
147th NY	430	60	144	92	296
56th PA	252	14	61	55	130
Total	2,090	128	509	363	1002
Less 7th IND	1,653	126	504	360	992 (60%)

* KIA/MW: killed in action/mortally wounded.
** WIA: wounded in action.

Several details are significant. Of all the Union and Confederate brigades that fought at Gettysburg, only five sustained combined casualties exceeding 1,000 men. The brigade commanders and casualty totals are as follows: Lewis Armistead (CSA, 1,191); Solomon Meredith's Iron Brigade (USA, 1,153); James J. Pettigrew (CSA, 1,105); Gabriel Paul (USA, 1,041), and Lysander Cutler (USA, 1,002). The five regiments of "Old Graybeard's" command lost the vast majority of their killed and wounded along the McPherson Ridge line on the morning of July 1. Probably fewer than 10% of the killed and wounded from these five regiments occurred after

3 Busey and Martin, *Regimental Strengths at Gettysburg*, p. 24; Tevis and Marquis, *The History of the Fighting Fourteenth*, p. 100; OR pt. 1, p. 173; *New York at Gettysburg*, pp. 108, 109, 213, 214, 221-223, 231; Cutler's Brigade Field Return, RG 393, Part 2, NARA. Since the publication of the second edition of *Cutler's Brigade at Gettysburg*, my research into the history of the 14th Brooklyn has identified 25 members of the regiment who were killed or mortally wounded during the battle. Another 111 chasseurs sustained battle wounds.

12:00 p.m. on July 1. This is only an estimate, however, because no day-to-day casualty figures exist.

Despite the early beating suffered during the brigade's first battle as a unit, Cutler capably reformed his men and effectively directed them throughout the remainder of the fighting. His brigade maintained its battlefield integrity despite the tremendous casualties of the first day. The men served splendidly along Seminary Ridge and atop Culp's Hill. In fact, Cutler's brigade was one of the few units actively engaged on all three days of the struggle. The command had a hand in repulsing or checking Confederate soldiers from the brigades of James J. Archer, Joseph Davis, Alfred Iverson, Junius Daniel, Alfred Scales, John M. Jones, J. M. Williams, George Steuart, and James A. Walker. The unusually high casualty totals sustained by the aforementioned Confederate brigades attests to the fighting prowess of Cutler's fine outfit.

It is fair to conclude that no soldiers fought better than the men of Lysander Cutler's brigade. Two weeks after the battle, a member of the outfit penned a letter in which he stated, "I have seen a great many hard battles but I believe that Gettysburg was the most desperate fight I ever saw. . . . I hope that I may never experience 3 more such days while I live."

The brigade deserves to be recognized for the valorous service it performed, and for the heroic sacrifices it made, on the battlefield at Gettysburg.[4]

---

4 OR pt. 1, pp. 168-194; OR pt. 2, pp. 338-346; J. L. Harding Letter, July 18, 1863, 7th Indiana Vertical File, Gettysburg National Military Park Library.

Brigadier General Lysander Cutler

Courtesy of David Cutler Ahlgren

POSTSCRIPT

The Aftermath

After the Battle of Gettysburg came to an end, rain and mud slowed the Army of the Potomac's cautious pursuit of the Army of Northern Virginia. High water in the Potomac River trapped General Lee's army at Williamsport, Maryland. Before General Meade could attack, the water level receded enough to allow Lee to slip his battered army across and escape. Lee's unchallenged departure from Maryland so chafed General Wadsworth that he temporarily left Meade's army. Lysander Cutler assumed command of the 1st Division during Wadsworth's absence, while Colonel Fowler took charge of Cutler's brigade.

Crippled by the enormous casualties suffered at Chancellorsville and Gettysburg, the two opposing Eastern armies reorganized and spent the rest of the summer and fall jockeying for an advantage. Other than a few relatively minor clashes across north-central Virginia, neither side gained a decided advantage. Fortunately for Cutler's former brigade, it missed those engagements.

The Army of the Potomac spent the winter of 1863-1864 bivouacked around Culpeper, Virginia. The extensive casualties sustained by the 1st Corps at Gettysburg led to the unit's disbandment just prior to the onset of the spring 1864 Overland Campaign. James Wadsworth returned to the army, replacing Cutler as commander of the 4th Division, 5th Corps. The deposed Cutler assumed leadership of the Iron Brigade, which now included the 7th Indiana, one of his old regiments. Brig. Gen. James C. Rice, one of the heroes of Gettysburg's Little Round Top, was assigned command of the five remaining regiments (56th

Pennsylvania, 14th Brooklyn, and 76th, 95th, and 147th New York) of Cutler's former brigade.

On March 2, 1864, President Lincoln promoted Ulysses S. Grant to the rank of lieutenant general and entrusted him with the command of all the Union armies. Instead of remaining in Washington, D.C., Grant decided to make his headquarters with the Army of the Potomac, but he retained Meade as commander of the army. That spring, Grant launched a multi-prong offensive in Virginia, Georgia, and elsewhere to bring about the final defeat of the Confederacy.

The initial fighting in Virginia took place in the heavy terrain of the Wilderness on May 5-6, which consisted of dense brush and tangled second-growth timber that limited visibility, disoriented the troops, and often left flanks vulnerable. The Confederates took advantage of these circumstances to launch counterattacks that thrashed the brigades led by Cutler and Rice. When a Rebel bullet mortally wounded Wadsworth on May 6, Cutler assumed command of the 4th Division.[1]

The shifting armies met again on May 8 around Spotsylvania Court House, where the fighting continued through May 19. The 14th Brooklyn reunited with its brigade for this phase of the campaign. Cutler's division, which included Rice's brigade, participated in several frontal assaults over open ground. These charges targeted formidable breastworks defended by veteran Southern infantry supported by well-placed Confederate artillery. The attacks failed. The only accomplishment of these foolhardy advances was a bulging casualty list that included a mortally wounded General Rice. A number of Brooklyn chasseurs, who had completed nearly three years of service, fell killed or wounded just days before their scheduled discharge.

The Army of the Potomac slid away from the Spotsylvania killing fields by moving once more around Lee's right flank. As the Union army marched south, the surviving original enlistees of the 14th Brooklyn left the ranks to start their journey home. The rest of the regiment joined the 5th New York Veteran Volunteers.

Colonel J. William Hofmann of the 56th Pennsylvania became the new brigade commander. The unit spent the spring and summer of 1864 enduring a steady cycle of marches interspersed with bloody combat. Losses mounted at North Anna, Cold Harbor, and the fighting around Petersburg, Virginia. Cutler's tenure in the field came to an end at the Battle of Globe Tavern (Second Weldon Railroad) on August 21 when a shell fragment struck him in the face. The injury

---

1 The 14th Brooklyn served as a wagon train guard and saw limited action in the battle.

severely disfigured the general. In September, he was relieved of active duty at his own request , effectively ending his service in the Army of the Potomac.[2]

Elements of the brigade saw the war to its bloody but successful end. Major James Coey of the 147th New York, who had received a brevet as lieutenant colonel for "conspicuous gallantry in the battles of the Wilderness and at Laurel Hill," elevated his heroism another notch at the battle at Hatcher's Run on February 6, 1865. There, his brigade (under the command of Henry A. Morrow) crossed an open field only to encounter heavy musketry from an enemy posted in a patch of timber. The troops refused to advance despite Morrow's pleas. At this critical moment, Coey seized his regiment's colors and headed for the enemy. "The effect was electrical," recalled one officer. "Color after color was advanced to the front, and the whole brigade line rose up and with a cheer advanced into the woods." A wide, deep ditch filled with water disrupted the charge, so Morrow ordered his men to retire. About this time, a Rebel musket ball struck Coey on the left side of his nose, just below the orbit of the eye, and exited behind his right ear. As two of his companions carried his body from the field, the Southerners launched a counterattack that threatened the Federal line. Somehow, a revived Coey not only survived the wound, but he mustered the strength to procure a horse from an ambulance sergeant. He mounted the animal with the help of his two friends and rallied his brigade a second time. For his conspicuous gallantry, James Coey received the Medal of Honor. He would live a long life before dying in 1918.[3]

When the war ended, Lysander Cutler resigned from the army to return to his Milwaukee home. The war had destroyed his "previously iron constitution." The pain caused by his Brawner's Farm wound had never subsided. An 1864 account by a 5th Corps aide to Maj. Gen. Gouverneur Warren hinted at Cutler's depleted condition. During the Battle of the Wilderness, just after Cutler's Iron Brigade had been outflanked and driven back, the aide came upon "Old Graybeard." He described Cutler as "an oldish, thin, earnest-looking Round-head sort of man, his light stubby beard and hair turning gray. He was bleeding from a wound across his

---

2 Jack D. Welsh, *Medical Histories of the Union Generals* (Kent State, OH, 1996), p. 89. Cutler spent the rest of the war performing administrative duty in Jackson, Michigan.

3 James Coey Medal of Honor Records, D-322-VS-1865, NARA. His full citation reads: "Seized the regimental colors at a critical moment and by a prompt advance on the enemy caused the entire brigade to follow him; and, after being himself severely wounded, he caused himself to be lifted into the saddle and a second time rallied the line in an attempt to check the enemy."

The 147th New York Monument

Steven Floyd

76th New York Reunion Ribbon

Author's Collection

upper lip, and looked ghastly, and I have no doubt felt worse, for he was a gallant man, and to lead his men back . . . must have been hard."[4]

Despite Cutler's ill health, Wisconsin Governor Lucius Fairchild (a former officer in the Iron Brigade) appointed the former general as state inspector of fish. The position required Cutler and his deputies to monitor the quality of fish being brined, packed in casks, and sold. Cutler's popularity in Wisconsin led to his selection as Grand Marshal of a parade on July 4, 1866, followed by the presentation of regimental battle flags to the state government. Cutler suffered a stroke three weeks later that left him paralyzed and helpless. He lingered but a few days before dying on July 30, 1866.[5]

The citizens of Wisconsin mourned the loss of their revered Lysander Cutler. "General Cutler

4 "A Brave Hero Gone," *Bangor Daily Whig and Courier*, August 4, 1866; Morris Schaff, *The Battle of the Wilderness* (Boston: Houghton Mifflin Company, 1910), p. 236.

5 "A State Fish Inspector," *The Daily Milwaukee News*, April 21, 1866; "The Flags of Wisconsin Regiments to be Presented to the State," *The Appleton Crescent*, June 9, 1866; "Independence Day at the Capital," *Semi-Weekly Wisconsin* (Milwaukee), July 11, 1866; "A Brave Hero Gone," *Bangor Daily Whig and Courier*, August 4, 1866.

was among the most efficient and best beloved of the soldiers from this state," proclaimed Governor Fairchild. "Distinguished for his service, covered with honorable scars, and filled with years and glory, he goes to his grave deeply mourned by the entire people of a sorrowing State." The flag above the state capitol building flew at half-mast on July 31 as a tribute to this lost warrior.[6]

After the war, J. William Hofmann became the unofficial spokesman for the brigade that had performed so gallantly at Gettysburg. His Gettysburg articles, which appeared in the *National Tribune* and the *Philadelphia Weekly Press*, praised the performances of the 56th Pennsylvania, 14th Brooklyn, 7th Indiana, and 76th, 95th, and 147th New York Regiments. Members of the Iron Brigade took exception to Hofmann's recollections. Many Westerners countered by claiming they had reached the field at Gettysburg first. They also claimed they had fired the first infantry volley, and that the 6th Wisconsin had acted alone in charging the railroad cut and capturing the prisoners. A lively correspondence ensued in the newspapers. Over time, the Iron Brigade veterans won the war of words. As a result, many modern historians still overlook the impact Lysander Cutler's brave band of men had on the Union victory at Gettysburg.

It is time for Cutler's brigade to receive the recognition it deserves for the crucial role it played during all three days of the fight.

---

6 "The Late Major-General Lysander Cutler," *The Evening Telegraph* (Philadelphia), August 6, 1866.

APPENDIX 1

Resupplying Ammunition

Authors have covered Civil War-related topics from eating habits to burial details. One subject that has received scant attention is how troops were resupplied with ammunition on the battlefield. The article below was written by a member of the Iron Brigade assigned to the 1st Corps ammunition train at Gettysburg. He delivered extra cartridges to the Iron Brigade during the afternoon of July 1. A portion of this ammunition may have been distributed to Cutler's men.

*   *   *

SOME ARMY SKETCHES

MILWAUKEE SUNDAY TELEGRAPH
July 30, 1882

by J. A. Watrous.

THE MULE TRAIN CHARGE AT GETTYSBURG

"I wonder why no one has written up that Mule Train Charge, at Gettysburg?"

The speaker was Sergeant Bert O'Connor, a member of the 7th Wisconsin, now a prosperous and respected resident of San Claire. (It is a notable fact that very few of the returned soldiers are other than respected citizens.)

"It was at the battle of Gettysburg, the first day, and a hot time it was, too, in more respects than one. The atmosphere was oppressive, and the sun poured out its hot rays without mercy, and Lee's army never fought better than it did at Gettysburg; so you see it was hot enough in two respects, at least.

At that time I was under the charge of Wadsworth's division ordnance sergeant. We had about forty wagon loads of infantry ammunition. Ours was the lead that 1st of July. We had heard the artillery firing for perhaps half an hour when the ordnance sergeant, who had received an order to take ten wagon loads of ammunition to the front as quickly as it was possible to get it there, came rushing down the line picking out the best teams, and, as he said, drivers who could be relied upon under any and all circumstances. He said, 'Bert, you run your team to the front.' I did so, and in a minute or two nine other teams rolled their heavy wagons behind mine. Ordering two men to get into each wagon, he then directed us to whip our mules into a keen run, and not to stop until he said so. It was a pretty good road, and you just bet we made those ten mule teams spin along.

Very soon we were on the outskirts of the town. It was down hill through town, so we increased the speed and fairly flew. It seemed as though those mules knew that glorious old Wadsworth's gallant men were getting short of ammunition, and that they must get it to them without a moment's delay. Reaching the street, well through town, which leads to the seminary, we turned to the left, shot out of town, and made direct for the line of battle, then a little beyond the seminary. That line did not prove to be Wadsworth's, and we ran through it. A major rode up to the ordnance sergeant and told him to 'stop that wagon train, as it would be captured,' but the sergeant told him he had been ordered to take ammunition to his division, and was going there with it, so we charged on through the field, half a dozen rebel guns opening on me at once, but we didn't halt a second until our boys were reached. Then the extra men in the wagons threw out the ammunition boxes, and the sergeant took an ax and chopped them open, and issued to the troops while they were fighting, what would make three wagon loads, or about 75,000 rounds.

All this time the rebels were shelling us to kill. Nearly every wagon cover was hit with a shell, solid shot or a minie ball while we were there. That work done, we were ordered to move back into town, and issue to such troops as were out, our ten loads being the only ammunition at the front for the First and Eleventh corps.

When we turned to obey that order, and got on to the turnpike, a perfect storm of shot, shell and bullets poured in that direction. The team next behind me was driven by an Indiana man. A solid shot struck his saddle mule, cutting off both of its hind legs. I shall never forget the look given by old "Indiana," as we called him, when the poor mule fell down on those stumps of legs. He was ordered to cut the harness and haul his load with the remaining three mules. One of the extra men shot the wounded animal. Before he did so, however, another shot made a flesh wound on the other wheel mule and still another shot away both hind wheels of the wagon. Just then a retreating regiment came along and took the ammunition from the disabled wagon, and "Indiana" drove into town with three mules hauling the front wheels and box of his wagon. Two other wagons were hit and considerably damaged, but none of the ammunition was lost.

We remained in town until the troops were in full retreat, and until many of them had passed through to Cemetery ridge. The sergeant made me take the rear in the retreat he riding by my side. When we turned to the right, leaving the seminary road, or street, the rebels were shelling the town right lively. The 11th corps had fallen back, and hearing a peculiar yell and the zip, zip, zipping of a shower of bullets, I looked back to see a rebel line of battle not fifteen rods behind us, moving into the city on a double-quick. They came so near that officers discharged their revolvers at them, and I imitated them.

About that time a New York regiment swung into line and gave the rebels a volley. The street was packed with troops, mounted officers, artillery and cavalry, and such confusion I never saw; but there was method enough in the confused crowd to push forward at a good pace for Cemetery ridge, where a halt was made. As our battered train, every wagon of which had been hit from one to a dozen times with solid shot, shell or bullets, passed over the ridge and down the hill out of range.

General Hancock, who had just come up, asked the sergeant where he had been 'with those wagons to get them shot up in that way?' 'Out to the line of battle, general, to supply the troops with ammunition,' responded the sergeant. 'Good,' said the general, 'but it is the first Mule Train Charge I ever knew anything about.' I guess it was the only charge of the kind during the war. I have been in some hard fights, both before and since that Gettysburg charge with a mule train, but was never in a tighter place than on that occasion. Five of our mules were shot and three of the extra men were wounded. I meet the old sergeant, who afterwards became adjutant general of a brigade and then colonel, once in a while, and we have a good laugh over the famous charge with a Mule Train at Gettysburg, and no matter where I am, or what I am doing, I never think of old "Indiana," as he appeared when his mule's legs were shot off, without laughing."

There were no braver men or better soldiers in Wadsworth's division than honest Bert O'Connor.

Appendix 2

Prisoners of War

The story of Union soldiers captured at Gettysburg and marched to Richmond has received little documentation. The following article by a member of the 147th New York provides information about the difficulties endured by the Federal captives.

* * *

GETTYSBURG PRISONERS

BRUTALITY AND INHUMANITY OF THE REBELS AND ROBBERS WHO WERE THEIR GUARDS ON THE MARCH AND IN PRISON.

National Tribune
August 11, 1904

by Orwin H. Balch.

Editor *National Tribune*: The following is a correct statement of facts, from notes taken on the spot, by Orwin H. Balch, 147th New York, to which I was an eyewitness, and I vouch for the truth of every word.

— Claus C. Claussen, Co. B, 82nd Illinois.

Annapolis, Md., Sept. 28, 1863

On the afternoon of July 1, there were about 3,000 of the First and Eleventh Corps taken prisoners, mostly in the village. Comrade Balch says:

I had been to work, until I was taken, in the hospitals, taking care of the wounded; was not allowed to take the parole there and left to take care of the wounded, as I always supposed was customary with all that were connected with the hospital, but was marched to the rear with the rest.

They enlarged our numbers the second and third days to over 4,000. On the third day we had our choice to take the parole and be sent to Carlisle, Pa., and take the responsibility of what view our Government might take of it, or go to Richmond and be legally exchanged.

The rebel officer also said he had understood that Gen. Halleck had issued an order that he would not accept any parole on the field; and if we were taken before we were lawfully exchanged, we would be shot or hanged, as sure as there was a God.

The most of our officers advised us not to accept of any parole on the field, as there was a great chance for our being recaptured before we crossed the Potomac.

About 1,500 took the parole there; the rest went to Richmond. We were all very hungry, for we had drawn no rations since we had been taken. This day, July 3, there was the hardest fighting. During the battle it was a continual roar of musketry and cannonading from morning until sometime after dark. We could see a change in the rebels' countenances towards night.

July 5. — This morning we were put on a double-quick and marched in the direction of the Potomac. The whole of Lee's army seemed to be on a retreat. At sundown we commenced passing through a mountain pass in one of the ranges of the South Mountains. Here we could see our cavalry making a dash on one of their trains, but we were guarded too sharply — the guard consisting of one division of infantry, one battery and a squadron of cavalry — to prevent us making any resistance, or attempt to escape. At 12 o'clock p. m. we arrived at a village called Spring Mountain, a small place. The roads were in an awful condition. Raining; no rations; men used up; no medicine for the sick, or wounded.

July 6. — A large number of officers and men agreed to take their parole. Maj. Fairfax commenced paroling all who wished, but at 9 a. m. Longstreet came to the house where the Major was engaged and stopped the business, saying that all would have to go to Richmond. This included the sick and wounded.

July 7. — At 10 o'clock a. m. reached Hagerstown, Md. Passed A. P. Hill's, Ewell's (late Jackson's) and Longstreet's Corps. The men of Hill's Corps gave our men a few hardtack. Along the whole route, it seemed, all the barns and outhouses had been taken possession of by the rebels for their wounded.

Passed through Hagerstown. Rebel guards used their bayonets on our men when getting water and trying to buy bread. The ladies of the town waved their handkerchiefs to us, and said: 'Cheer up, boys, we would give you bread, but the Chivalry of the South threaten to burn our houses if we do!' Encamped outside of town. Bread sent us by Union people was taken by the guards and distributed among their own men; Rations.

July 8. — Marched to Williamsport, Md., on the Potomac River. No person in town allowed to give or sell us bread. There had been a cavalry fight between Hagerstown and the River. Our dead lay, stripped of their clothing, in the field. Rebel pontoon bridges destroyed on the Potomac. The country around filled with wounded. Citizens of the town said over 15,000 wounded rebels had been set across the river. Our men had to trade their blankets and even take their shoes off their feet and gave them to the guards for bread. A guard would charge $3 in greenbacks for a small loaf of bread.

July 9. — Day occupied in crossing the Potomac in flatboats. River very high. Guards taking prisoners' money on pretense of buying something for them to eat, but never returning money or food. After crossing the river Imboden's Brigade took charge of the prisoners. Gen. Graham, with 125 officers and 4,000 men were now under Imboden, to be taken to Staunton.

July 10. — Finished crossing the Potomac and marched about two miles beyond Martinsburg. The most exciting scene on our march occurred while we were passing through the streets of this patriotic little village. I must say that the strongest sentiment was manifested in this place that I have been through during the time that, I have been in the service. It seemed that about every man, woman and child came into the streets, loaded with bread to feed the starving prisoners; but they met with a strong resistance from every officer and guard. Yet, in spite of all they could do to prevent our getting any of it, it was thrown into the ranks by cuts and loaves. Bakers' bread and great loaves of homemade bread, biscuits, crackers, cakes of all kinds, would come into the ranks, thrown from windows, doors and every by-place. They came like hailstones. They were not many pieces that struck the ground; for there were about 4,000 with raised hands, each eager to catch the bread.

One particular case I will relate, to show the feeling of the people of this little town. A man I took to be a baker came out of a small alley, his arms full of great cuts of bread, and rushed through the guards and scattered the bread through the ranks, then rushed back for more. The officers, a number of them, seeing that this was a dangerous man, rushed to this place to keep him from doing any more such horrible deeds as feeding starving men. They met him, his arms again full of bread, and with drawn swords they threatened his life, if he did not go back with the bread. He did not mind their threats or fear their swords, but rushed through their line and the line of guards and threw bread into our ranks. This was a true and brave man! I expected to see him shot down, but he was not while I was in sight of that place; but he was ordered under arrest, and went out of my sight with an officer and guards.

This village is 12 miles from the Potomac, and Williamsport, on the edge of West Virginia. The rebels were as much disappointed as we were elated at the strong Union sentiment that was manifested in the place. I was talking with one of the rebel officers. I told him that I was surprised to see the Union feeling that was in that place. He said I was no more surprised than he was, and that if he could have his way it would be Martinsburg no longer. 'You don't meant to say that you would destroy the place?' said I. 'Yes,' said he, 'for as I passed through the place the other day I tried to get a meal and I could not find a mouthful in the place! They said they had been robbed of all they had by our army!' He added that to see the abundance that they had for us made him feel as though he would, like to see every building laid in ashes. We encamped that night about two miles from this place.

July 12. — Reached Winchester and were hurried through the town. Encamped. Received rations — half pint of flour. The country on our route was a perfect waste — nothing having been planted. We had now 92 miles to march to Staunton. The march was commenced on July 13 and ended July 18. On the route large droves of horses and cattle passed. These had been stolen in Pennsylvania and Maryland. They were driven in the direction of Staunton. We fared no better as to rations, and as high as $5 in greenbacks was paid our guards for a small loaf of bread. The rebels officers said the men had undergone more hardships than any other prisoners taken since the war began. At Staunton the prisoners' gum blankets, shelter tents, and some private property was taken from them.

July 19. — The first lot of prisoners left for Richmond, 136 miles by rail, at which place they arrived on the morning of July 20. The prisoners were marched to a tobacco warehouse opposite a prison. The prisoners told our men through their grated windows, that since the battle of Gettysburg all deserters and other prisoners held there who would volunteer to the front, had been liberated.

BELLE ISLAND

On the afternoon of July 20, the prisoners who had arrived at Richmond were taken from the tobacco warehouse to Belle Island. Before they were taken they were searched, and everything of value, which could be found was taken from them.

The rations at the Island consisted of half a loaf of bread, weighing a half pound, one ounce of fresh meat, and a pint of water called bean soup. This was all a man received for his rations for one day. On Aug. 20 the Lieutenant of the Island had 800 men paroled for the purpose of being sent to Annapolis, Md. Aug. 21, 721 men were marched from the Island to Libby's Tobacco warehouse in Richmond and the following morning took the cars for City Point.

The following are the most important facts, which occurred during our six week's sojourn there:

Private Blass, 4th Regiment, Excelsior Brigade, took the oath of allegiance to the rebel government and shipped in their bogus navy.

Sept. 16 a lot of prisoners arrived. They had been taken at Charleston, S. C. These men, before leaving for Richmond, had their good clothing taken from them and old rebel suits given in exchange. This was the way the rebel government equipped its men in our uniforms around Richmond.

On the night of Aug. 12 a large party escaped, with a few of the guards, who belonged to the 42nd N. C.

At noon Aug. 14, Private John Donnelly, 91st Pa., who had that morning come to the Island, was standing near the bank that incloses the prisoners; the guard told him to go further back and as he was in the act of turning to comply the guard raised his gun and shot him down. This act was a cold-blooded murder. Donnelly lived in Philadelphia. The same ball that killed Donnelly struck Wm. Bayne, 82nd Ohio. The ball entered the breast of Bayne. His would was a painful one, but not dangerous. The guard was taken off his post for the day, but in two days he was back again, ready to shoot more unarmed Yankees.

On the morning Aug. 19 John Mahoney, 12 Mass., was shot dead by the guards. He was hurrying to the sink, being sick, when he was fired on and killed.

It was the custom to give each morning to every 100 men a little salt. Aug. 19 this was stopped, and the rebel Quartermaster gave the salt to a miserable prisoner to sell in camp at 25 cents for one small spoonful.

A number of the prisoners went to work for the rebels, outside the prisoners' inclosure. Their pay was extra rations. this they would bring inside, among the half-starved and sell. The most notorious individual at this business was a Sergeant by the name of Gavitt, 1st N. Y. Art. This Gavitt, when a squad was to be sent away, would select those who could give him $5 or $10.

There are still 3,200 men on the Island; some of these men are Tennesseans, taken as long ago as September '61. Others have now been held over 18 months.

A search was made among the men for money, in August, each man being examined separately. The result was that the Provost-Marshall of Richmond got a bucket full of greenbacks, watches, etc. No money was returned to the men on their departure.

The nights were very cold, and the men had nothing to cover themselves with. I am not capable of describing all the sufferings and scenes that I witnessed while on the Island.

The Stars and Stripes looked good, flying over the Steamer New York, that brought us safely to this place. Those who were able to go to College Green Barracks were taken there; the sick to St. John's College Hospital. I was among the latter. Here we got well washed up, received good, clean clothes — the old ones were thrown away. We felt like a set of new men after we got cleaned up and got rid of our Belle Island graybacks. They were very numerous in Richmond. The prisoners who have arrived here within the last few days state that the suffering of the prisoners increases daily."

APPENDIX 3

Hospital Duty

A third topic that has not received the coverage it deserves was the work performed by surgeons during the battle. Their efforts to establish field hospitals and to care for the wounded are rarely discussed. Below are two accounts by doctors who served in Wadsworth's division at Gettysburg. The first was written by a surgeon in the 7th Wisconsin and is included here primarily because it mentions the 14th Brooklyn. The second account, an excerpt from an article that appeared in the *National Tribune*, was penned by a surgeon in the 147th New York. Together, these accounts help fill a gap in the history of the battle.

ARMY REMINISCENCES

MILWAUKEE SUNDAY TELEGRAPH
September 30, 1883.

by Dr. D. Cooper Ayers

"I will never forget the first days of July, 1863 — eventful days in the history of our country. It was the beginning of the end of the war.

Early in the morning of July 1, 1863, the first corps was moving very rapidly toward Gettysburg. The cavalry was already engaged. When we deployed in line of battle the Iron brigade looked its best, and they went for the rebs, like an avalanche. At this point Gen. Reynolds, in whose command the corps was included, passed us at a rapid gait. A half an hour afterwards he had received a fatal wound, at the very front.

We drove the rebels nicely at first, yet, after a lull in the battle, although we were still in line it was evident that we could not hold the position. I saw them falling back, but I was a prisoner. Before this, I had seen old John Burns with his fusee, around among the boys.

My first duty after my capture was to attend the wounded. One of the hardest jobs I had was to tell Col. Stevens, of the 2nd Wis., his wound would result in death, and it did. We both shed tears. He mourned about his wife and children. From the seminary to town I went on foot, as I had sent my horses to the rear. Dr. Preston, of the 6th, was captured with me. They took us to a ware house, near the railroad track, where we had 145 patients and 80 attendants. The afternoon of the 1st we had a big job. There were five or six hospitals in town. We were fortunate in finding 27 barrels of flour in the ware house. We covered it up so as to keep it out of sight of the rebels. It was a bonanza to the wounded soldiers. I gave a rebel captain 2 pounds of it, and he went away happy.

There was joy amongst the prisoners and wounded on the 3rd, when the rebels were badly whipped and came flying back. "We are the boss this time" some of us said to the enemy.

While a prisoner I had many pleasant interchanges with rebel officers.

At dawn, the morning of the 14th of July, my host rushed to my room and said the rebels had gone. I bounced out of my room so as to charge on the bars in case they attempted to take me to Richmond. I saw the pickets and videttes moving away rapidly. My nurses were soldiers again. They flew to their guns and with white rags on their arms, gave them a volley as a parting salute. Some of the bullets took effect, as the line wavered and then sped on.

The rebel soldiers got plenty of whisky in those cold Pennsylvania cellars. General Early sent his compliments and asked Dr. Ayers if he wanted some whisky for his hospital. I sent back my compliments, accepting, with the remark, "Does a duck like to swim?" He sent two water pails full, and it revived many a poor men.

How happy we were to be free on that glorious Fourth of July. But the field was a terrible sight. Hundreds of dead were seen on a small space of ground where Pickett charged.

Our old brigade did nobly that 1st of July, but she had to fall back, while I had to stay. Dr. Ebersole, of the 19th Indiana, Dr. Stacy, of the 24th Michigan, and myself, were met by men who covered us with their guns and demanded immediate surrender. "Don't you see they are surgeons?" said a rebel captain. "Let them go and attend the wounded;" and the rebels left us. At another time a squad rode up to the hospital, and with revolvers in hand ordered us to surrender. "Don't you see we are surgeons at a hospital, doing our duty?" I said. "Then put up your flag, and have your men throw down their guns," they said. "Give us time," was my response. They were good men, and down went the guns. In the squad were many of our brigade and some of the 14th Brooklyn Zouaves. I was dressing a Georgian's wound when he said, "They always push our regiment against those big hat devils and the Zouaves," referring to our brigade and the Brooklyn boys.

On the 2nd of July they allowed us to go on the field and bring in our wounded. When they were brought in and were lying on the pavements, I heard my name called. Going to the man I found a member of the 7th whose eyes were hanging on his cheeks. He had been wounded the 1st, and had lain on the battle field all that time. He was strong, hearty and hungry. His first remark was, "a rebel had stolen his last $5."

Lieutenant, since Capt. L. E. Pond, of Co. E, 7th, was badly wounded and I thought the case hopeless. I secreted his sword in a merchant's house, and Pond had it returned to him.

Free on the 4th, and away on the march after Lee the 5th.

One by one of our noble column fall out, but the march is onward. The mighty column will soon stop for a final rest, and the camp fires will go out forever. Since we last met, General Kellogg has gone.

In closing, let me say that our camp fires are out, and we have gone to rest, and when the history of the war is written, there will be bright pages in it for the Iron Brigade.

FIGHTING THEM OVER

WHAT OUR VETERANS HAVE TO SAY ABOUT THEIR OLD CAMPAIGNS

THE 14th N. Y. ZOUAVES.

NATIONAL TRIBUNE
August 13, 1885.

by A. S. Coe.
Surgeon, 147th N. Y.

A FREE AND EASY REGIMENT WHICH DID GOOD SERVICE

. . . At the battle of Gettysburg July 1, 1863, the Surgeon of the 14th Brooklyn and myself selected a large hotel on the north side of the town, opposite to the railroad depot for a hospital. At the time we took possession of the building it was filled with guests, and no one seemed to expect much of a battle; but in a very short time the wounded were brought in in great numbers and the guests and proprietors left without much order in going, leaving us in quiet and undisputed possession, with abundance of bedding, provisions in the kitchen, and all kinds of liquors in the bar and cellar.

The building soon became filled with wounded of the two regiments (147th N. Y. and 14th Brooklyn), and we were obliged to take possession of the building adjoining on the south for the wounded who were brought in after the hotel became filled. The more seriously wounded occupied all of our attention, giving the slightly wounded freedom of the hotel. They found the liquor, to which they helped themselves freely.

About 3 o'clock p. m. I was called out to dress the wounds of some officers and men who had been brought in and left in a small tavern on a cross street just above the one on which the hotel was situated. I think the tavern was kept by a man by the name of Weaver. As I came out of the tavern to return to the hotel, I found that the enemy had taken the town and were driving our men through the streets. I came upon the advance line of the enemy as I reached the main street, and hurried past, and turned down toward the hospital without attracting attention. As I approached the hospital I found a line of about a dozen of the 14th Brooklyn men formed across the entrance, disputing possession of the building with about 20 rebels, who had their muskets to their shoulders about to shoot them down. I took in the situation at once, and called out sharply to them not to fire, as they were wounded men. The rebel officer in command of the squad thereupon ordered his men not to fire, and turned to me and said: "Doctor, have your men disarmed, or I will have them shot." I ordered the men to give up their arms and return into the hospital; all but four or five did so, and they were so crazed by liquor that they were wholly regardless of their fate. By dint of entreaty to the enemy, and personal effort in getting their arms away from them, I succeeded in saving all but one, who was shot through the heart.

Just as I had succeeded in disarming the 14th Brooklyn men I saw a mounted rebel officer on the opposite side of the street brandishing a pistol and declaring that he was going to have the hospital sacked, because his men had been fired at out of its windows. He about the same time spied me, and came riding across the street to show me his trophies that he had that day captured from the "d—d Yankees."

The opportunity afforded to satisfy his vanity in boasting of his exploits seemed to take the place of desire of wreaking his vengeance upon the hospital, and he soon quietly rode off without putting his threat into execution. Upon going into the hospital I found the cause of the disturbance. It seems that these Brooklyn men were looking out of the windows with their muskets in their hands when the enemy entered the town, and they discharged their guns out of the windows. The enemy returned a volley through the windows, knocking the plastering off the walls over the bar opposite. The Brooklyn men thereupon marched down and formed across the entrance, where I found them upon my return. All of them had been more or less severely wounded in the early part of the day. After the disturbance was quieted I found the Brooklyn men and the rebels, who a short time before were so anxious to shoot them, seated side by side on the curbstone, laughing at and joking each other as the best of friends. They seemed to be well acquainted; and had often met each other on the picketline and had a friendly game of cards or traded coffee for tobacco. Coffee was a rare luxury to the rebels in those days.

I was greatly indebted to the Brooklyn boys for their ingenuity and enterprise in obtaining food for our wounded in hospital during the three days we were within the rebel lines. We were in no way molested by the enemy, save by a guard placed in the hall of the hotel; but we were cut off from our own supplies and were dependent upon the enemy. In the confusion of the battles of the 2nd and 3rd of July I was unable to get the attention of the proper rebel officers to supply us, but the fertility of resources of the 14th Brooklyn was equal to the occasion, and the wounded did not want for anything. . . .

— A. S. Coe, Surgeon, 147th N. Y., Oswego, N. Y.

Appendix 4

Staff Officers

This list of staff officers was compiled by Robert L. Brake and appended by Kathy G. Harrison. A full listing can be found at the Gettysburg National Military Park Library.

Doubleday

Lieutenant-Colonel Chas. E. Livingston, AIG (76th NY)

Captain Eminel Potter Halsted (Halstead), AAG

Captain John Dunlap Adair, Commy. of Subs.

Captain Chandler Hall, AQM (42nd PA)

Captain Frank Hull Cowdrey, Asst. Commy. of Musters (95th NY)

First Lieutenant Henry Thos. Lee, ADC

Lieutenant Benj. T. Martin (Marten), ADC

First Lieutenant Meredith L. Jones, AADC (E, 149th PA)

Second Lieutenant James Harrison Lambdin, AADC (H, 121st PA)

First Lieutenant Jacob F. Slagle, AADC (D, 149th PA)

Lieutenant-Colonel Henry Carey Bankhead, IG

Captain Edward Baird, AAG

Surgeon W. T. Humphreys (149th PA)

Captain James Glenn, Provost Marshall (149th PA)

First Lieutenant Charles T. Shaw, Ordnance Officer (150th PA)

First Lieutenant John Huidekoper, Acting Topographical Officer (150th PA)

First Lieutenant George R. Snowden, Chief Ambulance Corps (142nd PA)

Lieutenant-Colonel Charles E. Livingston, AAIG (76th NY)

Cutler

First Lieutenant Homer Chisman, AIG (7th IN)

Captain Wm. Bloodgood, ADC (95th NY)

(Above): Lieutenant Stark Woodrow
(95th New York)

Woodrow served on Cutler's staff and was
dismounted three times when horses
he was riding were hit.

Courtesy of Lance Ingmire

(Below): First Lieutenant Thomas Miller
(55th Ohio Infantry)

Miller served as one of General Cutler's
volunteer staff officers.

Courtesy of Rick Carlisle

First Lieutenant Stark W. Woodrow, ADC (95th NY)
First Lieutenant Loren Burritt, ADC (K, 56th PA)
First Lieutenant Thomas W. Miller, ADC (55th OH)
Captain John A. Kellogg, AAAG (6th WI)
Captain Albert Walker, CS
Captain H. A. Laycock, AAQM (56th PA)
Surgeon George W. Metcalf (76th NY)

Meredith

Colonel John G. Stephenson, Volunteer Aide
Captain Hollon Richardson, AAIG (7th WI)
Captain John Azor Kellogg (6th WI)

First Lieutenant Dennis Burke Dailey (2nd WI)

First Lieutenant Gilbert M. Woodward, AADC (2nd WI)

Captain H. C. Holloway, ACS

Captain James D. Wood, AAG (D, 2nd WI)

First Lieutenant Sam. H. Meredith, ADC (19th IN - son)

Second Lieutenant Chas. C. Yemens, AADC (D, 24 MI - absent sick)

Surgeon A. W. Preston (6th WI)

Captain A. F. Maussin, AQM

First Lieutenant Wm. L. Ransom, AADC (95th NY — absent sick)

Wadsworth

Lieutenant-Colonel John Alex. Kress, AIG (94th NY)

Major Clinton Hanks Meneely, ADC

First Lieutenant Earl M. Rogers, Provost Marshall/? Ordnance Officer (6th WI)

Second Lieutenant Edw. Carrington, ADC (143rd NY)

Captain Chas. H. Ford, ADC (6th WI)

Captain Timothy Edwards Ellsworth, ADC/AAAG

Captain Chas. McClure, Commy. of Subs./Volunteer Aide-de-Camp

First Lieutenant Clayton E. Rogers, AADC (6th WI)

Surgeon George W. New (7th IN)

Captain W. H. Mandeville, AQM

Second Lieutenant Charles R. Robe, ACM (147th NY)

Appendix 5

The Hershel W. Pierce Letter

The following letter, written by Capt. Hershel W. Pierce of Company A, 76th New York, is from the collection of Dick Bridgeman. It is published with his permission.

* * *

Camp of the 76th N.Y. Vols.
In the Woods in Line of Battle, 1 1/2 Miles
from Antietam Creek, and 3 1/2 Miles from
Hagerstown, M.D. July 11th, 1863

Dear Brother

Having a few moments this morning unemployed I thought that I would drop you a few lines.

My health is good but I have been terribly fatigued during the last 4 weeks of severe marching and the 3 days hard fighting at Gettysburg P.A. Very many of our Dundee Boys fell in that terrific battle. Among those killed are B.F. Carpenter; Walter Wood and Young Bush of Barrington of the 76th N.Y. Vols. Henry Cook of Starkey and Young Basset of Barrington, (brother of Lieut. Basset) of the 126 N.Y. Vols. There may be others but these I know. There are some of the boys wounded. Albert L. Hilton of my company and Ed Conyell of the 126 N.Y. Vols. I escaped uninjured though present and hotly engaged during the whole battle. I have several bullet holes through my clothes but no blood drawn. Meads army now lies along Antietam creek and the Rebel army is supposed to occupy the opposite side from Hagerstown to the Potomac River. Yesterday we had a running fight with the enemy and drove them from Turners Gap in South Mountain through Boonesboro to Hagerstown. Up to this time (eight o'clock) this morning there has been no firing but the ball may open at any moment. I suppose that we are in as much doubt as to what the enemy intends to do as the folks in Dundee are and perhaps more. Our papers and letters come to us rather unsteady in consequence of our being constantly in motion and the interruptions caused by the tearing up of some of the rail roads. We have got the news of the surrender of Vicksburg and hope soon to hear of the capitulation of Port Hudson.

I have written to Mariet giving a list of the killed, wounded and missing of my company in the action at Gettysburg P.A. You can see the list by looking at it in her letter. As soon as I get time I will write Horatio. I do not know but that he feels already slighted if so I cannot help it. I have no time to write, and no conveniences for writing. It is only occasionally that I get ink. My writing is now mostly done with pencil. Our wagons do not come up, and we have nothing but what we carry. I have not been able to change my shirt for four weeks. I take off the one I have on and wash it, and then put it on again. This writing is very poor for the paper is poor, it is of Rebel Manufacture and I will enclose it in a Rebel Envelope. I have no stamped ones now. I sent one to Mariet as a curiosity. I took them from the knapsack of a dead Reb on the first day of July during the Battle. I do not wish to blow my own trumpet but I will just say that my carbine proved its worth during those three days fighting.

The color bearer of the 26th Alabama fell before it on the first day of July and on the 3rd no less than 4 of the enemies sharpshooters. In a pitched Battle the officers in command have all that they can do to see to their men and this leaves but little opportunity for them to attend to any individual enemy. But in these cases I took the opportunity. The Rebel Color Bearer he flaunted his defiant flag in the faces of our men about the time that Carpenter was shot. Both causes operated so strongly upon me that I could not resist any longer but unsling my carbine from my shoulder I shot him dead in his tracks. And I felt the better for doing it. The others I shot while on duty to the front in charge of the Pickets on the last day of the fight early in the morning. They were the enemies sharpshooters and were hidden behind rocks for the purpose of picking off our men. But it was a game that our men played at as successfully as the Rebels. But I cannot write you longer I hear the sound of artillery in the distance and ere long may again be engaged in this deadly strife.

Truly your Brother

H. W. Pierce

APPENDIX 6

The Edgar D. Haviland Letter

The following letter, written by Edgar D. Haviland, Company E, 76th New York, is from the collection of Paul Meuse. It is published with his permission.

* * *

Gen. Order

No. 184

Head Quarters 76th N.Y. Vols. near Rappahannock Station Va. Aug. the 11th 1863.

Dear Mother

I have just received your letter and was very happy the letter came fore I did not know whare to write and was very glad to hear you was well and had a good time in New York you said you was thare when the Riot Broke out I suppose you was most scared to death. I would like to have been thare with our Regiment those devils would thought that thare was no use talking fore a while we would not commenced with blank catridges on them but would give them the balls if they was so ancious for armies.

Now I will comence and tell you all about our Campaign this Summer. you know we was at Pratts Point last winter about two months. We recieved marching Orders for the Battle of Chanslersville and went thare in one day. It was a mighty hard march through the woods and over hills and through Vallies. We arrived on the Battle field about One O'clock thare was a great many men engaged when we come thare so we was on the reserve. The Fifth Forteenth and several other Regular Infantry Regiments ware in the front that day thare was the hardest musketry that I ever saw in my life the boys ware all ancious to get into it first then our old would break and run you brave fellows just open the ranks and let them through and take the . . . .

So we did not get in the musketry that time. Then about night we found out that the Rebs was leaving their Position and trying to get in the rear of us and then we fell back to the Rappahannock River and could see the rebs trying to cross but it was no go we went acrossed and headed them and drove them Back. Then we fell back to the Camp called Camp near White Oak Church thare we remainied thare for one month we heard after a while that the Johnneys ware in Pensilvania we receved marching Orders the next day to find them we marched night and Day for eight or ten days came mighty tough for us we arrived at Gettysburg on the first day of July and we had a grand celebration of fire works we was on the head of the colum that day and our Regiments was on the lead of all of the troops which caused us to get in the Battle the first day we had a great many killed and wounded from the cannons before we got into the Musketry after we got into the Musketry the men fell like sheep on all sides of me when we first came into line thare was a Corporal hit with a cannon Ball and fell wright back into my arms in such times a man dont have much time to take care of the men so I threw him down no sooner had I done. So I hastened to my command and just then we was Ordered to the rear to the woods the Major in Command of the Regiment Ordered me to give my Gun to one of the men in the ranks but that made me mad for I wanted to shoot with the rest of the boys and I asked him if he would not let me keep it and he said you must be a D—d fool you have your hands full now without a gun so he said you are a Brave little devil those are just the words he used and afterwards he was killed, he was a Gentleman and a Grand Officer his name was (A. J. Grover).

Now I will tell you all what I think I think I will get a Commision as a Second Lieutant what I have been working fore, fore three months dont tell Pop of this fore he will say it is all a dam lie. This is all at presant Write soon.

Your Son

E. D. Haviland

APPENDIX 7

The Peirre Thompson Letter

A couple of days after the Battle of Gettysburg, Peirre Thompson, 95th New York, wrote this letter to his mother explaining his participation in the fight. It is reproduced below, with all of its spelling and punctuation errors. Despite these flaws, it is a remarkable, primary account of the clash. His description provides another reminder that the 14th Brooklyn and his 95th New York participated in the charge on the railroad cut.[1]

* * *

Hospital, Gettysburgh, Penn
July 5th [1863]

My dear Ma———

I suppose you must be surprised and anxious at my long silence but I have been through so much and marching so constantly that I have not had an opportunity to write sooner. We arrived at this town on the 1st of July. Just before getting here the booming of cannon made us aware that the ball was opened for the first time since we crossed the River. We were ordered to load our pieces on the march and started on a Double quick into line of battle just out side of town.

We had hardly taken our position when we discovered the enemy advancing in several lines of battle deep on our right flank. We immediately opened on them and it began to be warm work the bullets flew like hail and men were dropping all around me. My colonel fell wounded in the breast my captain & lieutenant fell with 10 men of my company the rebs had got position of a Railroad and could lay there and pop us off without exposing

---

1 The letter can be found in Thompson's Pension File, NARA. Paragraphs were inserted to improve readability.

themselves. We finaly charged on them and took a whole Brigade prisoners. We were suddenly orders to fall back and did so pretty quickly. I was so much exhausted by fatigue that I could not go further than the town and I had hardly got there when the rebel cavalry came dashing in behind me discharging their carbines at our retreating forces. I knew there was no chance of escaping even if I was able so quietly surrendered and was detailed to stay in the Hospital and nurse the wounded of my division.

Our forces fell back just out side of the town and took a strong position on some hills and entrenched themselves and kept the enemy who were fully twice our number in check until they got reinforcements. The rebels had possession of the town for three days and after fighting all this time were compelled to evacuate it yesterday morning when our forces again took possession of it. Our officers and head doctors say we are not prisoners as the rebels did not parole us but merely took our names so I do not know how it will be—there was only my Core & part of the 11th Core fought the first day.

I cant see how it is you did not get the $18. I have not had a chance to speak to the Colonel about it yet. I have seen not Willie yet—address a letter to Gettysburgh, P.O. with my name and Regmt as I may be here some time. I am very busiey with the wounded but am quite well. The 95th lost half their men in this fight and is now no more than a good company. No more at present

From your affect Son
Peirre

Give my love to all the family.

Write soon and tell me if you have not got the money $18 yet—how did you spend the fourth.

Appendix 8

More on John Jochum

After the Civil War, John Jochum actively participated in the 14th Brooklyn's War Veterans' Association. As a member of the group, he served on the committees that designed the Gettysburg monuments dedicated to the regiment.

In 1893, Jochum wrote about his Gettysburg injury and his subsequent, but difficult, recovery. The story was serialized in newspapers throughout the country. Below is the version published by The *Buffalo Sunday Morning News* on April 23, 1893.

HIS BRAIN LAID BARE.
The Remarkable Experience of
a Gettysburg Veteran.
Alive With a Pierced Skull—Part of
His Head is in Washington
And Part is in New York

"A part of my head is in Washington." When I made this statement in the course of a conversation with some friends they looked at me very closely, as if to see whether I was really in my right mind. The explanation which followed I am sure convinced them that the statement I made was absolutely true, and at the request of a newspaper man who was present I repeat the story of my strange experience during the war, the result of which was to make my case one of the most remarkable in the annals of surgery.

I was born in 1837 and have lived in Brooklyn nearly all my life. I enlisted in 1862 in the 14th Regiment of Brooklyn. The peculiar and remarkable wound in my head was received about 11 o'clock of the first day of the battle of Gettysburg, just as the command was given to charge on Davis' Mississippi brigade along the railroad cut. I do not know whether a bullet or shell struck me, but I was probably shot by the sharpshooter in a neighboring barn who had mortally wounded Gen. Reynolds as he was standing beside me a moment before. The bullet, or shell, entered my head directly above the temple, taking a circuitous course to the base of my head, where it ploughed a hole through the skull just above the neck. At the present time there are several holes on each side of my head, each as large as a half dollar; they are like port holes in a fort.[1]

I lay unconscious probably half an hour, waking to find myself totally blind. I at once attributed my blindness to a shock to the optic nerves, for I remembered having read something on that subject. Fearful that I should be blind for life I wished that the shot had killed me on the spot.

I lay thus helpless about an hour, dimly realizing my terrible condition. Suddenly, I discovered, in rude outline, the features of the surrounding landscape. My joy can be imagined when I found my sight restored almost as quickly as it had been taken away.

In the meantime I had paid some attention to the wound in my head. I took off knapsack, tore a piece from my shelter tent, made a wad or compress of it and put it in the opening in my head. I suffered no pain, but afterward, when the shattered bone began to suppurate, I suffered as much as it is possible for a man to suffer and live. I also made a bandage from a piece of tent, placed it around my head and started off on a walk, not knowing exactly where I was going. I could see both lines of battle were getting ready for a general engagement. I soon received an intimation that I was going wrong. One of the soldiers of the Sixth Wisconsin shouted at me, at the same time making a motion for me to go back. I turned about, not knowing which direction to take, because I was out on the battlefield away from the roads. After three days' detention at Gettysburg I walked to Littlestown, a distance of 11 miles, which, it will be admitted, was a pretty severe undertaking, considering the character of my wound. Every now and then I would stop and rest under the shade of a tree, bathing my head with cold water from my canteen.

Just before this I had found my way to the Division Hospital, in charge of Dr. Farley. My wound was dressed and I was removed to the Philadelphia Hospital, then in charge of Dr. Hayes, famous in conjunction with the expedition to the North Pole. The hospital was terribly crowded, the patients were obliged to 'double up,' the atmosphere was horrible, and as a consequence I contracted the disease known as hospital gangrene.

---

1 Modern research refutes the possibility that Reynolds was struck by a sharpshooter; his mortal wound probably came from a volley fired by the 13th Alabama. Jochum would have been nowhere near Reynolds when the Rebel bullet hit the general.

Later on I was removed to the Ladies' Home Hospital, corner of Lexington avenue and Fifty-first street, New York. This might truly be called the sick man's paradise, for the treatment was the very best possible.

It was decided by the physicians that an operation should be performed on my head. The doctors in Philadelphia had arrived at the conclusion that I could not live, but Dr. Alexander Mott, in charge of the Ladies' Hospital, thought there was a chance for my recovery. In the meantime they kept up my strength. I not only had the best kind of food but drank daily, in alternation, 10 ounces of sherry wine, eight ounces of whiskey, eight ounces of brandy, two bottles of Guinness' stout, a quart of ale, eggnogs and milk punches.

Seven months after I had received the wound I submitted to an operation to remove the shattered pieces of skull. It was performed by Drs. Robi and Hinton, and lasted over an hour. I sat in a chair, resting my head in my left hand while the doctors worked. I refused to take an anaesthetic, because I was so much interested in my own case that I wanted to know exactly what they did. Already I had for months suffered the most intense pain, and I cannot say that the surgeon's knife added materially to my misery; in fact, it almost seemed to be a relief. As I say, although previous to the operation I had been well nourished, I never slept except under opiates.

It seems that the ball or shell which struck me had torn my scalp, carrying away the periosteum of the occipital bone and cracking the latter so that subsequent inflammation caused the expoliation[2] or throwing off of the bone. Portions of the inner table of the skull came away, but the inner periosteum remained intact; nature has provided new matter, which has formed a thin shell-like protection over my brain. At the time the bone was removed the surgeons could feel the pulsations of the brain, the inner periosteum having become visible.

After the bone was removed Prof. F. K. Hamilton, who attended President Garfield during his last illness, examined my wound and was so struck with the peculiarity of the fracture that he took me to Bellevue Hospital, where I furnished the subject of a lecture for the clinic. This lecture was published in the London Lancet for 1864.

At the clinic with me was a man named Monk, with a small hole in his head. That is, it appeared very small beside mine, though the lecturer intimated that his chances of surviving were not as good as mine.

---

2 Exfoliation.

Another interesting and not very cheerful feature of this experience was the fact that the lecturer brought from a cabinet a number of skulls, each one representing a phase of a fracture of the head. He would hold up one after another of these ghastly mementoes of the living, place it along side of my own cranium and say cheerfully, 'Now we may expect Mr. Jochum's skull to look like this after he is dead.' This was quite gruesome, but I consoled myself with the thought that I might be helping along medical science.

After this lecture many surgeons came to see me, traveling 200 or 300 miles for the purpose of studying my case. Dr. Van Buren, at that time a celebrated surgeon of New York, examined me, together with Dr. Mott. His experience with such surgical cases had been long, but he expressed great surprise at my recovery. I remember at the time he called a small handful of sutures which united the two bones had come out, and these were shown to him. The sutures had been picked out by the surgeon until there was quite a collection. They filled a tablespoon and looked like irregular, jagged pieces of ivory. They would slip off and work out through the hole in my head.

My case is mentioned in the 'Medical and Surgical History of the War,' and the piece of bone removed (3 ½ inches long by 2 ½ inches wide) is in the Medical Museum at Washington.

I daily attend to my regular business and have been interested in a number of public enterprises.

I am proud to have been a member of the 14th Regiment, which went to the war as a Brooklyn regiment, recruited as a Brooklyn regiment, fought as a Brooklyn regiment, and is a Brooklyn regiment today. But I am prouder still of the record I hold from the captain of my company: 'There could be no better soldier; always ready for duty, brave and courageous.'

"From the 76th [New York] Regiment"

I found this letter after the publication of the second edition of *Cutler's Brigade at Gettysburg.* The correspondence, written by a member of the 76th New York to his hometown newspaper, offers a vivid account of the experiences of the regiment during the march to Gettysburg and the beginning of the battle. The detailed casualty list at the end of the column provides a stark reminder of the human cost of victory.

* * *

"From the 76th Regiment"
Cherry Valley Gazette, Aug. 19, 1863

August, 1863

Friend Botsford:

Knowing the anxiety of those having friends in the 76th Regiment to hear from them, I take the liberty of sending the following list of killed and wounded of Co. H, at the terrible battle of Gettysburg. I also enclose a list of those of other companies, which, if you have space, you may publish, that our friends may see and feel justly proud of the 76th. If space would allow, I would rejoice to give a more minute account of its deeds of valor and endurance, from the time of leaving the old camp below Fredericksburg, June 12, until the great battles of the 1st, 2d, and 3d of July, at Gettysburg, but I must be denied that pleasure, as such an account, fully written, would fill a respectable volume. I will only say that our regiment was eight to ten miles from camp, on picket, when orders to march were received about 12 o'clock at night. Our line of six miles had to be called in and about daylight we were ready to march: At the word, off we go, and keep it up till late at night, making about twenty hours, and marching thirty miles or more. It was melting hot and so continued day after day till we crossed the Potomac, when it commenced to rain, and then it was mud and rain every day till we reached near Gettysburg about 175 miles from our starting point.

On the morning of the 1st, our regiment was in advance of the whole corps, which brought us on the extreme right when in line of battle. We marched six or seven miles that morning, moving cautiously, as we knew the enemy were not far ahead. About noon we came to the town of Gettysburg; we did not go through it, but turned to the left through the fields, and went about two and a half miles on double quick. Our batteries opened about this time, and shot and shell began to be quite plenty. Our regiment numbered nearly four hundred fit for duty that morning, and was under command of Maj. A. J. Grover; the Col. and Lieut. Col. being both absent on duty.

Passing swiftly on through fields, orchards, yards, and gardens, we soon met the enemy literally face to face, and before our line was fairly formed, we commenced a murderous fire and kept it up until completely outflanked by at least six times our number, when we slowly and in order fell back to a road and wall. Here we were soon reinforced by our friends, the gallant 2d Wisconsin[1] of the iron brigade. Now came a grand and bloody hand to hand fight, which the rebs could not stand and fell back in great disorder, leaving three hundred and fifty prisoners in our hands. We now held our first ground for a short time, and it was at this time that some of Co. H's noble boys carried Captain Story off to a place of safety: he being wounded before our first move back, consequently lying with the enemy until they were driven back.

The 76th, by this time, was reduced from four hundred to about one hundred: a few had gone back with the wounded but facts since show that about two hundred and fifty were killed and wounded; and all in a space of one or two hours, yet not a man went back or tried to do so except by orders. No words can express the true pluck of men under such terrible circumstances.

In the early part of the fight Major Grover was killed while gallantly encouraging and directing the men. The command then fell on Capt. J[ohn] E. Cook who led though the day and escaped injury.

Out of twenty four officers present at the commencement eighteen were killed or wounded: two or three slightly but most of them very severely. Both color bearers fell, but corporals Stevens and Powers of Co. H, soon had the fallen colors off the ground, and "Jack" sticks to his up to the present time.

---

1 The 6th Wisconsin, not the 2nd Wisconsin, bolstered the Union right flank.

The enemy were kept back so much by our corps, although we faced their whole army, that the position they were so anxious to gain, was lost to them: we keeping them from it until dark, and by daylight next morning our other corps had come up, and all know the final result, which would have been different, had the first corps flinched the first day.

Co. A—Corp'l Benj. F. Carpenter, Cor'p. Herman D. Smith, Privates Wm. C. Fox, James Edwards, Wm. H. Cranston, Chas. F. Smith, killed, Wounded 1st Lieut. N. G. Harmon, leg, 1st Sergt. Ira C. Potter, hip, slight. Privates Wm. H. Bloomer, leg, David E. Johnson, ankle, Albert L. Hilton, side, Melvin O. Smith, throat, John W. Seeber, leg amputated. Missing—Privates M. O. Byington, Frank E. Arnold, Wm. Collier, Wm. Craig, Mus. N. G. Barnum, Bugler O. Hutchins.

Co. B—Killed—Private Ansom M. Johnson. Wounded—Capt. Robert Story, since dead: 1st Lieut. B. Button, leg, 2d Lieut. A. L. Carter, foot, 1st sergt. Wm. Cahill, leg, Sergt, Chas. V. Fuller, leg, slightly, Sergt. A. J. Wildman, ankle. Corp'l. Lorenzo Cotton, leg, Benj. F. Eaton, arm. Everett Fuller, leg, Horace G. Fabian. Privates Daniel Fox, leg, Lewis Fox, arm. James W. Burch, leg, Jerome W. Frink, leg. Geo. Thornton, groin, seriously. Chas. A. Hyde, groin, seriously, Daniel J. Hill, both feet, Daniel B. Forry, leg, Joseph M Lane, hip, John Eber, back, James Parks, Christopher Heffron, leg—Missing—John Wood, Robert Parke, Thadeus Bradley, William Thompkins, Edward Greeson, George Cross.

Co. C—Killed—Corp'ls Henry D. Weaver, Daniel Bradley, Privates Hannibal Howel, Lorenzo Tousley. Wounded—2d Lieut. Lucius Davis, hand. Sergt's Charles Howard, leg, Peter Catheart, leg, Corp'ls Daniel P. Griswold, leg, Privates Charles Hughs, leg, Alvin Wyckoff, leg, slight, John Orland, hand, Dexter Eldridge, foot, Conwell R. Horton, leg, Charles Thompkins, leg. Thomas M. Cor____, hand, Henry Ryan, leg. Missing—Daniel Raymond, Amos Hicks, Hugh Patterson.

Co. D—Killed—Thomas Colvin. Wounded—2d Lieut. Wm. Buchanan, shoulder, 1st Sergt. Wm. H. Talbell, both legs. Privates John Evans, Simon Tarbell, arm, Geo. Norton, Michael Quinliven, Samuel T. Spencer, leg amputated, Horace Stewart, leg— Missing—John Lanigan, Lyman Satterly, M. Stevens, M. Van Beathusen.

Co. E——Killed——Sergt. Walter B. Wood, Charles E. Persons, Wounded——Corp'ls George L. Northrup, leg, slight, Lorenzo Beaver, head, Thomas Powers, leg, R. E. Spicer, face. Privates—James B. Bush, leg, Barney Hill, leg, Henry B. Kenyoa, shoulder, Lewis Torango, leg amputated. Missing—Sergt. Newton Smith. Privates James Ash, Peter Ambirk, Eli S. Berry, Peter Cody, Oscar Gibson, Warren Holbrook, Valda S. Kellogg, George Lamphere.

Co. F—Killed——Corp'l Benj. F. Holden, Hiram Gilbert, Patrick Smith. 1st Lieut. John W. Fisher, arm broken, 2d Lieut. Rob't G. Noxon, leg, 1st Sergt. D. _. Montgomery, hand and shoulder, Sergt. Ralph E. Tucker, thigh, Corp'ls Geo. H. Peters, hand, Amos Coyswell, side, dangerous, Martin Hoy, Mason Myers, leg broken, Rulandus Pitts, ankle and shoulder, Scepter Rindgo, leg, Geo. W. Smith, leg and foot. Missing——Philip Faisch.

Co. G——Killed——Sergt. Franklin Gay, Corp'l Chapin W. Menick, Lyman G. Scriven. Wounded——2d Lieut. Samuel E. Sanders, foot, Sergts. Geo. W. Steel, leg, Wm. Miller, hip, Corp'l John L. Seeber, both legs, Privates Henry Cooper, ankle, James Cowlin, arm broken, Wm. H. Galpin, hand, Daniel M. Lane, thigh, Albert Hollenbeck, thigh, Favette Pender, do., Wm. Pooler, leg, Geo. Sweeting, arm broken, John Tripp, breast, mortal, Wm. Yolk, head, slight, Wm. Webbie, do., Jas. Weatherhead, arm broken, Orrin Zufelt, hip. Missing——Wm. H. Rankin, bugler.

Co. H——Killed——George Bosworth, Lewis Blackman. Wounded——Capt. Swan, breast and arm; Lieut. Swan, shoulder, Sergt. I. Baker, leg, H. Brown, knee. Corp'ls Wm. Wait, leg, P. Brown. Privates M. P. Bishop, side, J. Dorson, arm and side, mortally; J. Hickey, groin, C. Hoag, H. Lake, John Michar, lungs, mortally; W. Mahana, groin, H. Mickel, back, M. O'Brien, leg, J. O'Donnel, J. Rarick, leg; J. Van Buren, shoulder, breast, and arm, J. Welsh, hand, A. Embrige——22. There are three or four, in addition to the above list, still missing, whose fate is uncertain. Six were taken prisoners at the hospitals while assisting the wounded, viz: Sol. Howe, J. Hudson, P. Brown, A. Embrige, J. George, Jas. O'Brien. Four others missing and unaccounted for, sums up the thirty-two killed, wounded, and missing, out of thirty-eight or thirty-nine that went into the action in co. H !

Co. I——Killed——Sergt. E. J. Efner, Corp. J. H. Hammond, David Lynes, Uriah Young, Wounded——2d Lieut. Peter S. Clark, slight, Sergt. John Kerney, leg amputated, Corp'ls John J. Rice, John W. Coons, Durius C. Barton, Privates Henry

Sperveck, John D. Catur, Chas. S. Mattison, arm amputated, Abram Vausburg, Calvin Traver. Missing—-William Momley.

Co. K—-Killed—-Wm. E. Powell. Wounded—-Capt. John W. Young, leg. 2d Lieut. Michael Long, leg. 1st Sergt. Thomas Weldon, hand. Corp'ls. Charles Smith, side and leg, Alfred Chapman, hand and leg, seriously. Privates John C. Buchanan, leg, Francis Chapman, arm and shoulder, Francis Eggensberry, leg, Nathan Parrish, Geo. Young, leg, Wm. V. Hopkins, hand, Thos. Nichols, leg. Missing—-James Yager, Geo. W. Devoe, Joseph Phelps, Walter Watkins, E. H. Whitemore, John Ward, John Buchanan, Augustus Sonhart.

Bibliography

Archival Sources

Gettysburg National Military Park Library

Bachelder Papers Typescripts, Gettysburg National Military Park. This may be the most important collection of Gettysburg data in existence. The originals are located at the New Hampshire Historical Society.

Vertical Files

Burning of E. Harmon Farm, Human Interest File.

Davis Brigade, Vertical File 7-CS8b. This file contains two letters written by W. B. Murphy of the 2nd Mississippi Vol.

8th Illinois Cavalry, Vertical File 6-I8. This file contains a letter from Colonel Gamble to W. S. Church, dated March 10, 1864; a handwritten transcript of an article in the July 1, 1913 *New York Times* concerning the reception given Buford's cavalrymen; and a booklet entitled *Marcellus E. Jones, Captain, 8th Illinois Cavalry*.

56th Pennsylvania, Vertical File. This file contains The Civil War Journal of Samuel Healy, 1862-1863. He was a 1st Lieutenant in Co. I, 56th Pennsylvania Infantry.

James Wadsworth Papers, Vertical File 5-24a. This file contains a collection of papers from the manuscript division of the Library of Congress. The author is unidentified but is possibly E. P. Halstead.

July 1: McPherson Farm Area Action, Vertical File 4-9c. This file contains a letter from Chas. H. Veil to D. McConaughy, April 7, 1864.

July 1st Battle General Information, Vertical File 4-9a. This file contains a transcript of a letter written by Rev. Dr. Jacobs that appeared in the July 30, 1885 issue of *The Star and Sentinel*. It discusses weather conditions during the battle.

Major General Abner Doubleday, Vertical File 5-40.

North Carolina Troops: Personal Accounts, Vertical File 7-CS9b. This file contains "Fifty-fifth North Carolina: History of Regiment and Officers-Positions Occupied at Gettysburg." *The Galveston Daily News*. July 21, 1896.

147th New York, Vertical File. This file contains the Lyman Diary and the John Bartlett letter.

2nd Wisconsin, Vertical File 4-9c. This file contains the Cornelius Wheeler Papers.

7th Indiana, Vertical File. This file contains a letter written by J. L. Harding, dated July 18, 1863.

Tennessee Troops, Vertical File 7-CS11.

3rd Indiana Cavalry, Vertical File 6-IN3. This file contains a typescript of Colonel George Henry Chapman's diary and a typescript of a diary kept by F. J. Bellamy.

Tilberg, Frederick to Alan T. Nolan, March 3, 1960.

Tilberg, Frederick to Warren W. Hassler, February 23, 1951.

National Archives and Records Administration

James Coey, Medal of Honor Records, DD-322-VS-1865.

Lysander Cutler, Pension File.

Court-martial Record, Colonel Ira Grover, RG 153, Box 1510, NN-0072

Field Returns for Cutler's Brigade, RG 393, Part 2, Entries 3715, 3718, 3722, and 3729 Bound Together.

John Jochum (14th Brooklyn) Compiled Service Records and Pension File.

Francis Miller (147th New York) Pension File.

Peirre Thompson (95th New York) Pension File.

Various Collections

76th New York Newspaper Clippings File, New York State Military Museum

Abner Doubleday Papers, New York Historical Society.

Fry, B. D., Letter to John Bachelder, February 10, 1878. Author's Collection.
Haviland, E. E. (76th New York), Letter to his mother, August 11, 1863, Paul Meuse Collection.

Headquarter Records of the 14th Brooklyn, 1863, Brooklyn Historical Society.

Henry Harrison Lyman Collection, Oswego County Historical Society.

John Vliet Letters, 1861-1864, Brooklyn Historical Society. The majority of Vliet's letters, edited by David M. Cory, appeared in four issues of *The Journal of Long Island History* [Vol. II, Spring, 1962, No. 1; Vol. II, Fall, 1962, No. 2; Vol. III, Fall, 1963, No. 2; and Vol. IV, Summer, 1964, No. 3].

Pierce, H. W. (76th New York), Letter to his brother, July 11, 1863, Dick Bridgeman Collection.

Robert Brake Collection, U. S. Army Military History Institute. Two primary accounts were used from this collection. They were Franklin F. Pratt's letter to his parents, July 4, 1863 [76th New York] and Colonel George Henry Chapman's diary [3rd Indiana Cavalry].

File on Joseph R. Davis, Robert K. Krick Collection.

Society Small Collection, The Historical Society of Pennsylvania. This collection contains numerous communications between veterans and John William Hofmann.

Uberto A. Burnham Papers, New York State Library Manuscripts Collections. Burnham served in the 76th New York. This collection contains 4 letters pertaining to Gettysburg.

Newspaper Articles

"A Brave Hero Gone." *Bangor Daily Whig and Courier*, August 4, 1866.

"A Chaplain at Gettysburg." *Gettysburg Newspaper Clippings Relating to the Battle*. Gettysburg National Military Park.

"A Settled Question." *Milwaukee Sunday Telegraph*. July 29, 1883.

"An Interesting Statement. The Story of a Member of the 14th Captured at Gettysburg." *Brooklyn Daily Eagle*. July 7, 1863.

"At Gettysburg. How a Proposed Night Attack by the Enemy Was Foiled." *National Tribune*. February 11, 1886.

Ayers, Dr. D. Cooper. "Army Reminiscences." *Milwaukee Sunday Telegraph*. September 30, 1883.

Bachelder, Col. John B. "Hall's Maine and Calef's U. S. Batteries at Gettysburg." *Grand Army Scout and Soldiers Mail*. December 26, 1885.

Balch, Orwin. "Gettysburg Prisoners." *National Tribune*. August 11, 1904.

"Battle 42 Years Ago." *Gettysburg Compiler*, July 5, 1905.

"The Battle Field at Gettysburg." *Brooklyn Daily Eagle*. July 15, 1863.

Beale, James. "The First Day's Fight." *Philadelphia Weekly Times*. April 27, 1878.

Bentley, W. G. "Opening the Battle at Gettysburg." *National Tribune.*   October 16, 1913.

Beveridge, John. "First Shot at Gettysburg. General Beveridge Claims Honor for Captain Jones, 8th Illinois Cavalry." *National Tribune*. July 31, 1902.

Bishop, C. B. "Starting the Gettysburg Fight." *Philadelphia Weekly Times*. June 2, 1910.

Boland, E. T. "Death of General Reynolds. An Ex-Confederate Who Was a Witness Describes the Event." *National Tribune*. May 20, 1915.

"The Capture at the Railroad Cut." *National Tribune*. September 1, 1910.

Coe, A. S. "The 14th New York Zouaves." *National Tribune*. August 13, 1885.

Coey, James. "Cutler's Brigade. The 147th New York's Magnificent Fight on the First Day at Gettysburg." *National Tribune*. July 15, 1915.

Cook, C. W. "A Day at Gettysburg." *National Tribune*. April 7, 1898.

Cook, C. W. "The 76th New York at Gettysburg." *National Tribune*. May 19, 1887.

Cook, C. W. "Who Opened Gettysburg." *National Tribune*. November 24, 1892.

Dawes, Rufus. "A Clincher." *Milwaukee Sunday Telegraph*. August 12, 1883.

Dawes, Rufus. "Align on the Colors. A Graphic Description of a Gettysburg Charge." *Milwaukee Sunday Telegraph*. April 27, 1890.

Day, T. G. "First Shot at Gettysburg." *National Tribune*. October 30, 1902.

Day, Thomas G. "Opening the Battle. A Cavalryman's Recollections of the First Day's Fight at Gettysburg." *National Tribune*. July 30, 1903.

"Death of Colonel Pye." *Peeksville Messenger*, June 23, 1864.

Dickson, D. J. "At Culp's Hill, Gallant Fighting by the First Corps." *National Tribune*. April 15, 1915.

Ditzler, O. H. "The First Gun at Gettysburg." *National Tribune*. May 22, 1902.

Dodge, H. O. "Opening the Battle. Lieutenant Jones the 8th Illinois Cavalryman Fired the First Shot at Gettysburg." *National Tribune*. September 24, 1891.

"The Flags of Wisconsin Regiments to be Presented to the State." *The Appleton Crescent*, June 9, 1866.

Fowler, E. B. "The Fourteenth Regiment." *Brooklyn Daily Eagle*. July 6, 1863.

Fowler, E. B. "The Fourteenth Regiment. Official From Colonel Fowler." *Brooklyn Daily Eagle*. July 11, 1863.

"From the 76th New York." *Cherry Valley Gazette*, August 19, 1863.

"From General John B. Callis." *Milwaukee Sunday Telegraph*. July 15, 1883.

"General Cutler at Gettysburg." *Milwaukee Sunday Telegraph*. March 18, 1883.

"Gettysburg Again." *Milwaukee Sunday Telegraph*. May 6, 1883.

Hofmann, J. W. "Gettysburg Again." *National Tribune*. June 5, 1884.

Hofmann, J. W. "Gettysburg. General Hofmann Replies to the 2nd Wisconsin Claim." *National Tribune*. June 19, 1884.

Hofmann, J. W. "The 56th Pennsylvania at Gettysburg." *National Tribune*. March 20, 1884.

Hofmann, Bvt.-Gen. J. W. "The Fifty-sixth Pennsylvania Volunteers in the Gettysburg Campaign." *Philadelphia Weekly Press*. January 13, 1886.

Hopkins, T. S. "Death of General Reynolds. It Came From a Volley and Not a Sharpshooter." *National Tribune*. April 4, 1910.

Hubbard, J. N. "Cutler's Brigade Led." *National Tribune*. September 1, 1910.

Hubbard, J. N. "Gettysburg, Wadsworth's Division on Culp's Hill." *National Tribune*. March 15, 1915.

Huber, A. H. "At Gettysburg. Cutler's Brigade First and the Iron Brigade Next on the Field." *National Tribune*. December 8, 1892.

Hughes, Morgan. "People of Gettysburg. How They Inspired the Cavalry…." *National Tribune*. March 24, 1892.

"Independence Day at the Capital." *Semi-Weekly Wisconsin*, July 11, 1866.

Jochum, John. "His Brain Laid Bare, The Remarkable Experience of a Gettysburg Veteran." *The Buffalo Sunday Morning News*, April 23, 1893.

"John Jochum's Death." *The Brooklyn Daily Eagle*, January 16, 1894.

Jones, Jesse. "Cutler and the 2nd Brigade." *National Tribune*. September 1, 1910.

Kelley, Benton. "Gettysburg. An Account of Who Opened the Battle by One Who Was There." *National Tribune*. December 31, 1891.

Ketcheson, John C. "The First Shot at Gettysburg." *National Tribune*. December 25, 1913.

Kress, John A. "Tales of the War. Thrilling Description of Scenes and Incidents at Gettysburg." *Missouri Republican*. December 4, 1886.

"The Late Major-General Lysander Cutler." *The Evening Telegraph* (Philadelphia), August 6, 1866.

Lyman, H. H. "At Gettysburg. Cutler's Brigade Opened the Battle — Claim of Iron Brigade Refuted." *National Tribune*. October 13, 1892.

Lyman, H. H. "Battle of Gettysburg. Opened by Cutler's Brigade and Not by Any Single Regiment." *National Tribune*. August 25, 1887.

Mickey of Company K. "The Charge at Gettysburg." *Milwaukee Sunday Telegraph*. January 20, 1884.

Mix, A. R. "Experiences at Gettysburg." *National Tribune*. February 22, 1934.

Moore, J. H. "The Battle of Gettysburg." *Philadelphia Weekly Times*. November 4, 1882.

Okey, C. W. "Echoes of Gettysburg. After That Flag." *Milwaukee Sunday Telegraph*. April 29, 1883.

Parkhurst, B. E. "At Gettysburg. Heroism of the 147th New York." *National Tribune*. November 1, 1888.

Parkhurst, Burns E., "Dear Parents." *Mexico Independent*, July 23, 1863.

Pierce, J. V. "Gettysburg. Last Words as to 'What Regiment Opened the Battle'." *National Tribune.* April 3, 1884.

"Playing Parson." *National Tribune,* October 4, 1888.

Reed, E. R. "The 2nd Wisconsin Sticks to Its Claim." *National Tribune.* March 20, 1884.

Robertson, John. "Opening the Battle. How I Saw the First Shot Fired at Gettysburg." *National Tribune.* April 2, 1903.

Rogers, Earl. "The Second, or Fifty-Sixth — Which?" *Milwaukee Sunday Telegraph.* June 22, 1884.

Sherman, Edward. "Iron Brigade Medals." *National Tribune.* August 11, 1904.

"A State Fish Inspector." *The Daily Milwaukee News,* April 21, 1866.

"The Story of a Member of the 14th Captured at Gettysburg." *Brooklyn Daily Eagle.* July 7, 1863.

Stubbs, Charles. "2nd Maine Battery at Gettysburg." *National Tribune.* June 2, 1910.

Swett, Joel B. "The 8th New York Cavalry at Gettysburg." *National Tribune.* April 3, 1884.

Tripp, B. H. "At Gettysburg. Substantiating the Claim That the Iron Brigade Opened the Battle." *National Tribune.* September 22, 1892.

Tripp, B. H. "The Iron Brigade. They Opened the Battle of Gettysburg." *National Tribune.* June 18, 1891.

Truitt, P. "The 7th Indiana Fighters at Gettysburg." *National Tribune.* November 19, 1925.

Watrous, J. A. "Some Army Sketches." *Milwaukee Sunday Telegraph.* July 30, 1882.

Whitney, M. M. "The 76th New York, How It Opened the Fight on the First Day at Gettysburg." *National Tribune.* July 21, 1887.

Willett, Frank. "Another Gettysburg. A Comrade Who Says the 8th New York." *National Tribune.* December 1, 1892.

"With Reference to the 95th." *Rockland County Messenger.* June 1, 1893. Lance Ingmire Collection.

Magazine and Journal Articles

Ashe, Capt. S. A. "The First Day at Gettysburg." Confederate Veteran, Vol. 38. 1930.

Belo, Col. A. H. "The Battle of Gettysburg." *Confederate Veteran, Vol. 8.* 1900

Boland, Pvt. E. T. "Beginning of the Battle of Gettysburg." *Confederate Veteran, Vol. 14.* 1906.

"Brig.-Gen. James T. Archer." *Confederate Veteran, Vol. 8.* 1900.

Calef, Col. John H. "Gettysburg Notes: The Opening Gun." *Journal of the Military Service Institute, Vol. 40.* 1907.

Clark, Augustus. "The 6th New York Cavalry, Its Movement and Service at the Battle of Gettysburg." *United Service Magazine, Vol. 16.* 1896.

Colston, Capt. F. M. "Gettysburg As I Saw It." *Confederate Veteran, Vol. 5.* 1897.

"14th Regiment New York State Militia, 1861-1864." *Military Collector and Historian, Vol. 10, No. 3.* Fall 1958.

Fulton, Capt. W. F. "The Fifth Alabama Battalion at Gettysburg." *Confederate Veteran, Vol. 31.* 1923.

Hankins, Samuel. "Simple Story of a Soldier, VII, VIII." *Confederate Veteran, Vol. 21.* 1913.

Harris, T. C. "The 2nd Mississippi at Gettysburg." *Confederate Veteran, Vol. 25.* 1917.

Hartwig, D. Scott. "Guts and Good Leadership; The Action at the Railroad Cut, July 1, 1863." *Gettysburg: Historical Articles of Lasting Interest, Issue No. 1.* 1989.

Haskins, Benjamin. "General James Archer." *Confederate Veteran, Vol. 2.* 1894.

Heenehan, "Correcting the Error: The Court-Martial and Acquittal of Col. Ira Grover, 7th Indiana Infantry." *The Gettysburg Magazine, Issue Number 45* (July 2011).

Herdegen, Lance. "Old Soldiers and War Talk" *The Gettysburg Magazine, Issue No. 2.* 1990.

Herdegen, Lance and William Beaudot. "With the Iron Brigade Guard at Gettysburg." *Gettysburg: Historical Articles of Lasting Interest, Issue No. 1.* 1989.

"Heth's Division at Gettysburg." *The Southern Bivouac, Vol. 3.* May 1885.

Jones, Dr. Gordon W. "Surgery in the Civil War." *Civil War Times Illustrated, Vol. 2, No. 2.* May 1963.

Kimble, J. "Tennesseans at Gettysburg. The Retreat." *Confederate Veteran, Vol. 28.* 1910.

Long, Roger. "A Mississippian in the Railroad Cut." *The Gettysburg Magazine, Issue No. 4.* 1991.

Love, William A. "Mississippi at Gettysburg." *Publications of the Mississippi Historical Society.* Oxford, Mississippi: Printed for the Society, 1906.

M'Farland, Baxter. "Casualties of the Eleventh Mississippi Regiment at Gettysburg." *Confederate Veteran, Vol. 24.* 1916.

M'Farland, Baxter. "Losses of the Eleventh Mississippi Regiment at Gettysburg." *Confederate Veteran, Vol. 31.* 1923.

Marye, John L. "The First Gun at Gettysburg." *American Historical Register, Vol. 2.* 1895.

McLean, Jr., James L. "The Execution of John Wood on the March to Gettysburg." *The Gettysburg Magazine, Issue No. 45.* July, 2011.

McLean, Jr., James L. "The First Union Shot at Gettysburg." *Lincoln Herald, Vol. 82, No. 1.* Spring 1980.

Moon, W. H. "Beginning the Battle of Gettysburg." *Confederate Veteran, Vol. 33.* 1925.

Moore, Capt. J. H. "Heroism in the Battle of Gettysburg." *Confederate Veteran, Vol. 9.* 1901.

Purifoy, John. "Battle of Gettysburg, July 1, 1863." *Confederate Veteran, Vol. 31.* 1923.

Purifoy, John. "Battle of Gettysburg, July 2, 1863." *Confederate Veteran, Vol. 31.* 1923.

Purifoy, John. "Ewell's Attack at Gettysburg, July 2, 1863." *Confederate Veteran, Vol. 31.* 1923.

Sledge, Robert W. "The Railroad Cut Reconsidered." *The Gettysburg Magazine, Issue Number 52.* January, 2015.

Storch, Mark and Beth Storch. "'What a Deadly Trap We Were In': Archer's Brigade on July 1, 1863." *The Gettysburg Magazine, Issue No. 6.* 1992.

Strain, J. H. "Heroic Henry McPherson." *Confederate Veteran, Vol. 31.* 1923.

Turney, J. B. "The First Tennessee at Gettysburg." *Confederate Veteran, Vol. 8.* 1900.

Winschel, Terrence. "Heavy Was Their Loss: Joe Davis' Brigade at Gettysburg." *The Gettysburg Magazine, Issue No. 2.* 1990.

Winschel, Terrence. "Heavy Was Their Loss: Joe Davis' Brigade at Gettysburg, Part 2." *Gettysburg: Historical Articles of Lasting Interest, Issue No. 3.* 1990.

Books and Pamphlets

Addresses Delivered Before the Historical Society of Pennsylvania Upon the Occasion of the Presentation of a Portrait of Major-General John F. Reynolds. Philadelphia: J. B. Lippincott and Co., 1880.

Aroostook War, Historical Sketch and Roster of Commissioned Officers and Enlisted Men Called into Service for the Protection of the Northeastern Frontier of Maine. Augusta: Kennebec Journal Print, 1904.

Ashhurst, R. L. *First Day's Fight at Gettysburg.* Philadelphia: Press of Allen, Lane, and Scott, 1897.

Bandy, Ken and Florence Freeland. *The Gettysburg Papers,* 2 *Vol.* Dayton: Press of Morningside Bookshop, 1978.

Bates, Samuel P. *The Battle of Gettysburg.* Philadelphia: T. H. Davis & Co., 1875.

Bates, Samuel. *History of the Pennsylvania Volunteers, 1861-1865, Vol. 2.* Harrisburg: B. Singerly, State Printer, 1897.

Beale, James. *The Statements of Time on July 1 at Gettysburg, Pennsylvania, 1863.* Philadelphia: James Beale Printer, 1897.

Bellah, James Warner. *Soldiers' Battle: Gettysburg.* New York: David McKay Co., Inc., 1962.

Bigelow, John. *The Peach Orchard, July 2, 1863.* Minneapolis: Kimball-Storer, 1910.

Boatner, Mark Mayo. *The Civil War Dictionary.* New York: David McKay Co., Inc., 1959.

Broadhead, Sarah. *The Diary of a Lady of Gettysburg.* Hershey, 1990 reprint of 1863 edition.

Busey, John W. and David G. Martin. *Regimental Strengths at Gettysburg.* Baltimore: Gateway Press, Inc., 1982.

Busey, John W. and David G. Martin. *Regimental Strengths and Losses at Gettysburg, Fourth Edition*. Hightstown: Longstreet House, 2005.

Busey, Travis W. and John W. Busey. *Union Casualties at Gettysburg, A Comprehensive Record*, 3 vols. Jefferson: McFarland Publishing, 2011.

Catton, Bruce. *Mr. Lincoln's Army*. New York: Doubleday and Co., Inc., 1951.

Cheek, Phillip and Mair Pointon. *History of the Sauk County Riflemen Known as Company "A", Sixth Wisconsin Veteran Volunteer Infantry, 1861-1865*. Gaithersburg: Butternut Press, 1984.

Cheney, Newel. *History of the Ninth Regiment New York Volunteer Cavalry*. Jamestown: Poland Center, 1901.

Clark, Walter, ed. *Histories of the Several Regiments and Battalions From North Carolina in the Great War, 1861-1865*. 5 vol. Raleigh, 1901.

Cleaves, Freeman. *Meade of Gettysburg*. Norman: Univ. of Oklahoma Press, 1901.

Coddington, Edwin B. *The Gettysburg Campaign: A Study in Command*. New York: Charles Scribner's Sons, 1968.

Commager, Henry Steele, ed. *The Blue and the Gray, Vol. 2*. New York: The Bobbs-Merrill Co., 1950.

Cook, Lt.-Col. Benjamin F. *History of the 12th Massachusetts Vol. (Webster Regiment)*. Boston: Twelfth Regiment Association, 1882.

Cowles, Capt. Calvin D., compiler. *Atlas to Accompany the Official Records of the Union and Confederate Armies*. New York: Gramercy Books, 1983.

Dawes, Rufus. *Service With the Sixth Wisconsin*. Dayton: Morningside House, Inc., 1984.

Doubleday, Abner. *Chancellorsville and Gettysburg*. New York: Charles Scribner's Sons, 1882.

Dowdey, Clifford. *Death of a Nation*. New York: Alfred A. Knopf, 1958.

Downey, Fairfax. *The Guns at Gettysburg*. New York: David McKay Co., Inc., 1958.

Dyer, Frederick H. *A Compendium of the War of the Rebellion*. New York: Thomas Yoseloff, 1959.

Eddy, Richard. *History of the 60th Regiment, New York State Volunteers*. Philadelphia: Crissy & Markley, 1864.

Easley, Jerry M., ed. *1863 Civil War Diary, James M. Hart, 7th Indiana Volunteer Infantry*. n. p., n. d..

Foote, Shelby. *The Civil War: Fredericksburg to the Meridian*. New York: Random House, 1963.

Fox, William Freeman. *Regimental Losses in the American Civil War, 1861-1865*. Albany: Albany Publishing Company, 1889.

Freeman, Douglas Southall. *Lee's Lieutenants: A Study in Command, Vol. 3*. New York: Charles Scribner's Sons, 1944.

Fulton, William Frierson. *The War Reminiscences of William Frierson Fulton II, 5th Alabama Battalion, Archer's Brigade*. Gaithersburg: Butternut Press, 1986.

Gallagher, Gary ed. *The First Day at Gettysburg: Essays on Confederate and Union Leadership*. Kent: The Kent State University Press, 1992.

Georg, Kathleen R. *Edward McPherson Farm: Historical Study*. Unpublished manuscript at GNMP Library.

Gottfried, Bradley M. *The Maps of Gettysburg: An Atlas of the Gettysburg Campaign, June 3-July 13, 1863*. El Dorado Hills: Savas Beatie LLC, 2007.

Glazier, Capt. Willard. *Three Years in the Federal Cavalry*. New York: R. H. Ferguson and Co., 1874.

Goldsborough, W. W. *The Maryland Line in the Confederate Army, 1861-1865*. Darnestown: Butternut Press, 1983.

Guelzo, Allen. *Gettysburg, The Last Invasion*. New York: Alfred A. Knopf, 2013.

Hall, Isaac. *History of the 97th Regiment New York Volunteers in the War for the Union*. Utica: Press of L. C. Childs and Son, 1890.

Hard, Abner. *History of the Eighth Cavalry Regiment Illinois Volunteers During the Great Rebellion*. Aurora, 1868.

Harwell, Richard, ed. *Two Views of Gettysburg*. Chicago: R. R. Donnelley and Sons Co., 1964.

Harwell, Richard. *The Union Reader.* New York: Longmans, Green and Co., 1958.

Hassler, Warren W. *Crisis at the Crossroads: The First Day at Gettysburg.* University: Univ. of Alabama Press, 1970.

Haupt, Herman. *Reminiscences of General Herman Haupt.* Milwaukee: Wright and Joys Co., 1901.

Herdegen, Lance J. and William J. K. Beaudot. *In the Bloody Railroad Cut at Gettysburg.* Dayton: Morningside House, Inc., 1990.

History of the 6th New York Cavalry, Second Ira Harris Guard. Worcester: The Blanchard Press, 1908.

Hofmann, Bvt. Brig.-Gen. J. Wm. *Remarks on the Battle of Gettysburg.* Philadelphia: A. W. Auner, Printer, 1880.

Hoke, Jacob. *The Great Invasion of 1863, or General Lee in Pennsylvania.* New York: Thomas Yoseloff, 1959.

Howard, Oliver O. *Autobiography of Oliver Otis Howard.* 2 vol. New York: Baker and Taylor Co., 1908.

Illinois Monuments at Gettysburg. Springfield: H. W. Rokker, State Printer and Binder, 1892.

Imhof, John. *Gettysburg: Day 2, A Study in Maps.* Baltimore: Butternut and Blue, 1999.

In Memoriam, George Sears Greene, Brevet Major-General, U. S. Vol., 1801-1899. Albany: J. B. Lyon Co., State Printers, 1909.

In Memoriam, James Samuel Wadsworth, 1807-1864. Albany: J. B. Lyon Co., State Printers, 1916.

Jacobs, Michael. *Notes on the Rebel Invasion of Maryland and Pennsylvania and the Battle of Gettysburg, July 1, 2 and 3, Accompanied by an Explanatory Map.* Gettysburg, 1909 reprint of an earlier edition.

Johnson, Robert Underwood and Clarence Clough Buel, ed. *Battles and Leaders of the Civil War, Vol. 2, North to Antietam* and *Vol. 3, Retreat from Gettysburg.* New York: Castle Books, 1956.

Ladd, David and Audrey Ladd, ed. *The Bachelder Papers, Volume 1.* Dayton: Morningside House, Inc., 1994.

Ladd, David and Aubrey Ladd, ed. *John Bachelder's History of the Battle of Gettysburg.* Dayton: Press of Morningside, 1997.

Laino, Philip. *Gettysburg Campaign Atlas: 421 Maps Encompassing the March to Gettysburg, the Battle, and the Retreat.* Dayton: Gatehouse Press, 2009.

Lindsley, John Berrien, ed. *The Military Annals of Tennessee, Confederate.* Nashville: J. M. Lindsley and Co., Publishers, 1886.

Lord, Francis and Arthur Wise. *Uniforms of the Civil War.* New York: Thomas Yoseloff, 1970.

McBrien, Joe Bennett. *The Tennessee Brigade.* Chattanooga: Hudson Printing and Lithographing Co., 1977.

McClure, Alexander K., ed. *The Annals of the War.* Philadelphia: The Times Publishing Co., 1879.

McIntosh, David Gregg. *Review of the Gettysburg Campaign.* Falls Church: Confederate Printers, 1984.

Maine at Gettysburg, Report of the Maine Commissioners Prepared by the Executive Committee. Portland: The Lakeside Press, 1898.

Meade, George Gordon. *With Meade at Gettysburg.* Philadelphia: John C. Winston Co., 1930.

The Medical and Surgical History of the War of the Rebellion. Washington: Government Printing Office, 1870-1888.

Memoirs of Colonel John A. Fite, 7th Tennessee Infantry, C. S. A.. This undated manuscript was dictated by Fite to his niece in 1910. A copy of this document can be found at the Gettysburg NMP Library.

Miers, Earl S. and Richard A. Brown. *Gettysburg.* New Brunswick: Rutgers Univ. Press, 1948.

Military Record of Brevet Brigadier-General John William Hofmann, United States Volunteers. Philadelphia: A. W. Auner, Printer, 1884.

Minnigh, Luther. *Gettysburg: "What They Did Here."* Gettysburg: Tipton and Blocher, 1924.

Montgomery, James Stuart. *The Shaping of a Battle: Gettysburg.* New York: Chilton Co., 1959.

Moyer, H. P. *History of the 17th Regiment Pennsylvania Volunteer Cavalry….* Lebanon: Sowers Printing Co., 1911.

Mulholland, St. Clair A. *Percentage Losses at Gettysburg Greatest in History.* Gettysburg: W. H. Tipton, 1911.

Nevins, Allan, ed. *A Diary of Battle: The Personal Journals of Colonel Charles S. Wainwright, 1861-1865.* New York: Harcourt, Brace and World, Inc., 1962.

New York Monuments Commission for the Battlefields of Gettysburg and Chattanooga, Final Report of the Battlefield of Gettysburg. 3 vol. Albany: J. B. Lyon Co., Printers, 1900.

Nolan, Alan T. *The Iron Brigade: A Military History.* Madison: The State Historical Society of Wisconsin, 1975.

Norton, Oliver. *The Attack and Defense of Little Round Top.* New York: The Neale Publishing Company, 1913.

O'Sullivan, Richard. *History of the 13th Alabama, Part 8: The Gettysburg Campaign.* Typescript mailed to author, August 24, 1990.

Paul, Jr., L. B. *Paul's Brigade at Gettysburg, July 1, 1863.* 1966.

Pearson, Henry Greenleaf. *James S. Wadsworth of Geneseo, Brevet Major-General of United States Volunteers.* New York: Charles Scribner's Sons, 1913.

Pennsylvania at Gettysburg, Ceremonies at the Dedication of the Monuments Erected by the Commonwealth of Pennsylvania. 2 Vol. Harrisburg: Wm. Stanley Ray, State Printer, 1904.

Pennypacker, Isaac R. *General Meade.* New York: D. Appleton and Co., 1901.

Pfanz, Harry. *Gettysburg: Culp's Hill and Cemetery Hill.* Chapel Hill: The University of North Carolina Press, 1993.

Pfanz, Harry. *Gettysburg—The First Day.* Chapel Hill: The University of North Carolina Press, 2001.

Phisterer, Frederick, comp. *New York in the War of the Rebellion.* 5 vol. Albany: J. B. Lyon Co., State Publishers, 1912.

Pickerill, W. N., ed. and comp. *Indiana at the Fiftieth Anniversary of the Battle of Gettysburg.* 1913.

Presentation of Flags of New York Volunteer Regiments…July 4, 1865. Albany: Weed, Parsons and Company, Printers, 1865.

Raus, Edmund. *A Generation on the March: The Union Army at Gettysburg.* Lynchburg: H. E. Howard, Inc., 1987.

Reardon, Carol and Tom Vossler. *A Field Guide to Gettysburg: Experiencing the Battlefield Through its History, Places, and People.* Chapel Hill: The University of North Carolina Press, 2013.

Riggs, David. *East of Gettysburg: Stuart versus Custer.* Bellevue: Old Army Press, 1970.

Report of the Adjutant General of the State of Indiana, Vol. 2. Indianapolis: W. R. Holloway, State Printer, 1865.

Rosengarten, J. G. *Reynolds Memorial Address, March 8, 1880.* Historical Society of Pennsylvania.

Sauers, Richard Allen. *Advance the Colors, Volume 1.* Harrisburg: Commonwealth of Pennsylvania, 1987.

Sauers, Richard Allen. *The Gettysburg Campaign, June 3-August 1, 1863: A Comprehensive, Selectively Annotated Bibliography.* Westport: Greenwood Press, 1982.

Sauers, Richard Allen. *The Gettysburg Campaign, June 3-August 1, 1863: A Comprehensive, Selectively Annotated Bibliography, Second Edition.* Baltimore: Butternut and Blue, 2004.

Schaff, Morris. *The Battle of the Wilderness.* Boston: Houghton Mifflin Company, 1910.

Scott, James K. P. *The Story of the Battles at Gettysburg.* Harrisburg: The Telegraph Press, 1927.

Smith, Adam. *History of the 76th Regiment New York Volunteers.* Cortland: Truair, Smith and Miles, Printers, 1867.

Snyder, Charles. *Oswego County, New York in the Civil War.* 1962 Yearbook of the Oswego County Historical Society and the Oswego County Civil War Centennial Committee.

Stewart, George R. *Pickett's Charge: A Microhistory of the Final Attack at Gettysburg, July 3, 1863.* Boston: Houghton-Mifflin Company, 1959.

Stine, J. H. *History of the Army of the Potomac.* Philadelphia: J. B. Rodgers Printing Co., 1892.

Swinton, William. *Campaigns of the Army of the Potomac.* New York: Univ. Publishing Co., 1871.

Swinton, William. *The Twelve Decisive Battles of the War.* New York: Dick and Fitzgerald, 1867.

Taylor, Frank H. *Philadelphia in the Civil War.* Philadelphia, 1913.

Tevis, C. V. and D. R. Marquis. *The History of the Fighting Fourteenth.* New York: Brooklyn Eagle Press, 1911.

Thomson, Orville. *Narrative of the Service of the Seventh Indiana Infantry in the War for the Union.* n. p., n. d.

Toombs, Samuel. *New Jersey Troops in the Gettysburg Campaign....* Orange: The Evening Mail Publishing House, 1888.

Tregaskis, John, comp. *The Battlefield of Gettysburg: The Men Who Fought and the Monuments Dedicated.* New York: Tregaskis and Co., 1888.

Tucker, Glenn. *High Tide at Gettysburg: The Campaign in Pennsylvania.* Dayton: Morningside Bookshop, 1973.

Vanderslice, John M. *Gettysburg: Then and Now.* Dayton: Morningside Bookshop, 1983.

Vautier, John D. *History of the 88th Pennsylvania Volunteers in the War for the Union, 1861-1865.* Philadelphia: J. B. Lippincott Co., 1894.

Warner, Ezra J. *Generals in Blue, Lives of the Union Commanders.* New Orleans: Louisiana State Univ. Press, 1964.

Warner, Ezra J. *Generals in Gray, Lives of the Confederate Commanders.* New Orleans: Louisiana State Univ. Press, 1959.

War of the Rebellion: Official Records of the Union and Confederate Armies, Vol. 27, 3 Parts. Dayton: Morningside Bookshop, 1981.

Welsh, Jack D. *Medical Histories of the Union Generals.* Kent State, OH, 1996.

Wilson, LeGrand. *The Confederate Soldier.* Memphis: Memphis State University Press, 1973.

Wise, Jennings C. *The Long Arm of Lee, The History of the Artillery of the Army of Northern Virginia.* Lynchburg: J. P. Bell Co., 1915.

Young, Jesse Bowman. *The Battle of Gettysburg: A Comprehensive Narrative.* New York: Harper and Brothers Publishers, 1913.

INDEX